Concurrency in Ada

Concurrency in Ada

Alan Burns and Andy Wellings
University of York

CAMBRIDGE
UNIVERSITY PRESS

Published by the Press Syndicate of the University of Cambridge
The Pitt Building, Trumpington Street, Cambridge CB2 1RP
40 West 20th Street, New York, NY 10011-4211, USA
10 Stamford Road, Oakleigh, Melbourne 3166, Australia

© Cambridge University Press 1995

First published 1995

Printed in Great Britain at Biddles Ltd, Guildford and Kings Lynn

A catalogue record of this book is available from the British Library

Library of Congress cataloguing in publication data

ISBN 0 521 41471 7 hardback

Contents

Foreword

Much has changed in the ten years since Alan Burns wrote the book entitled *Concurrent Programming in Ada* which in many ways was the forerunner to *Concurrency in Ada* which you are now reading.

That ten years has seen solid use of the original version of Ada, which we can refer to as Ada 83. That ten years has also brought a great deal of understanding regarding the theories of scheduling. Ten years ago few had a personal computer, now they are ubiquitous. Ten years ago, few had heard of Object Oriented Programming; now it is all the fashion. And ten years has brought a new Standard language, Ada 95, building on the strengths of the old Ada 83 and incorporating changes to meet the new demands for the future.

Ada 83 was the first International Standard to include concurrency as an intrinsic feature in the language. It was a bold step and, as one would expect, not without problems. It certainly enabled the description of parallel activities in an abstract way and introduced the rendezvous as a high level means of communication. However, it did not provide any specific facilities for shared data access, believing that data manager tasks and the rendezvous would provide an appropriate technique. Moreover, it took a very rigid view regarding priority scheduling. There were also sneaky little problems regarding race conditions that were not thoroughly understood; symptoms of something not quite right.

Nevertheless, Ada 83 provided and continues to provide a good framework for the development of many embedded applications especially in areas such as avionics (both civil and military), railroad signaling, process control and so on. Experiences with those applications and theoretical understanding, especially from the Software Engineering Institute, have resulted in Ada 95 having much improved facilities for concurrency in both practical and theoretical terms.

The protected object provides a highly efficient feature for shared data access. Indeed, although a high level concept and thus amenable to proof through clarity, it has the potential for greater efficiency than raw semaphores. Other advantages are that, being passive, there are no associated termination problems such as can occur with manager tasks. Protected objects also provide a better paradigm for the expression of interrupt handling.

More flexibility for scheduling is incorporated by the provision of various pragmas enabling the application to select appropriate strategies. Priority inversion can thus be overcome, rate monotonic scheduling used and so on. Those particularly inclined to use their own techniques in certain areas are catered for by packages for synchronous and asynchronous control.

The problems of race conditions mentioned above are now understood as requiring preference control. Ada 95 provides preference control by the requeue statement which enables a service to be provided in parts with old clients taking preference over new clients where appropriate.

Better timing control is also provided through the "delay until" statement giving absolute timing (relative delay can exhibit a form of race condition). There is also a guaranteed monotonic Clock for embedded applications where the clock in the package Calendar is not appropriate.

Of course Ada 95 is not just Ada 83 with much better concurrency. Ada 95 also includes full OOP with dynamic polymorphism, a hierarchical naming structure at the top level for the development of independent subsystems, and greater flexibility for communication with external systems.

Many will consider the new OOP facilities as the most important improvement over Ada 83. Hindsight may well prove this not to be the case. Certainly OOP is important and has a role to play, indeed it has useful interactions with concurrency. But for those whose concerns are for the development of reliable embedded applications, the new concurrency model must surely be one of the great strengths of Ada 95.

Having a new standard language is not enough, practitioners need to know how the facilities should be used in real situations and this is where this book by Alan Burns and Andy Wellings is so valuable. Not only does it cover the whole of the concurrency model in real depth but it also contains myriads of canonical examples illustrating the various features and especially the interactions between them.

This book is thus a very welcome addition to the literature on Ada in particular and to concurrency in general. Alan and Andy are to be congratulated on their efforts.

John Barnes
January 1995
Reading

Preface

The development of the Ada programming language forms a unique and, at times, intriguing contribution to the history of computer languages. As all users of Ada must know, the original language design was a result of competition between a number of organisations, each of which attempted to give a complete language definition in response to a series of requirements documents. This gave rise to Ada 83. Following ten years of use, Ada was subject to a complete overhaul. The resulting language, Ada 95, is defined by the *Ada Language Reference Manual* (ARM, 1995). During this overall the language was known colloquially as Ada 9X.

An important aspect of the new Ada language is the model it presents for providing *concurrent* or parallel programming. This model is both complex and new. It builds upon the original language features but provides many additional facilities required to meet the challenges of modern systems development. Many of the criticisms that were levelled at Ada 83 have been addressed; but as a result Ada 95 is much more extensive.

This book gives a detailed description and an assessment of that part of the Ada language that is concerned with concurrent programming. No prior knowledge of concurrent programming (in general) or Ada tasking (in particular) is assumed in this book. However, readers should have a good understanding of at least one high level sequential programming language.

This book is aimed both at professional software engineers and students of computer science (and other related disciplines). Already, many millions of lines of Ada 83 code have been produced world wide, and over the next decade a wide range of applications will be designed with Ada 95 in mind as the target language. It is important that Ada programmers do not restrict themselves to a sequential subset of the language on the dubious assumption that tasking is not appropriate to their work, or for fear that the tasking model is too complex and expensive. Tasking is an integral part of the language, and programmers must be familiar with, if not experienced in, its use. Due to space considerations, books that describe the entire language may not deal adequately with the tasking model; this book therefore concentrates, exclusively, on this model.

Students studying real-time programming, software engineering, concurrent programming or language design should find this book useful in that it gives a comprehensive description of the features that one language provides. Ada is not merely a product of academic research (as are many concurrent programming languages) but is a language intended for actual use in the information technology industry. Its model of tasking has therefore had to be integrated into the entire language design, and the interactions between tasking and non-tasking features carefully defined. Consequently, the study of Ada's model of concurrency should be included in those advanced courses mentioned above. However, this does not imply that the tasking model is free from controversy, has a proven semantic basis or is amenable to efficient implementation. The nature of these areas of 'discussion' are dealt with, as they arise, in this book.

Unlike Ada 83, which defined a single language, the Ada 95 definition has a core language design plus a number of domain specific annexes. A compiler need not support all the Annexes but it must support the core language. Most of the tasking features are contained in the core definition. But there are relevant annexes that address systems programming, real-time programming and distributed systems programming. These issues are also addressed in later parts of this book.

The first chapter gives a brief overview of the important non-concurrent features of the language. No attempt is made to be exhaustive, and readers completely unfamiliar with Ada are recommended to supplement this book with some appropriate text (there are many to choose from, for example Barnes, 1994).

Chapters 2 and 3 look, in detail, at the uses of concurrent programming and the inherent difficulties of providing inter-process communication. There is, as yet, no agreement on which primitives a concurrent programming language should support and, as a consequence, many different styles and forms exist. In order to understand the Ada tasking model fully, it is necessary to appreciate these different approaches and the problems faced by the user of any language that supports multi-processing.

The Ada task is introduced in Chapter 4 and the rendezvous and the important select statement are considered in the following two chapters. The rendezvous provides a synchronous communication mechanism. Data-oriented asynchronous communication is considered in Chapter 7, together with the important abstraction of a protected object. This provides a passive means of encapsulating data and providing mutual exclusion. An effective way of increasing the expressive power of the communication primitives is the requeue facility. This is described, with many examples given, in Chapter 8. The importance of protected objects as building blocks for concurrent programs is addressed in Chapter 9. The relationship between tasks and exceptions is dealt with in Chapter 10. This chapter also covers the means by which one task can affect the behaviour of another task asynchronously.

As indicated earlier, a number of the ARM annexes deal with issues of relevance to concurrent programming. Chapter 11 considers systems programming (including support for low level programming). Real-time issues are focused upon in Chapter 12.

In addition to its support for concurrent programming, Ada also facilitates the use of object-oriented programming. Chapter 13 considers the interactions between these two important abstractions.

Chapter 14 considers the programming of distributed systems. This gives an overview of the material presented in the distribution annex of the ARM and presents paradigms for programming distributed systems. Clearly, there is an interaction between concurrency issues and distribution. A number of open issues remain, and these are reviewed in this chapter.

The material presented in this book reflects the authors' experience in both using and teaching Ada tasking. Teaching experience has been obtained by writing and presenting courses at the University of York (UK) and by developing educational material and training.

Braille copies

Braille copies of this book, on paper or versabraille cassette, can be made available. Enquires should be addressed to Professor Alan Burns, Department of Computer Science, University of York, UK.

Real-time Systems Research at York

Alan Burns and Andy Wellings are members of the Real-Time Systems Research Group in the Department of Computer Science at the University of York (UK). This group undertakes research into all aspects of the design, implementation and analysis of real-time systems. Specifically, the group is addressing: formal and structured methods for development, scheduling theories, reuse, language design, kernel design, communication protocols, distributed and parallel architectures, and program code analysis. The aim of the group is to undertake fundamental research, and to bring into engineering practice modern techniques, methods and tools. Areas of application of our work include space and avionic systems, engine controllers, vehicle control and multi-media systems. Further information about the group's activities can be found via our WWW page:

http://dcpu1.cs.york.ac.uk:6666/real-time/

Many of our reports and papers can also be obtained directly from our ftp site. The address of the site is:

minster.york.ac.uk

(if the name is not recognised then a numeric name can be used: 144.32.128.41)

The reports and papers are located in the directory:

/pub/realtime/papers

Acknowledgements

The authors would like to thank the following individuals and groups who have, directly or indirectly, helped during the preparation of this book. Firstly we would like to thank the Ada 9X Mapping Team for answering all our questions on the new language. In particular, Offer Pazy has been very patient with our continual questioning of language semantics, and Tucker Taft has helped us understand the nuances of the object-oriented programming model.

Several people have read and commented on chapters of the book, and we are very grateful for their constructive criticism. In particular, we would like to thank Rob Allen, Geoff Davies, Mike Kamrad and Pat Rogers. Anthony Gargaro also gave us valuable insight into the Ada Distribution Model.

Finally, we would like to thank the GNAT project team for all their efforts to produce a public domain Ada 95 compiler. Writing a book for a new language is very difficult when there are no validated compilers to help test the code. Access to the GNAT system has provided us with more confidence that the code given in this book is at least syntactically correct! We would also like to thank Dan Johnson for his help in installing and using GNAT.

Chapter 1 ————————————————————

The Ada Language

Designing, implementing and maintaining software for large systems is a non-trivial exercise and one which is fraught with difficulties. These difficulties relate to the management of the software production process itself, as well as to the size and complexity of the software components. Ada is a general purpose programming language which has been designed to address the needs of large-scale system development, especially real-time and embedded systems. A major aspect of the language, and the one that is described comprehensively in this book, is its support for concurrent programming. Before examing the concurrency model in detail, however, a brief overview of the non-concurrent features of the language will be given in this chapter. The goal is to provide background material for the remainder of the book. For a more detailed discussion on the sequential aspect of Ada the reader is referred to Barnes (1994). Here, it is assumed that the reader is familiar with Pascal-like languages.

In considering the features of high level languages, it is useful to distinguish between those that aid the decomposition process and those that facilitate the programming of well-defined components. These two sets of features have been described as:

* support for programming in the small;
* support for programming in the large.

Section 1.1 first considers those aspects of Ada that are useful for programming components. Section 1.2 then considers the Ada package, which provides the basic support for programming in the large. This is followed, in Section 1.3, by a discussion on generic units which provide additional support for large-scale software development. Finally, Section 1.4 considers exception handling and the general issue of type security and error classification in Ada.

1.1   Programming in the small

1.1.1   Blocks and data structures

Ada is a strongly typed language with conventional Pascal-like data structures (it lacks only the set construct). Control structures are also similar to Pascal, with Ada possessing a more flexible loop construct that allows exit from the loop at any point within it. The first major distinction between the two languages comes from Ada's block structure. An Ada block consists of (i) the declaration of any entities (types, objects, procedures, etc.) that are local to the block (if there are no such entities, then this declaration part may be omitted), (ii) a sequence of statements and (iii) a collection of exception handlers (these handlers may be omitted and are considered later in this chapter):

```
declare
   <declarative part>
begin
   <sequence of statements>
exception
   <exception handlers>
end;
```

A block itself may be declared at any place in the program where a statement may be written. Blocks, which may be named, can contain other blocks and they therefore form a useful method of providing decomposition within a program unit. When a block is executed, the declarative part is said to be elaborated and the sequence of statements executed; in both operations it may be necessary to evaluate expressions.

The scope rules for blocks in Ada are somewhat different from those in other languages. They can be described informally as follows:

1.   The scope of an identifier is the block in which it is declared and all blocks enclosed within.

2.   An identifier is in scope immediately following its declaration.

3.   The visibility of an identifier matches its scope unless an identical identifier is declared in an inner block, in which case the original identifier is not directly visible.

A simple example will indicate the nature of Ada's block structure:

```
Top: declare -- a named block
   -- Top is NOT a destination label for a goto statement
   A : Integer := 42;     -- initial values can be
```

```
                                -- given to most objects.
      B : Integer := A + 3;   -- A is visible.
    begin
      A := A + B;              -- A equals 87
      declare                  -- an inner anonymous block
        A : Integer := 10;
        C : Integer;
      begin
        C := B;      -- C equals 45.
        C := A;      -- C equals 10.
        C := Top.A;  -- C now equal to 87.
      end;
      B := A;        -- B equals 87 and C is now out of scope.
    end Top;
```

The predefined scalar types in Ada are Integer, Character, Wide_Character, Boolean, Float and Duration (for use with real-time as shown in the next chapter); from these it is possible to derive new types. A type may also be constructed by defining all allowable values which objects of that type may take (these are called enumeration types). With all data types it is permissible to define a subtype that restricts the range of values of the parent type. It is not permitted, however, to use a subtype to restrict the operators that are associated with that type. The following illustrates the use of types, derived types and subtypes:

```
declare
    type Penny is range 1 .. 100;
       -- a new type constructed from the
       -- underlying (Universal) integer type
    type New_Int is new Integer;
       -- a new type derived from Integer
    type Small_Int is new Integer range -32 .. +31;
       -- a new constrained type derived from Integer
    type Day is (Monday, Tuesday, Wednesday, Thursday, Friday,
                 Saturday, Sunday); -- an enumeration type
    subtype Pos_Int is New_Int range 1 .. New_Int'Last;
    subtype Weekday is Day range Monday .. Friday;
    Start : Day := Monday;
    A : New_Int;
    B : Pos_Int;
    C : Integer;
begin
    A := B; -- legal.
    B := A; -- legal, but the value may be out of range
            -- and cause an exception to be raised
            -- during execution.
    A := C; -- illegal, this is a type clash as A and C
            -- are different types: A is New_Int
            -- and C is Integer.
    ...
end;
```

Note, the declaration of Small_Int defines an anonymous derived type and a subtype that restricts its range to -32 to 31.

In the above example, an attribute ('Last) is employed to represent the largest integer supported. Attributes are used throughout the language to provide information about types and objects.

Array and record types are declared in a straightforward way, for example

```
type Hour is new Integer range 1 .. 24;
type Event_Entry is
  record
    Start_Time : Hour;
    Activity : String(1 .. 40);
  end record;

type Day is (Sunday, Monday, Tuesday, Wednesday,
             Thursday, Friday, Saturday);

type Day_Diary is array (Hour) of Event_Entry;

type Weekly_Diary is array (Day) of Day_Diary;

Week1 : Weekly_Diary;
```

This example uses a predefined type called String which is an array of Characters. The size of the string is set to 40. An alternative formulation could pass the size of the string as a parameter to the type definition. Such a parameter is called a *discriminant*:

```
type Event_Entry (Size : Positive := 40) is
  record
    Start_Time : Hour;
    Activity : String(1 .. Size);
  end record;

One_Event : Event_Entry; -- uses the default size of 40
Verbose_Event : Event_Entry(100);
```

1.1.2   Type extensions and object-oriented programming

Ada facilitates object-oriented programming by providing a form of inheritance (via type extension) and run-time polymorphism (via run-time dispatching operations). If a type is to be extended, it must be declared as being a *tagged* record type (or a tagged private type — see below):

```
type Coordinates is tagged
  record
```

```
     X : Float;
     Y : Float;
  end record;
```

This type can then be extended:

```
type Three_D is new Coordinates with
  record
     Z : Float;
  end record;

Point : Three_D := (X => 1.0, Y => 1.0, Z => 0.0);
```

All types derived in this way (including the original *root*) are said to belong to the same *class* hierarchy. When a type is extended, it automatically inherits any primitive operations (those defined with the type) available for the parent type. However, these may be overridden with new versions. So, for example, if a Move procedure was defined with Coordinates, then a new version of Move could be defined with Three_D. Examples of the use of inheritance and run-time dispatching will be given in Chapter 13, where some of the interactions of object-oriented and concurrent programming are explored.

Further support for object-oriented programming is provided by *controlled* types. With these types it is possible to define subprograms that are called (automatically) when objects of the type:

* are created — *initialize*;

* cease to exist — *finalize*;

* are assigned a new value — *adjust*.

To gain access to these features, the type must be derived from Controlled, a predefined type declared in the library package Ada.Finalization, that is, it must be part of the Controlled class hierarchy. The package Ada.Finalization defines procedures for Initialize, Finalize and Adjust. When a type is derived from Controlled these procedure may be overridden. As objects typically cease to exist when they go out of scope, the exiting of a block may involve a number of calls of Finalize.

1.1.3 Subprograms

Procedures and functions are known collectively as subprograms. They are specified by giving a name, a complete description of the parameters and, if the subprogram is a function, the type of the returned object:

```
procedure Quadratic(A,B,C  : in Float;
                    R1,R2   : out Float;
```

```
OK        : out Boolean);
```

```
function  Minimum(X,Y,Z : Integer) return Integer;
```

The parameters must have their type and their mode specified. Three such modes are allowed:

*   **in** — within the subprogram the parameter acts as a local constant — a value is assigned to the formal parameter on entry to the procedure or function. This is the only mode allowed for functions. It is the default mode.

*   **out** — within the subprogram the value of the parameter can be written and read — a value is assigned to the calling parameter upon termination of the subprogram.

*   **in out** — within the subprogram the parameter acts as a variable — upon entry to the subprogram a value is assigned to the formal parameter; upon termination the value attained is passed back to the calling parameter.

Interestingly, these parameter modes do not dictate the method of implementation, which could be either by copy or by reference. There are, however, some restrictions. Non-composite types (e.g. scalars such as integers and booleans) must be passed "by copy". Also, certain more complex types (e.g. tasks and protected types) must be passed "by reference".

A subprogram body consists of a repeat of the specification plus whatever declarations and statements are needed to 'implement' the specification:

```
function Minimum(X,Y,Z : Integer) return Integer is
begin
  if X <= Y then
    if X < Z then
      return X;
    else
      return Z;
    end if;
  elsif Y <= Z then return Y;
    else return Z;
  end if;
end Minimum;
```

```
procedure Quadratic(A,B,C  : in Float;
                    R1, R2 : out Float;
                    OK     : out Boolean) is
  Z : constant Float := B**2 - 4.0*A*C;
begin
  if Z < 0.0 or A = 0.0 then
    OK := False;
```

```
            R1 := 0.0; -- arbitrary value.
            R2 := 0.0;
            return;   -- return from procedure before
                      -- reaching physical end.
         end if;
         OK := True;
         R1 := (-B + Sqrt(Z))/(2.0*A);
         R2 := (-B - Sqrt(Z))/(2.0*A);
      end Quadratic;
```

Parameters of mode 'in' can have default expressions, the values of which are used if a call of the subprogram does not contain an actual matching parameter. Calls, in general, can make use of the usual positional notation or employ named notation to remove positional errors and increase readability:

```
   function Wage(Grade    : University_Post;
                 Hours    : Float := 40.0;
                 Overtime : Float := 0.0) return Float;
```

Calls to this function could take the form

```
   Pay := Wage(Secretary, 40.0, 0.0);
   Pay := Wage(Secretary);               -- uses default values.
   Pay := Wage(Grade => Secretary);  -- uses name notation.
   Pay := Wage(Professor, Hours => 80.0);
   Pay := Wage(Grade => Lecturer, Overtime => 25.0);
```

All subprograms can be called recursively and are reentrant.

1.1.4 Access types

Indirect access to program entities (i.e. objects and subprograms) can be obtained through the use of access types. Such types can be used to access subprograms, ordinary objects and objects created by allocators. Some examples should illustrate these various uses of access types. First consider accesses to subprograms:

```
   type Ptr is access procedure (I : out Integer; L : in List);

   procedure Sum(I : out Integer; L : in List) is
   begin
      ...
   end Sum;

   S : Ptr := Sum'Access;
   -- 'Access is an attribute which returns an access pointer

      ...
```

```
procedure Min(I : out Integer; L : in List) is
begin
   ...
end Min;

S := Min'Access;
```

One of the useful applications of this feature is the ability to pass subprograms (via access types) as parameters to other subprograms.

Dynamic object creation comes from the use of an access type and an allocator:

```
type Some_Data is
  record
    ...
  end record;

type Some_Data_Pointer is access Some_Data;

Srp : Some_Data_Pointer;
   -- the 'value' of Srp is null

Srp := new Some_Data;
   -- a new data object is created;
   -- it is identified as Srp.all
```

This access type is restricted to only pointing to objects created by the 'new' allocator. It is, however, also possible to have an access type that allows ordinary objects to be so referenced:

```
Object : aliased Some_Type;
   -- aliased to say that it may be
   -- referenced by an access type

type General_Ptr is access all Some_Type;
   -- access all indicates that an access variable of this
   -- type can point to either static or dynamic objects

Gp : General_Ptr := Object'Access;
   -- assigns reference to Object to Gp
```

A final form of access type definition allows a read-only restriction to be imposed on the use of accesses:

```
Object1 : aliased Some_Type;
Object2 : aliased constant Some_Type := ...;

type General_Ptr is access constant Some_Type;

Gp1 : General_Ptr := Object1'Access;
   -- Gp1 can now only read the value of Object1
```

```
Gp2 : General_Ptr := Object2'Access;
  -- Gp2 is a reference to a constant
```

Access types can be passed as parameters to subprograms in a straightforward way:

```
type T is ...
type A is access T;

procedure P1(O : in out A);
procedure P2(O : A);
```

In procedure P2, the object is passed with 'in' mode; hence O must remain pointing to the same object (of type T). The object designated by O can, however, change its value.

In addition to defining standard access types as parameter types, it is also possible to define an anonymous "access parameter":

```
procedure P(A : access T);
```

A call of P can pass any object of an access type who accessed type is T. It is also possible to use "access discriminants":

```
type Rec(A : access T) is
  record
    ...
  end record;
```

See Section 4.1. for an example of their use with tasks.

1.2 Packages and library units

The package is the single most important construct in Ada. It serves as the logical building block of large, complex programs and is the most natural unit of separate compilation. In addition, the package provides for data hiding and the definition of abstract data types. A package definition has two parts, the specification (which itself may consist of a private as well as a visible part) and the body. The body contains the code necessary to implement the specification. Its inner details are hidden from the rest of the program, and, in terms of program development, the body of a package will often be constructed later and take the form of a separately compiled unit. The general form of a package is

```
package <Name> is
  -- visible declarations of constants, types,
  -- variables and subprograms
```

```
private
  -- hidden type and constant declarations, if any
end <Name>;

package body <Name> is
  -- internal declarations
begin
  -- sequence of statements for initialising the package
end <Name>;
```

If the sequence of statements in the package body consists only of the null statement, then the package body need only contain the bodies of units specified in the package specification. An example of the use of a package to define an abstract data type is one that provides complex arithmetic for the rest of the program. This package specifies the type Complex, the usual arithmetic operations and a set of functions for converting from type Float to Complex and vice versa:

```
package Complex_Arithmetic is
  type Complex is private;
  function "+"(X,Y : Complex) return Complex;
  function "-"(X,Y : Complex) return Complex;
  function "*"(X,Y : Complex) return Complex;
  function "/"(X,Y : Complex) return Complex;
  function Comp(A,B : Float)    return Complex;
  function Real_Part(X : Complex) return Float;
  function Imag_Part(X : Complex) return Float;
private
  type Complex is
    record
      Real : Float;
      Imag : Float;
    end record;
end Complex_Arithmetic;
```

This package defines operators, ("+", "-", "*" and "/" for objects of type Complex. These operators are said to *overload* the usual operators. Overloading is allowed for all subprograms in Ada as long as the meaning is unambiguous.

By defining Complex to be private, no assumption can be made (outside this package) about the structure of the type; in this example it is implemented as a record; however it could just as easily have been constructed as a two-component array. If a type has been designated as being private, then the following operations are allowed in the rest of the program where the package is in scope:

1.   Objects of that type can be declared.

2.   Subprograms supplied with the type can be called.

3.   Two objects of that type can be compared for equality.

4.   Values of that type can be assigned to objects.

5.   Subprograms can be defined with parameters of the type.

If it is desirable to remove the possibility of assignment and (predefined) equality tests, then the type can be declared as being "limited private". If the type is to be extended, it may be defined as "tagged private" or "tagged limited private" (see Chapter 13).

The body of the above package would have the structure

```
package body Complex_Arithmetic is

   function "+"(X,Y : Complex) return Complex is
   begin
      return (X.Real + Y.Real, X.Imag + Y.Imag);
   end "+";

   function "-"(X,Y : Complex) return Complex is
   begin
      return (X.Real - Y.Real, X.Imag - Y.Imag);
   end "-";

   -- similarly for "*" and "/".

   function Comp(A,B : Float) return Complex is
   begin
      return (A,B);
   end Comp;

   function Real_Part(X : Complex) return Float is
   begin
      return X.Real;
   end Real_Part;

   -- similarly for Imag_Part.

end Complex_Arithmetic;
```

The clear distinction between specification and body should imply that the private part of a package specification is contained in the body, where it would be appropriately hidden. This would, however, make implementation very difficult due to the rules of separate compilation in Ada which allow a package specification to be used prior to the completion of the corresponding body.

If Complex_Arithmetic is a precompiled library unit, then an example of the use of the package takes the form:

```
with Complex_Arithmetic; use Complex_Arithmetic;
procedure Main is
   A,B,C : Complex;
```

```
      Signal : array (1..10) of Complex;
   begin
      A := Comp(0.0,1.0);
      B := A + Comp(1.0,1.0);
      C := (A + B)/A;
      -- note, A.Real := 1.0 would be illegal.
   end Main; --
```

The 'with' clause names the precompiled library unit (or units) upon which
Main is dependent. Only those units upon which there is a direct dependence
should be specified. Library units can themselves have 'with' clauses, thereby
supporting a hierarchy of dependencies. Clearly, the recompilation of any
unit necessitates the recompilation of all units that depend upon it.

   The 'use' clause provides direct visibility of declarations that appear in
the visible part of the named package. If the 'use' clause were omitted from
the above example, then the names of all objects from the package would
need to be prefixed by the package name, for example

```
   A,B,C : Complex_Arithmetic.Complex;
```

Separate compilation can also be achieved by the use of subunits which are
either package, subprogram, task (or protected object) bodies. A subunit is
removed from its immediate surrounding unit and compiled later:

```
   package body Complex_Arithmetic is
      function Comp(A,B : Float) return Complex is separate;
      ...
```

The separate compilation of this subunit (which must name its parent unit)
would take the form

```
   separate (Complex_Arithmetic)
   function Comp(A,B : Float) return Complex is
   begin
      return (A,B);
   end Comp;
```

Subunits provide for the top-down construction of programs; they also have
the facility for providing access to additional library units:

```
   with Lib_Unit;
   separate(Parent)
   procedure Inner(...) is
      ...
   end Inner;
```

Unless explicitly stated, no other part of Parent will have access to Lib_Unit.

The above is one example of child/parent relationships between library units. There is also an explicit parent/child structure. Given the declaration of a package with a private part, a child package is allowed access to these private declarations. Consider the package for complex arithmetic given above. If this is a library package, and it is necessary to add some I/O routines, a child package could be used:

```
package Complex_Arithmetic.IO is
  -- note name is parent.extension
  procedure put(C : Complex);
  procedure get(C : out Complex);
end Complex_Arithmetic.IO;
-- the body of this package has access
-- to the concrete representation of the
-- type in the private part of the parent
```

Note that by using a child package, extensive recompilation of client packages is not necessary.

The package construct provides both for decomposition and abstraction and it therefore has an important role in any design method. Module specification will invariably lead to package specification, and the 'implementation' of package bodies gives a natural partition to project work. The link between package specification and implementation is, however, merely a syntactical one: there are no formal means by which the semantics of the implementation can be specified using standard Ada. This shortcoming has led to the development of a number of methods for specifying the semantics of package and subprogram bodies. Two general approaches have been suggested: one involves the use of formal comments, the other uses additional subprograms to state precondition, postcondition and invariant properties of the implementation. Formal comments are, in effect, extensions to the language definition and may use Ada-like syntax or algebraic axioms. Subprograms have the advantage that they can be used during unit testing to check that the intended conditions are satisfied.

No book on concurrent programming would be complete without the bounded buffer example, and this book will be no exception. This example not only illustrates the use of packages and, later, generics but it is also relevant as the use of buffers is an important feature in concurrent programming. A bounded buffer is constructed as an array with two indices; one index indicates the next free slot on the array, the other indicates the slot containing the next object to be removed. As the array is of a fixed finite size, the indices must wrap around the array. For this reason, the structure is often called a *circular buffer*. Consider, first, a package that defines appropriate operations for a single buffer object (let Data be some type defined in library package Data_Decs):

```
with Data_Decs; use Data_Decs;
```

```
package Store is
  procedure Give(R : Data);
  procedure Take(R : out Data);
end Store;


package body Store is

  Size    : constant := 128;    -- size of buffer.
  subtype Vector_Range is Integer range 0 .. Size-1;
  Vector : array (Vector_Range) of Data;
  Top     : Vector_Range := 1; -- next free slot.
  Base    : Vector_Range := 1; -- slot containing next
                               -- Data to be removed.

  procedure Give(R : Data) is
  begin
    Vector(Top) := R;
    Top := (Top + 1) mod Size;
  end Give;

  procedure Take(R : out Data ) is
  begin
    R := Vector(Base);
    Base := (Base + 1) mod Size;
  end Take;

end Store;
```

This example clearly shows the data hiding properties of packages; neither
Vector, Top nor Base is accessible from outside the package. Only procedures
Give and Take are defined to be visible and therefore callable. As it stands,
the above code is unreliable, as attempts to take from an empty buffer or
place into a full one are not trapped. However, before considering exception
handling, the package specification will be expanded so that it allows more
than one buffer to be declared:

```
with Data_Decs; use Data_Decs;
package Store is
  type Buffer is limited private;
  procedure Give(R : Data; B : in out Buffer);
  procedure Take(R : out Data; B : in out Buffer);

private
  Size : constant := 128;
  subtype Vector_Range is Integer range 0..Size-1;
  type Vec is array (Vector_Range) of Data;
  type Buffer is
    record
      Vector : Vec;
      Top     : Vector_Range := 1;
```

```
         Base    : Vector_Range := 1;
      end record;
   end Store;
```

```
   package body Store is
      procedure Give(R : Data; B : in out Buffer) is
      begin
         B.Vector(B.Top) := R;
         B.Top := (B.Top + 1) mod Size;
      end Give;

      procedure Take(R : out Data; B : in out Buffer) is
      begin
         R := B.Vector(B.Base);
         B.Base := (B.Base + 1) mod Size;
      end Take;
   end Store;
```

Buffers can then be declared and used as follows:

```
   with Data_Decs;  use Data_Decs;
   with Store;  use Store;
   procedure Main is
      Buff1, Buff2 : Buffer;
      Buffers : array(1..64) of Buffer;
      Client : Data;
   begin
      -- produce value for Client
      Give(Client,Buff2);
      -- etc
   end Main;
```

As the above example shows, the package is a means of encapsulating related objects in a program. It is, nevertheless, a static and passive construct; it is strictly a compile-time facility that should exhibit no run-time overheads. The idea of a package is not new in programming languages. In fact, the class construct in SIMULA is probably the first example of such an abstraction mechanism. Following SIMULA, a number of Pascal derivatives have introduced some form of class/module structure; for example, Modula-2 has a module structure. The main criticism that can be levelled at the Ada package is its use of open scope rules, whereby all objects visible at the point of package declaration are automatically accessible outside the package. This is to be compared with Modula-2, where, in a module specification, all external objects that are used in the module have to be named explicitly in an "import list".

1.3   Generics

An essential feature of library units should be a generality which will allow them to be used over a wide range of applications. This generality can be achieved in a limited sense by the appropriate choice of subprogram parameters (with default values). However, the strong typing model of Ada prevents flexibility. Generics and type extensibility make possible the production of reusable software components and they represent important features of the Ada language.

A generic is a template (with parameters) from which instances of subprograms and packages can be constructed. This construction, or *instantiation* as it is usually called, involves the association of formal and calling parameters at compile time.

Generic instantiation is more powerful than mere macro expansion. A detailed analysis of the Ada model is, however, of only tangential significance to this book and will therefore not be undertaken. Rather, the bounded buffer example will be expanded so that the type Data becomes a generic parameter. Within the package Store, the only property of Data that is used is assignment and, therefore, within the package, Data acts as a private type; the specification of the generic package is thus

```
generic
   type Data is private;
package Store is
   type Buffer is limited private;
   procedure Give(R : Data; B : in out Buffer);
   procedure Take(R : out Data; B : in out Buffer);
private
   -- as before
end Store;
package body Store is separate; -- as before
```

From this generic specification, a package may be instantiated for any type other than one that is limited private:

```
type Date is
   record
      Day   : Integer range 1..31;
      Month : Integer range 1..12;
      Year  : Integer range 1066..2066;
   end record;
package Date_Store is new Store(Data => Date);
package Int_Store is new Store(Data => Integer);
Buff1, Buff2 : Int_Store.Buffer; -- two integer buffers
In_Tray : Date_Store.Buffer;     -- a single Date buffer
```

Buffer structures are important in concurrent programs and a generic package is a useful program component. However, in the above form it is unreliable for all but sequential programs as it does not protect itself against concurrent access.

1.4 Exception handling and type security

During the execution of a program, events or conditions may occur which might be considered 'exceptional'. With commercial or numerical computing, such conditions can be catered for by an appropriate run-time error message followed by program termination. This is not acceptable with embedded systems, where the software should be tolerant of both hardware and software faults. Two broad classifications of exception can be isolated:

- *Error conditions* — arithmetic overflow, storage exhaustion, array-bound violation, subrange violations, peripheral time-outs, etc.

- *Abnormal program condition* — errors in user input data, need for special algorithms to deal with singularities, etc.

In order to deal with error conditions, the run-time system must bring such errors to the program's attention — predefined exceptions are said to be raised. With abnormal program conditions, it is usual to raise exceptions explicitly within the software:

```
if Condition then raise Exception_Name; end if;
```

For both these situations, it is necessary for control to pass to a specified sequence of statements which is called the "exception handler". These exception handlers are separated, textually, from the place at which the error is raised so that the normal behaviour of the program is not obscured. The raised exception is, therefore, an up-market goto statement in many ways, and its widespread use can lead to the kind of unmaintainable spaghetti code that high level languages are designed to avoid. Because of this, Ada contains a limited form of exception handling that should really be used only for error conditions. For example, the Ada model of exceptions does not allow for an automatic return to the point of the error from within the exception handler.

Any program block (or subprogram) in Ada may contain handlers that can catch exceptions raised during the execution of that block, for example

```
declare
   Bad_Data : exception;  -- user-defined exception
begin
   -- sequence of statements containing:
   if Condition then raise Bad_Data; end if;
exception
   when Bad_Data =>
```

```
                    -- sequence of statements to be
                    -- executed if this exception is raised
              when Constraint_Error =>
                    -- handler for predefined exception
              when others => -- handler for all other exceptions
           end;
```

The optional handler 'others' is guaranteed to catch all exceptions raised
in the block (excluding those already mentioned and therefore explicitly
handled). Exception occurrences can then be used to find out which exception
has been raised (by calling some predefined routines in the library package
Ada.Exceptions):

```
        with Ada.Exceptions; use Ada.Exceptions;
        package body Example is
          procedure P is
          begin
             . . .

          exception
             -- Error is a defining identifier for an
             -- Exception_Occurrence; its scope is the
             -- associated handler
             when Error : others =>
                -- all these functions return a string value
                Put(Exception_Name(Error));
                Put(Exception_Message(Error));
                Put(Exception_Information(Error));
          end;
             . . .
        end Example;
```

When an exception is raised, the appropriate exception handler is executed
and the block terminates. If no handler is to be found in the local block,
then the exception is propagated to containing blocks (in the absence of
subprogram calls) until it is handled or, if there is no such handler in the
main program block (or task), the program (or task) itself terminates. Where
an exception is raised and not handled in a subprogram, the subprogram
is terminated and the named exception is raised again at the point of call
of that subprogram. In this way, the exception is propagated through the
dynamic chain of subprogram calls. If a user-defined exception goes out of
scope due to its propagation, then the exception becomes anonymous and
can only be caught with an 'others' handler.
    The bounded buffer example can now be expanded so that buffer over-
flow and underflow are managed by the use of exceptions. The package
specification now becomes

```
        package Store is
          type Buffer is limited private;
```

```
procedure Give(R : Data; B : in out Buffer);
procedure Take(R : out Data; B : in out Buffer);
Overflow, Underflow : exception;

private
  Size: constant := 128;
  subtype Vector_Range is Integer range 0..Size-1;
  type Vec is array (Vector_Range) of Data;
  type Buffer is
    record
      Vector     : Vec;
      Top, Base  : Vector_Range := 1;
      Contents   : Integer range 0..Size := 0;
    end record;
end Store;
```

Within the body of Store, the procedures Give and Take would now have the form:

```
procedure Give(R : Data; B : in out Buffer) is
begin
  if B.Contents = Size then raise Overflow; end if;
  B.Vector(B.Top) := R;
  B.Top := (B.Top + 1) mod Size;
  B.Contents := B.Contents + 1;
end Give;

procedure Take(R : out Data; B : in out Buffer) is
begin
  if B.Contents = 0 then raise Underflow; end if;
  R := B.Vector(B.Base);
  B.Base := (B.Base + 1) mod Size;
  B.Contents := B.Contents - 1;
end Take;
```

It is thus the responsibility of the user of this package to trap overflow and underflow exceptions:

```
declare
  A_Data : Data := ...;
  Temp_Data : Data;
    -- if the buffer is full, an element
    -- will be taken off and ''thrown away"
begin
  Store.Give(A_Data,A_Buffer);
exception
  when Store.Overflow =>
    Store.Take(Temp_Data,A_Buffer);
    Store.Give(A_Data,A_Buffer);
end;
```

The package Store illustrates an interesting 'feature' of the interaction between exceptions and packages. In the specification of Store there are

two subprograms and two exceptions and yet without some comments it is
not possible to know which exceptions can be raised by which subprograms
unless one looks into the body of the package. This is clearly against the
philosophy of packages and is a genuine problem with large library units.
For example, Text_IO (the predefined library package for file-oriented input
and output) has over eighty subprograms and eight exceptions. Obviously,
not all exceptions can be raised by each subprogram but unless 'others' is
used to catch all exceptions, an overelaborate handler must be associated
with all subprogram calls.

1.4.1   Type security and errors

One of the objectives of a strongly-typed language is to ensure that all
programmer errors are detected prior to execution. Typically, the compiler
will reject all programs that fail to conform to the language definition. Good
compilers will, in addition, give some indication as to why compilation has
failed. Although it is clearly beneficial to ensure that the maximum number
of errors are detected in this way, it is not possible to catch all software
faults at compile time. For run-time errors, Ada recognises three separate
classes:

- those that must raise an exception;
- those that have a bounded number of possible effects; and
- those that can lead to totally erroneous behaviour.

Most errors, such as divide by zero, subrange violation, etc., give rise to
exceptions. If all executions of some program are bound to cause an
exception to be raised, then a good compiler should provide a warning, but
it must still generate code for the program.

Bounded errors may not be recognised at run-time but the effects of the
error are limited, and are defined on a per error basis. For example, it is
a bounded error to raise an unhandled exception during finalisation of a
controlled type. If this happens, then an implementation must define the
possible consequences. One of the allowable behaviours is the raising of the
exception Program_Error; others are allowed but must be defined.

Unfortunately, there is still a class of errors that cannot be bounded. If they
occur then all bets are off: the effect is not predictable. Ada has, however,
attempted to reduce to an absolute minimum the number of situations that
can give rise to erroneous program behaviour.

Of course, there is a further type of error — the program works perfectly
(at least in language terms) but produces incorrect results! Although a
language definition cannot prevent the production of such programs, having
sufficient expressive power, and ease of use, within the language will reduce
the frequency with which they occur. Concurrent programming is perhaps

more susceptible than other forms of programming to error-prone program design. The tasking model of Ada is intended to facilitate correct concurrent programming. This book is intended to facilitate a correct understanding of the tasking model.

1.5 Further reading

J.G.P. Barnes, *Programming in Ada Plus an Overview of Ada 9X*, 4th Edition, Addison-Wesley, Wokingham, 1994.
J. Skansholm, *Ada from the Beginning*, 2nd edition, Addison-Wesley, Workingham, 1994.

Chapter 2

The Nature and Uses of Concurrent Programming

Any language, natural or computer, has the dual property of enabling expression whilst at the same time limiting the framework within which that expressive power may be applied. If a language does not support a particular notion or concept, then those that use the language cannot apply that notion and may even be totally unaware of its existence. Pascal, FORTRAN and COBOL share the common property of being sequential languages. Programs written in these languages have a single thread of control. They start executing in some state and then proceed, by executing one statement at a time, until the program terminates. The path through the program may differ due to variations in input data, but for any particular execution of the program there is only one path.

A modern computer system will, by comparison, consist of one or more central processors and many I/O devices, all of which are operating in parallel. Moreover, an operating system that provides for interactive use will always support many executing programs (called processes), in the sense that they are being time-sliced onto the available processors. The effect of fast process switching is to give behaviour that is almost indistinguishable from true parallelism. In the programming of embedded systems, one must deal with the inherent parallelism of the larger system. A real-time language must therefore provide some facility for multi-programming. This can be achieved by specifying a standard interface to a multi-processing operating system or by allowing multiple process systems to be expressed in the language itself.

Ada provides for the direct programming of parallel activities. Within an Ada program there may be a number of tasks, each of which has its own thread of control. It is thus possible to match the parallel nature of the application area with syntactical forms that reflect these structures. This has proved to be an invaluable aid in the production of clear and correct software. Languages whose conceptual framework includes parallelism are known as *concurrent programming languages*. Ada is such a language but it is by no means the first (or last!); for example Modula, CHILL, Mesa, CSP, PEARL, occam and LINDA all deal with concurrency, although in radically different ways. In addition to these procedural languages there are also functional, logic-based and data-flow languages available for the specification and implementation of concurrent systems.

In general, each individual thread of control within a concurrent program is known as a *process*, although Ada uses the term *task*. No distinction is made, in this book, between tasks and processes. The execution of a process usually takes one of three forms:

1. All processes may share a single processor.

2. Each process may have its own processor and the processors share common memory.

3. Each process may have its own processor and the processors are distributed (i.e. they are connected by a communications network).

Hybrids of these three methods are also evident. Ada is designed for all the above situations. Because of the different implementation methods, the term *concurrent*, rather then *parallel*, is of more use in this area of computing. Two processes are said to be executing in *parallel* if at any instant they are both executing. Therefore, in the above classifications only cases 2 and 3 are truly parallel.

By comparison, two processes are said to be *concurrent* if they have the potential for executing in parallel. A concurrent program is thus one that has more than one thread of control. Execution of this program will, if processors are available, run each of these threads of control in parallel. Otherwise each of the threads will be interleaved. The important concept is therefore concurrency (as it encompasses all three of the above cases) rather than whether, or not, the implementation of concurrency involves parallelism or pseudo-parallelism. A correct concurrent program will execute in accordance with its functional specification on all three platforms. Only its performance should change, perhaps dramatically, as the nature of the hardware is altered:

> Concurrent programming is the name given to programming notation and techniques for expressing potential parallelism and for solving the resulting synchronisation and communication problems. Implementation of parallelism is a topic in computer systems (hardware and software) that is essentially independent of concurrent programming. Concurrent programming is important because it provides an abstract setting in which to study parallelism without getting bogged down in the implementation details. (Ben-Ari, 1982)

The problems of synchronisation and communication are considered in the next chapter.

2.1   Uses of concurrent programming

Concurrency is used extensively in the programming of embedded systems. A system is also *real-time* if its specification has time-dependent features. Virtually all embedded systems are inherently parallel; the software must therefore control the simultaneous operations of the coexisting hardware components. Typically, this is achieved by associating with each external device a process that controls the input and output operations of that device. These processes, together with the necessary internal data management processes, comprise the software model. Embedded systems themselves are to be found in a wide variety of applications, for example:

*   process control;

*   air traffic control;

*   avionics systems;

*   industrial robots;

*   engine controllers;

*   domestic appliances;

*   environmental monitors;

*   command and control systems.

The implementation of these multi-task systems can be achieved by integrating sequential programs, but this necessitates the support of an underlying operating system that will map the programs onto the processes and allow data communication. The use of a concurrent programming language may, however, preclude operating system support, in which case the run-time system of the language implementation must control scheduling, and data communication (plus synchronisation) is programmed directly in the language.

Concurrency is also of value in mapping software efficiently onto multi-processor hardware to exploit the properties of concurrent algorithms. For instance, the need to sort 10,000 objects (a standard sequential problem) may be more effectively undertaken as ten parallel processes, each sorting 1,000 objects, followed by a merge operation. Here the distinction between true and pseudo-parallelism is important: the above algorithm will almost certainly be less efficient than a standard approach if the processes are time-sliced onto a single processor. The hardware architecture can therefore have a serious effect upon certain non-functional aspects of the portability of concurrent programs.

It should be noted that concurrent programming is not the only way of exploiting parallel hardware. Array and vector processors are better utilised by having access to concurrent operators such as vector addition. Also, certain dataflow machines require a completely different computational model. None the less, concurrent programming does represent one of the main ways of gaining access to standard multi-processor hardware.

Software engineering principles indicate that the implementation languages should, wherever possible, mimic the structure of the application domain. If the application contains inherent parallelism, then the design and construction of the software product will be less error-prone, easier to prove correct and easier to adapt if concurrency is available in the design and implementation languages. Two examples of this type of use of Ada are in the development of information processing system prototypes and dialogue control systems. In the first of these, a data-flow description of an information processing system consists, primarily, of tasks (where information is processed) and data-flows which link these tasks. The transformation of this description into a series of sequential programs is time consuming and error-prone. With a concurrent language such as Ada, the implementation is straightforward and can be undertaken almost automatically.

A dialogue control system, DCS, enables the application software (which may be multi-tasking) and the user interface implementation to be designed separately and programmed as concurrent objects. The DCS provides a flexible multi-levelled interface, which can be used by the application software to interact with the human users of the system. This is achieved by allowing the tasks in the application software to communicate, in a controlled way, with the tasks in the DCS. This logic naturally extends to viewing the software, the interface and the user as concurrent elements of the same system.

These two quite different examples indicate that concurrent programming is not just concerned with coding embedded systems but is quite a fundamental language structure. The wide availability and use of Ada will allow programmers from many differing application domains to have available, if necessary, concurrent programming facilities. It is therefore important that all users of Ada understand the tasking model.

2.2 Program entities

The object-oriented programming paradigm encourages system (and program) builders to consider the artifact under construction as a collection of co-operating objects (or, to use a more neutral term, *entities*). Within this paradigm it is constructive to consider two kinds of object — active and reactive. Active objects undertake spontaneous actions (with the help of a processor): they enable the computation to proceed. Reactive objects, by comparison, only perform actions when 'invoked' by an active object. Other programming paradigms, such as data-flow or real-time networks, identify active agents and passive data.

The Ada language itself does not prescribe a specific programming paradigm, and it is not the intention of this book to present just a single model. Rather, we take a more abstract view: an Ada program is deemed to consist of (be populated by) active entities, resource entities and passive entities.

Only active entities give rise to spontaneous actions. Resources are reactive but can control access to their internal states (and any real resources they control). Some resources can only be used by one agent at a time; in other cases the operations that can be carried out at a given time depend on the resources' current states. A common example of the latter is a data buffer whose elements cannot be extracted if it is empty. The term *passive* will be used to indicate a reactive entity that can allow open access.

The implementation of resource entities requires some form of control agent. If the control agent is itself passive (such as a semaphore), then the resource is said to be protected. Alternatively, if an active agent is required to program the correct level of control, then the resource is in some sense active. The term *server* will be used to identify this type of entity, and the term *protected resource* to indicate the passive kind. These, together with *active* and *passive*, are the four abstract program entities used in this book.

In a concurrent programming language, active entities are represented by processes. Passive entities can be represented either directly as data variables or they can be encapsulated by some module/package construct that provides a procedural interface. Protected resources may also be encapsulated in a module-like construct and require the availability of a low level synchronisation facility. Servers, because they need to program the control agent, require a process.

A key question for language designers is whether to support primitives for both protected resources and servers. Resources, because they typically use a low level control agent, are normally efficient (at least on single-processor systems). But they can be inflexible and lead to poor program structures for some classes of problem (this is discussed further in the next chapter). Servers, because the control agent is programmed using a process, are eminently flexible. The drawback of this approach is that it can lead to proliferation of processes, with a resulting high number of context switches during execution. This is particularly problematic if the language does not support protected resources and hence servers must be used for all such entities.

Ada 83 only supported the single notion of a **task**; thus active and all control entities were encoded in tasks. The current version of Ada, by comparison, has introduced a new abstraction for resource entities — the **protected type**. An object of such a type can control access to the data it protects but does not have a thread of control. Thus resources should be coded as protected objects, with tasks being used for active objects and servers. The design of a concurrent Ada program must therefore incorporate early recognition of the key active, passive, resource (protected) and server entities and use the appropriate Ada language features for representing their required behaviour directly.

2.3 Process representation

Various notations are used to specify the concurrent components of a program, and different methods are also employed to indicate when a process should start executing and when it should terminate. Coroutines were one of the first methods of expressing concurrency, although the coroutines themselves cannot actually execute in parallel. A coroutine is structured like a procedure; at any one time a single coroutine is executing, with control being passed to another coroutine by means of the **resume** statement. The scheduling of the coroutines is therefore explicitly expressed in the program. A resumed coroutine continues executing, from its last executing state, until it again encounters a resume statement. The resume statement itself names the coroutine to be resumed.

Coroutines have been used, primarily, in discrete event simulation languages such as SIMULA, although they are also supported in Modula-2. Because coroutines are not adequate for true parallel processing they are not available in Ada. Instead, Ada, like many other concurrent programming languages, uses a direct representation of process which, as has been noted, is called a task. Moreover, the execution of a task is started, in effect, by the scope rules of the language. This is in contrast to languages such a Algol68, CSP and occam where execution is started by a *cobegin .. coend* or *Par* structure, for example

```
cobegin
    P1; P2; P3;
coend;
```

will cause the concurrent execution of processes P1, P2 and P3.

A detailed examination of task declaration is given in Chapter 4. However, a more informal description will be of use at this stage. Consider the following program skeleton:

```
procedure Main is
    task A;
    task B; -- two tasks have been declared and named.
    .
    .
    .
    task body A is separate; -- implementation of task A.
    task body B is separate;

begin
```

```
      -- A and B are now both executing concurrently.
         .
         .
         .
      end Main;
```

The task has a similar syntactical structure to that of the package. In the sequence of statements of procedure Main, three concurrent objects are executing: the two tasks (A and B) and the statements of the procedure. The procedure will itself only terminate when all these statements have been executed and the two tasks have terminated. Execution of tasks A and B is deemed to commence immediately after **begin**, that is, before any of the statements of Main.

2.4   A simple embedded system

In order to illustrate some of the advantages and disadvantages of concurrent programming, a simple embedded system will now be considered. Figure 2.1 outlines this simple system: a process T takes readings from a set of thermocouples (via an analogue to digital converter, ADC) and makes appropriate changes to a heater (via a digitally controlled switch). Process P has a similar function, but for pressure (it uses a digital to analogue converter, DAC). Both T and P must communicate data to S, which presents measurements to an operator via a screen. Note that P and T are active entities; S is a resource (it just responds to requests from T and P): it may be implemented as a protected resource or a server if it interacts more extensively with the user.

The overall objective of this embedded system is to keep the temperature and pressure of some chemical process within defined limits. A real system of this type would clearly be more complex — allowing, for example, the operator to change the limits. However, even for this simple system, implementation could take one of three forms:

1.   A single program is used which ignores the logical concurrency of T, P and S. No operating system support is required.

2.   T, P and S are written in a sequential programming language (either as separate programs or distinct procedures in the same program) and operating system primitives are used for program/process creation and interaction.

3.   A single concurrent program is used which retains the logical structure of T, P and S. No direct operating system support is required by the program although a run-time support system is needed.

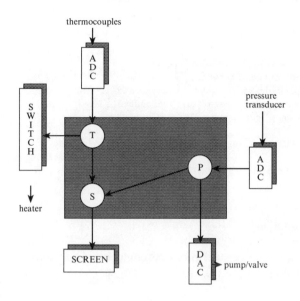

Figure 2.1: A Simple Embedded System

To illustrate these solutions consider the Ada code to implement the simple embedded system. In order to simplify the structure of the control software, the following passive packages will be assumed to have been implemented:

```
package Data_Types is
   -- necessary type definitions
   type Temp_Reading is new Integer range 10..500;
   type Pressure_Reading is new Integer range 0..750;
   type Heater_Setting is (On, Off);
   type Pressure_Setting is new Integer range 0..9;
end Data_Types;
```

```
with Data_Types; use Data_Types;
package IO is
   -- procedures for data exchange with the environment
   procedure Read(TR : out Temp_Reading); -- from ADC
   procedure Read(PR : out Pressure_Reading);
      -- note, this is an example of overloading; two reads
      -- are defined but they have a different parameter type;
      -- this is also the case with the following writes
   procedure Write(HS : Heater_Setting);   -- to switch.
   procedure Write(PS : Pressure_Setting); -- to DAC
```

```
      procedure Write(TR : Temp_Reading);      -- to screen
      procedure Write(PR : Pressure_Reading); -- to screen
   end IO;
```

```
   with Data_Types; use Data_Types;
   package Control_Procedures is
      -- procedures for converting a reading into
      -- an appropriate setting for output.
      procedure Temp_Convert(TR : Temp_Reading;
                             HS : out Heater_Setting);
      procedure Pressure_Convert(PR : Pressure_Reading;
                                 PS : out Pressure_Setting);
   end Control_Procedures;
```

Sequential solution

A simple sequential control program could have the following structure (it is known as a *cyclic executive*):

```
   with Data_Types; use Data_Types;
   with IO; use IO;
   with Control_Procedures; use Control_Procedures;
   procedure Controller is
      TR : Temp_Reading;
      PR : Pressure_Reading;
      HS : Heater_Setting;
      PS : Pressure_Setting;
   begin
      loop
         Read(TR);      -- from ADC.
         Temp_Convert(TR,HS); -- convert reading to setting
         Write(HS);     -- to switch.
         Write(TR);     -- to screen.
         Read(PR);      -- as above for pressure
         Pressure_Convert(PR,PS);
         Write(PS);
         Write(PR);
      end loop; -- infinite loop, common in embedded software
   end Controller;
```

This code has the immediate handicap that temperature and pressure readings must be taken at the same rate, which may not be in accordance with requirements. The use of counters and appropriate **if** statements will improve the situation, but it may still be necessary to split the computationally intensive sections (the conversion procedures Temp_Convert and Pressure_Convert) into a number of distinct actions, and interleave these actions so as to meet a required balance of work. Even if this were done, there remains a serious drawback with this program structure: while waiting to read a temperature no attention can be given to pressure (and vice versa). Moreover, if there is a system failure that results in, say, control never returning from the temperature Read, then in addition to this problem no further pressure Reads would be taken.

An improvement on this sequential program can be made by including two boolean functions in the package IO, Ready_Temp and Ready_Pres, to indicate the availability of an item to read. The control program then becomes

```
with Data_Types; use Data_Types;
with IO; use IO;
with Control_Procedures; use Control_Procedures;
procedure Controller is
  TR : Temp_Reading;
  PR : Pressure_Reading;
  HS : Heater_Setting;
  PS : Pressure_Setting;
  Ready_Temp, Ready_Pres : Boolean;
begin
  loop
    ...
    if Ready_Temp then
      Read(TR);
      Temp_Convert(TR,HS);
      Write(HS);    -- assuming write to be reliable.
      Write(TR);
    end if;
    if Ready_Pres then
      Read(PR);
      Pressure_Convert(PR,PS);
      Write(PS);
      Write(PR);
    end if;
  end loop;
end Controller;
```

This solution is more reliable; unfortunately the program now spends a high proportion of its time in a 'busy loop' polling the input devices to see if they are ready. Busy-waits are, in general, unacceptably inefficient. They tie up the processor and make it very difficult to impose a queue discipline on waiting requests. Moreover, programs that rely on busy-waiting are difficult to design, understand or prove correct.

The major criticism that can be levelled at the sequential program is that no recognition is given to the fact that the pressure and temperature cycles are entirely independent subsystems.

Using operating system primitives

All operating systems provide facilities for creating concurrent processes. Usually, these processes execute a single sequential program; however in recent years there has been a tendency to provide the facilities for processes to be created from within programs. Modern operating systems allow processes created from within the same program to have unrestricted access to shared memory (such processes are often called *threads*).

Consider a simple operating system which allows a new process/thread to be created and started by calling the following subprograms:

```
package Operating_System_Interface is
  type Thread_ID is private;
  type Thread is access procedure;

  function Create_Thread(Code : Thread) return Thread_ID;
  procedure Start(ID : Thread_ID);
  -- other subprograms for thread interaction
private
  type Thread_ID is ...;
end Operating_System_Interface;
```

The simple embedded system can now be implemented as follows:

```
with Data_Types; use Data_Types;
with IO; use IO;
with Control_Procedures; use Control_Procedures;
with Operating_System_Interface;
use Operating_System_Interface;
procedure Controller is

  TC, PC : Thread_ID;

  procedure Temp_Controller is
    TR : Temp_Reading; HS : Heater_Setting;
  begin
    loop
      Read(TR);
      Temp_Convert(TR,HS);
      Write(HS);
      Write(TR);
    end loop;
  end Temp_Controller;

  procedure Pressure_Controller is
    PR : Pressure_Reading; PS : Pressure_Setting;
  begin
    loop
      Read(PR);
      Pressure_Convert(PR,PS);
```

```
        Write(PS);
        Write(PR);
      end loop;
    end Pressure_Controller;

begin
    TC := Create_Thread(Temp_Controller'Access);
    PC := Create_Thread(Pressure_Controller'Access);
    Start(TC);
    Start(PC);
end Controller;
```

Procedures Temp_Controller and Pressure_Controller execute concurrently and each contains an indefinite loop within which the control cycle is defined. While one thread is suspended waiting for a read, the other may be executing; if they are both suspended a busy loop is not executed.

Although this solution does have advantages over the cyclic executive solution, the lack of language support for expressing concurrency means that the program can become difficult to write and maintain. For the simple example given above, the added complexity is manageable. However, for large systems with many concurrent processes and potentially complex interactions between them, having a procedural interface obscures the structure of the program. For example, it is not obvious which procedures are really procedures or which ones are intended to be concurrent activities.

Using a concurrent programming language

In a concurrent programming language, concurrent activities can be identified explicitly in the code:

```
with Data_Types; use Data_Types;
with IO; use IO;
with Control_Procedures; use Control_Procedures;
procedure Controller is
    task Temp_Controller;
    task Pressure_Controller;

    task body Temp_Controller is
      TR : Temp_Reading; HS : Heater_Setting;
    begin
      loop
        Read(TR);
        Temp_Convert(TR,HS);
        Write(HS);
        Write(TR);
      end loop;
    end Temp_Controller;

    task body Pressure_Controller is
```

```
       PR : Pressure_Reading; PS : Pressure_Setting;
    begin
      loop
        Read(PR);
        Pressure_Convert(PR,PS);
        Write(PS);
        Write(PR);
      end loop;
    end Pressure_Controller;

  begin
    null;    -- Temp_Controller and Pressure_Controller
             -- have started their executions
  end Controller;
```

The logic of the application is now reflected in the code; the inherent parallelism of the domain is represented by concurrently executing tasks in the program. Note that if the Read operations are non-blocking (e.g. they involve only the reading of a memory mapped register), then each task can be defined to work at a specific rate. A refinement to the code to achieve this is illustrated at the end of this chapter.

Although an improvement, one major problem remains with this two-task solution. Both Temp_Controller and Pressure_Controller send data to the screen, but the screen is a resource that can only sensibly be accessed by one process at a time. In Figure 2.1, control over the screen was given to a third entity (S) which will need a representation in the program — Screen_Controller. This entity may be a server or a protected resource (depending on the complete definition of the required behaviour of Screen_Controller). This has transposed the problem from one of concurrent access to a non-concurrent resource to one of inter-task communication, or at least communication between a task and some other concurrency primitive. It is necessary for tasks Temp_Controller and Pressure_Controller to pass data to Screen_Controller. Moreover, Screen_Controller must ensure that it deals with only one request at a time. These requirements and difficulties are of primary importance in the design of concurrent programming languages. Therefore, before considering in detail how Ada faces these problems, the next chapter will concentrate on inter-process communication and what structures other concurrent languages have employed.

Operating systems defined versus language defined concurrency

There has been a long debate amongst programmers, language designers and operating system designers as to whether it is appropriate to provide support for concurrency in a language or whether this should be provided by the operating system only. Arguments in favour of including concurrency in the programming languages include the following:

1.   It leads to more readable and maintainable programs.

2. There are many different types of operating system; defining the concurrency in the language makes the program more. portable

3. An embedded computer may not have any resident operating system available.

Arguments against concurrency in a language include the following:

1. Different languages have different models of concurrency; it is easier to compose programs from different languages if they all use the same operating system model of concurrency.

2. it may be difficult to implement a language's model of concurrency efficiently on top of an operating system's model.

3. Operating system standards are beginning to merge and therefore programs become more portable.

This debate will no doubt continue for some time. The Ada philosophy is that the advantages outweigh the disadvantages, and it therefore supports concurrency directly at the language level.

2.5   Clocks and time

This chapter concludes with a discussion of clocks and time. Many embedded systems need to coordinate their executions with the natural time of the environment in which they are executing. To do this they use a hardware clock that approximates the passage of real-time. For long running programs (i.e. years of non-stop execution) this clock may need to be resynchronised to some external authority (such as International Atomic Time) but from the program's point of view the clock is the source of *real* time.

Ada provides access to this clock by providing two packages. The main section of the ARM (Ada Reference Manual) defines a compulsory library package called Ada.Calendar that provides an abstraction for "wall clock" time that recognises leap years, leap seconds and other adjustments. In the Real-Time Systems Annex, a second representation is given that defines a monotonic (i.e. non-decreasing) regular clock (package Ada.Real_Time). Both these representations should map down to the same hardware clock but cater for different application needs.

First consider package Ada.Calendar:

```
package Ada.Calendar is

   type Time is private;

   subtype Year_Number is Integer range 1901..2099;
   subtype Month_Number is Integer range 1..12;
```

```
subtype Day_Number is Integer range 1..31;
subtype Day_Duration is Duration range 0.0..86_400.0;

function Clock return Time;

function Year(Date:Time) return Year_Number;
function Month(Date:Time) return Month_Number;
function Day(Date:Time) return Day_Number;
function Seconds(Date:Time) return Day_Duration;

procedure Split(Date:in Time; Year:out Year_Number;
                Month:out Month_Number; Day:out Day_Number;
                Seconds:out Day_Duration);

function Time_Of(Year:Year_Number; Month:Month_Number;
                Day:Day_Number;
                Seconds:Day_Duration := 0.0) return Time;

function "+"(Left:Time;Right:Duration) return Time;
function "+"(Left:Duration;Right:Time) return Time;
function "-"(Left:Time;Right:Duration) return Time;
function "-"(Left:Time;Right:Time) return Duration;

function "<"(Left,Right:Time) return Boolean;
function "<="(Left,Right:Time) return Boolean;
function ">"(Left,Right:Time) return Boolean;
function ">="(Left,Right:Time) return Boolean;

Time_Error:exception;
-- Time_Error may be raised by
-- Time_Of, Split, Year, "+" and "-"

private
   -- implementation-dependent
end Ada.Calendar;
```

A value of the private type Time is a combination of the date and the time of day, where the time of day is given in seconds from midnight. Seconds are described in terms of a subtype Day_Duration which is, in turn, defined by means of Duration. This fixed point type Duration is one of the predefined Scalar types and has a range which, although implementation dependent, must be at least -86_400.0 .. +86_400.0. The value 86_400 is the number of seconds in a day. The accuracy of Duration is also implementation dependent but the smallest representable value (Duration'Small) must not be greater than 20 milliseconds (it is recommended that it is no greater than 100 microseconds).

The current time is returned by the function Clock. Conversion between Time and program accessible types such as Year_Number is provided by subprograms Split and Time_Of. In addition, some arithmetic and boolean operations are specified. Package Calendar therefore defines an appropriate

structure for an abstract data type for time.
The other package has a similar form:

```
package Ada.Real_Time is
  type Time is private;
  Time_First: constant Time;
  Time_Last: constant Time;
  Time_Unit: constant := -- implementation-defined-real-number;

  type Time_Span is private;
  Time_Span_First: constant Time_Span;
  Time_Span_Last: constant Time_Span;
  Time_Span_Zero: constant Time_Span;
  Time_Span_Unit: constant Time_Span;

  Tick: constant Time_Span;
  function Clock return Time;

  function "+" (Left: Time; Right: Time_Span) return Time;
  function "+" (Left: Time_Span; Right: Time) return Time;
  function "-" (Left: Time; Right: Time_Span) return Time;
  function "-" (Left: Time; Right: Time) return Time_Span;

  function "<" (Left, Right: Time) return Boolean;
  function "<="(Left, Right: Time) return Boolean;
  function ">" (Left, Right: Time) return Boolean;
  function ">="(Left, Right: Time) return Boolean;

  function "+" (Left, Right: Time_Span) return Time_Span;
  function "-" (Left, Right: Time_Span) return Time_Span;
  function "-" (Right: Time_Span) return Time_Span;
  function "/" (Left,Right : Time_Span) return Integer;
  function "/" (Left : Time_Span; Right : Integer)
          return Time_Span;
  function "*" (Left : Time_Span; Right : Integer)
          return Time_Span;
  function "*" (Left : Integer; Right : Time_Span)
          return Time_Span;

  function "<" (Left, Right: Time_Span) return Boolean;
  function "<="(Left, Right: Time_Span) return Boolean;
  function ">" (Left, Right: Time_Span) return Boolean;
  function ">="(Left, Right: Time_Span) return Boolean;

  function "abs"(Right : Time_Span) return Time_Span;

  function To_Duration (Ts : Time_Span) return Duration;
  function To_Time_Span (D : Duration) return Time_Span;

  function Nanoseconds  (Ns: Integer) return Time_Span;
  function Microseconds (Us: Integer) return Time_Span;
  function Milliseconds (Ms: Integer) return Time_Span;
```

```
type Seconds_Count is range -- implementation-defined

procedure Split(T : in Time; Sc: out Seconds_Count;
                Ts : out Time_Span);
   function Time_Of(Sc: Seconds_Count; Ts: Time_Span) return Time;

private
   -- not specified by the language
end Ada.Real_Time;
```

The Real_Time.Time type represents real time values as they are returned
by Real_Time.Clock. The constant Time_Unit is the smallest amount of
time representable by the Time type. The value of Tick must be no greater
than one millisecond; the range of Time (from the epoch that represents the
program's start-up) must be at least fifty years. Other important features of
this time abstraction are described in the Real-Time Systems Annex; it is
not necessary, for our purposes, to consider them in detail here.

In summary; both packages provide an abstractions for time and clock. In
addition, Calendar uses conversions to type Duration, whereas Real_Time
uses Time_Span.

To illustrate how these packages could be used, consider the following
code which tests to see if some time-critical sequence of statements executes
within 1.7 seconds:

```
declare
   Start, Finish : Time;   -- Ada.Calendar.Time
   Interval : Duration := 1.7;
begin
   Start := Clock;
   -- sequence of statements.
   Finish := Clock;
   if Finish - Start > Interval then
      raise Overrun_Error;   -- a user-defined exception.
   end if;
end;
```

The above code fragment would also execute correctly with the real-time
clock if Interval were declared as follows:

```
Interval : Time_Span := To_Time_Span(1.7);
             -- for use with Ada.Real_Time.Time
```

2.5.1   Delay primitives

As well as having access to a real-time clock, tasks must also be able to
delay themselves for a period of time. This enables a task to be queued on
some future event rather than busy-wait on calls to a Clock function:

```
-- busy-wait to delay ten seconds.
Start := Clock;
loop
   exit when Clock - Start > 10.0; -- or To_Time_Span(10.0)
end loop;
```

Ada provides an explicit *delay statement*:

```
delay 10.0;
```

The expression following 'delay' must yield a value of the predefined type Duration. It is important to appreciate that 'delay' is an approximate time construct, the inclusion of which in a task indicates that the task will be delayed by at least the amount specified. There is no upper bound given on the actual delay, although it may be possible to calculate one from an understanding of the implementation of delay and the clock. The significant point is that the delay cannot be less than that given in the delay statement.

The use of delay supports a relative time period (i.e. ten seconds from now). If a delay to an absolute time is required, then the *delay until* statement should be used. For example, if an action should take place ten seconds after the start of some other action, then the following code should be used (with Ada.Calendar):

```
Start := Clock;
First_Action;
Start := Start + 10.0;
delay until Start;
Second_Action;
```

Note that this is *not* the same as

```
Start := Clock;
First_Action;
Start := Start + 10.0;
delay 10.0 - (Clock - Start);
Second_Action;
```

In order for this second formulation to have the same behaviour as the first, then

```
delay 10.0 - (Clock - Start);
```

would have to be an uninterruptible action, which it is not. For example, if First_Action took two seconds to complete, then

```
10.0 - (Clock - Start);
```

would equate to eight seconds. But after having calculated this value, if the task involved is preempted by some other task it could be three seconds (say) before it next executes. At that time it will delay for eight seconds rather than five. The delay_until formulation does not suffer from this problem, and it can be used with time values from either clock package.

As with delay, delay_until is accurate only in its lower bound. The task involved will not be released before the current time has reached that specified in the statement but it may be released later.

2.5.2   Periodic activities

Another temporal issue concerns repeated (or periodic) activities. Consider task T:

```
task body T is
begin
  loop
     Action;
     delay 5.0;
  end loop;
end T;
```

Here Action must not be called twice in any five-second interval. Two subsequent calls may, however, be separated by any time interval greater than this value. If a five-second interval is desired, the time overrun is called *local drift* — it cannot be eliminated using normal Ada constructs. The time taken to execute the above loop in task T consists of, at least, five seconds plus the execution time of Action plus a small overhead for the loop (a jump instruction). If Action should be called at regular five-second intervals, then on each iteration of the loop there will be an addition to a *cumulative drift*. This can be eliminated by using **delay until** to delay for less than five seconds following an overrun (again using Ada.Calendar):

```
task body T is
   Interval : constant Duration := 5.0;
   Next_Time : Time;
begin
   Next_Time := Clock + Interval;
   loop
      Action;
      delay until Next_Time;
      Next_Time := Next_Time + Interval;
   end loop;
end T;
```

This removes cumulative drift but not local drift.

Consider the simple embedded system example described earlier. Assume that the sensor reads are non-blocking and that the controllers should execute periodically. Let the pressure controller, Pressure_Controller, have a required period of 30ms; as the temperature in the environment changes slowly, a period of 70ms is adequate for the temperature controller, Temp_Controller. The code (without Screen_Controller) is as follows:

```
with Ada.Real_Time;
with Data_Types; use Data_Types;
with IO; use IO;
with Control_Procedures; use Control_Procedures;
procedure Controller is
  task Temp_Controller;
  task Pressure_Controller;

  task body Temp_Controller is
    TR : Temp_Reading; HS : Heater_Setting;
    Next : Ada.Real_Time.Time;
    Interval : Ada.Real_Time.Time_Span := To_Time_Span(0.03);
  begin
    Next := Ada.Real_Time.Clock;   -- start time
    loop
      Read(TR);
      Temp_Convert(TR,HS);
      Write(HS);
      Write(TR);
      Next := Next + Interval;
      delay until Next;
    end loop;
  end Temp_Controller;


  task body Pressure_Controller is
    PR : Pressure_Reading; PS : Pressure_Setting;
    Next : Ada.Real_Time.Time;
    Interval : Ada.Real_Time.Time_Span := To_Time_Span(0.07);
  begin
    Next := Ada.Real_Time.Clock;   -- start time
    loop
      Read(PR);
      Pressure_Convert(PR,PS);
      Write(PS);
      Write(PR);
      Next := Next + Interval;
      delay until Next;
    end loop;
  end Pressure_Controller;
begin
  null;
end Controller;
```

2.6   Summary

A definition of concurrency has been given in this chapter, and a comparison has been made between concurrency and parallelism. Many uses of concurrency have been outlined. A model of a concurrent program has been given, in which active, passive, protected and server entities are defined. Issues of process representation and implementation have been illustrated by the use of an example of an embedded real-time system.

The chapter was concluded by a discussion of clocks and time. Ada provides a standard package for access to a clock function and an abstract data type for time. An implementation may also support a real-time package that supports a monotonic, fine grain clock. Ada also defines a delay statement that allows a task to delay itself for an absolute or relative period of time.

Chapter 3 ———————————————

Inter-Process Communication

The major difficulties associated with concurrent programming arise from process interaction. Rarely are processes as independent of one another as they were in the simple examples of the previous chapter. One of the main objectives of embedded systems design is to specify those activities that should be represented as processes (i.e. active entities and servers), those that are more accurately represented as protected entities (i.e. resources). It is also critically important to indicate the nature of the interfaces between these concurrent objects. This chapter reviews several historically significant inter-process communication primitives: shared variables, semaphores, monitors and message passing. Before considering language primitives, however, it is necessary to discuss the inherent properties of inter-process communication. This discussion will be structured using the following headings:

- Data communication
- Synchronisation
- Deadlocks and indefinite postponements
- System performance, correctness and reliability

These are the themes that have influenced the design of the Ada tasking model.

As this model directly represents active and protected entities, there are two possible forms of communication between active tasks:

(a) direct — task to task communication;

(b) indirect — communication via a protected resource.

Both these models are appropriate in Ada programs. In the following sections, however, we start by considering the problems of communicating indirectly by the use of only passive entities.

3.1 Data communication

The partitioning of a system into tasks invariably leads to the requirement that these tasks exchange data in order for the system to function correctly.

For example, a device driver (a process with sole control over an external device) needs to receive requests and return data (if it is an input request) from other processes.

Data communication is, in general, based upon either shared variables or message passing. Shared variables are passive entities to which more than one process has access; communication can therefore proceed by each process referencing these variables when appropriate. Message passing involves the explicit exchange of data between two processes by means of a message that passes from one process to the other. Ada provides for shared variables and a type of message passing structure (called a rendezvous).

Although shared variables are a straightforward means of passing information between processes their unrestricted use is unreliable and unsafe. Consider the following assignment:

```
X := X + 1;
```

This will most probably be implemented in three stages:

1.   Copy value of X into some local register.

2.   Add 1 to register.

3.   Store the value of the register in the address for X.

If two or more processes are assigning values to X (called multiple update), it is possible from the nature of the concurrency for unexpected values to be given to the shared variable. For example, let processes P1 and P2 execute the above assignment concurrently; a possible sequence of actions is (let X be zero initially):

1.   P1 copies value of X into its register $(X(P1) = 0)$.

2.   P1 adds 1 to its register $(X(P1) = 1)$.

3.   P2 copies value of X into its register $(X(P2) = 0)$.

4.   P2 adds 1 to its register $(X(P2) = 1)$.

5.   P2 stores its value of X $(X = 1)$.

6.   P1 stores its value of X $(X = 1)$.

This interleaving of the executions of P1 and P2 results in X having the final value of 1 rather than the expected value 2. Only if the assignment statement for X is an indivisible operation would the integrity of the variable be assured. Because of this multiple update problem shared variables are usually only employed in concert with operators that give indivisible actions (see Section 3.7). Otherwise, the shared variable must be implemented as a protected resource.

3.2 Synchronisation

Although processes execute essentially independently, there are situations where it is necessary for two or more processes to coordinate their executions. For example, in order for a process to receive a message it is necessary for another process to have first sent this message. Synchronisation can be defined simply as one process possessing knowledge about the state of another process. In most instances, data communication will necessitate synchronisation. Indeed, with the Ada rendezvous, communication and synchronisation are closely related in the same basic mechanism.

With languages that allow communication through shared objects, there are two particularly important classes of synchronisation: *mutual exclusion* and *condition synchronisation*. The execution of a program implies the use of resources (files, devices, memory locations), many of which can only be safely used by one process at a time. A shared variable is itself an example of such a resource. Mutual exclusion is a synchronisation that ensures that while one process is accessing a shared variable (or other such resource), no other process can possibly gain access. The sequence of statements that manipulates the shared resource is called a *critical section*. It may be a single assignment (such as the X := X + 1 described above) or it may be more complex (e.g. a file update). One means of defining mutual exclusion is to treat a critical section as an indivisible operation. The complete actions on the resource must therefore have been performed before any other process could execute any, possibly corrupting, action.

Condition synchronisation is necessary when a process wishes to perform an operation that can only sensibly or safely be performed if another task has itself taken some action or is in some defined state. If two processes are communicating via a shared variable, then the receiver of the data must be able to know that the sender has made the appropriate assignment to this variable. In this case, the sender does not need to synchronise with the receiver; in other cases, the data communication may be in both directions or the sender may wish to know that the receiver has taken the data. Here, both processes must perform condition synchronisation.

Another example of condition synchronisation comes with the use of buffers as described in Chapter 1. Two processes that pass data between them may perform better if the communication is not direct but, rather, via a buffer. This has the advantage of de-coupling the processes and allows for small fluctuations in the speeds at which the two processes are working. The use of this structure (two processes communicating via a buffer) is commonplace in concurrent programs and is known as the *producer-consumer* system. Two condition synchronisations are necessary if a finite buffer is used. Firstly, the producer process must not attempt to deposit data onto the buffer if the buffer is full. Secondly, the consumer process cannot be allowed to extract objects from the buffer if the buffer is empty. If the buffer is serving more than one producer or consumer, then mutual exclusion over the buffer elements themselves will also be needed.

3.3   Deadlocks and indefinite postponements

The above synchronisations, although necessary, lead to difficulties that must be considered in the design of concurrent programs (rather than in the design of concurrent languages — in which it is impracticable to remove the possibility of these difficulties arising). A deadlocks is the most serious condition and entails a set of processes being in a state from which it is impossible for any of the processes to proceed. Consider two processes P1 and P2 and two resources R1 and R2, each of which must be accessed without interference. Access to the resources must be via critical sections that preclude further access. Let P1 have access to R1 and P2 have access to R2; the program structure may then allow the following interleaving:

```
P1 retains access to R1 but also requires R2

P2 retains access to R2 but also requires R1
```

Mutual exclusion will ensure that concurrent access does not take place, but unfortunately both P1 and P2 are deadlocked as a consequence: neither can proceed.

Four necessary conditions must hold if deadlock is to occur:

1.   *Mutual exclusion* — only one process can use a resource at once.

2.   *Hold and wait* — there must exist processes which are holding resources while waiting for others.

3.   *No preemption* — a resource can only be released voluntarily by a process.

4.   *Circular wait* — a circular chain of processes must exist such that each process holds resources which are being requested by the next process in the chain.

The testing of software rarely removes other than the most obvious deadlocks; they can occur infrequently but with devastating results. Two distinct approaches to the deadlock problem can be taken. One can attempt to prove that deadlocks are not possible in the particular program under investigation. Although difficult, this is clearly the correct approach to take and is helped by programming in an appropriate style. Alternatively, one can attempt to avoid deadlocks whilst having contingency plans available if they do occur. These actions can be grouped together under three headings:

(a)   deadlock avoidance;

(b)   deadlock detection;

(c)   recovery from deadlock.

Avoidance algorithms attempt to look ahead and stop the system moving into a state that will potentially lead to a deadlock. Detection and recovery is never painless and must involve, for real-time systems, the aborting (or backing off) of at least one process with the preemptive removal of resources from that process. Deadlocks are a particular problem with operating systems and considerable analysis has been undertaken on deadlocks within this context (see, e.g., almost any book on operating systems).

Indefinite postponement (sometimes called *lockout* or *starvation*) is a less severe condition whereby a process that wishes to gain access to a resource, via a critical section, is never allowed to do so because there are always other processes gaining access before it. If entry to a critical section is in the order of the requests that have been made, then indefinite postponement is not possible. However, if processes have priorities, and if the order of entry is dependent on these priorities, then a low priority process may be postponed indefinitely by the existence of higher priority requests. Even if the postponement is not indefinite, but indeterminate, it may not be possible to make assertions about the program's behaviour.

An alternative view of indefinite postponements is obtained by considering the opposite criterion, namely that of *fairness*, which may be defined as an equal chance for equal priority processes, or *liveness*. This latter property implies that if a process wishes to perform some action, then it will, eventually, be allowed to do so. In particular, if a process requests access to a critical section, then it will gain access in some finite time . If requests are being actively processed and there is a defined upper limit on how long a process will be delayed, then the synchronisation mechanism is said to be *bounded fair*. This property is needed in 'hard' real-time programs where static analysis must be able to determine the worst case response time of all actions that have deadlines imposed upon them.

3.4   System performance, correctness and reliability

Both mutual exclusion and condition synchronisation give rise to situations in which a process must be delayed; it cannot be allowed to continue its execution until some future event has occurred. Message-based systems similarly require processes to be suspended. A receiver process must wait until a message arrives and, in other circumstances, a sender process may wish to have it confirmed that the message has reached its destination before proceeding.

One method of "holding back" a process would be to have it execute a busy-wait loop testing a continuation flag. This approach was criticised in the previous chapter as being grossly inefficient. What is more, fairness is impossible to prove on a system using busy-waits. Rather, what is required is a mechanism by which a process is "put to sleep", only to be awakened when circumstances are right for it to proceed. As this future event may be waited upon by a number of processes (although only one may proceed when it occurs, e.g. access to a critical section), it is necessary to queue processes and to have an appropriate run-time support system for managing this queue. The combination of fairness and process queues gives the foundation for an acceptable system performance. Particular communication methods, and implementation techniques, will nevertheless have varying effects upon this performance.

Given that the run-time performance of a concurrent program is heavily dependent upon the techniques used for implementation, it is important to reiterate that the functional correctness of a program should not depend on these issues. Two informal notions may help to clarify this point:

1.   The execution environment (hardware and run-time support system) is *minimal* if the program eventually undertakes all the input and output activities that are required of it.

2.   A program is functionally correct if when running on any minimal execution environment it produces output that conforms to that defined by the program's functional specification.

The topic of program specification, although crucially important, is outside the scope of this book.

A minimal execution environment may, of course, not be sufficient for a real-time system (where each system transaction may have a deadline defined). Its average performance may also not be satisfactory.

The notion of correctness applies across all minimal execution environments: single-processor with priority-based scheduling, single-processor with round-robin scheduling, multi-processor shared-memory systems, and distributed systems. This makes comprehensive testing difficult. With an incorrect program, it may not be possible to produce invalid results on the available platform for testing. But it may fail on another platform or when the 'current' hardware is enhanced. It is therefore critically important that many of the known problems of concurrent programs are tackled during design. For example, the following simple program will probably produce the correct result ("N = 40") on most single-processor implementations (because they do not arbitrarily interleave task execution). Nevertheless, the program is incorrect as there is no protection against multiple updates;

```
with Simple_IO; use Simple_IO;
procedure Main is
  N : Integer := 0;
  task type Simple;
```

```
T1, T2 : Simple; -- two tasks defined, both
                  -- execute according to the same body
task body Simple is
begin
  for I in 1 .. 20 loop
    N := N + 1;
  end loop;
end Simple;
begin
  delay 60.0;
  -- any minimal system is assumed to have completed
  -- the two tasks in one minute
  Put("N = "); Put(N);
end Main;
```

Reliability is of paramount importance with embedded systems, where software failure may be costly or dangerous. With inter-process communication, the model to be adopted in a language should be both reliable in itself and lead to the production of reliable programs. The possibility of misinterpreting parts of the model should be eliminated, and implementation factors should not infringe upon the semantics of the language.

One aspect of reliability is of general significance: the effect of a single process failure upon the rest of the process system. Failure may be due to internal errors or to external circumstances (i.e. being aborted); in both cases the impact on all other processes should be minimal. A reliable model will allow a process to terminate without any effect upon existing processes. However, attempts to communicate or synchronise with a terminated process must be catered for. A process failing whilst executing a critical section presents particular difficulties. A graceful termination may still lead to deadlock if it does not release its mutual exclusive hold over the critical section.

With pure message-based languages, reliability implies that systems should be resilient not only to process failure but also to message loss. This can be difficult. If process P1 sends a message to process P2, and expects a reply, what action should it take if the reply has not materialised? Does it assume that the original message was lost, or that the reply is lost, or that P2 has failed? An easy approach for the language is to assume that the run-time system implements a completely reliable communication system. This may take the form of an *atomic transaction*. An atomic transaction is either fully executed or it is not executed at all. Therefore, if the reply message is received P2 has acted, once, upon the request; if a reply is not received then P2 has taken no action — it is as if P2 never received the original request. Implementation of atomic transactions is, however, expensive in distributed systems.

3.5   Dining philosophers problem

The dining philosophers problem concerns a system, which does not contain computers, whose behaviour illustrates well the points made in the above sections. Five Chinese philosophers are seated, permanently, around a circular table; between each pair of philosophers there is a single chopstick (so there are only five chopsticks). Each philosopher can be considered as an active concurrent process whose existence is entirely made up of either eating or thinking (Cogito ergo sum: ergo deinde consumo!).

Even though each philosopher is well versed in Chinese culture, they find it impossible to eat with only one chopstick. Therefore, at most two philosophers can be eating at any one time. The chopsticks are a scarce protected resource (i.e. they cannot be broken in two!). It is assumed that philosophers are too polite to lean across the table to obtain a chopstick (and too engrossed in thought to leave and find more) and thus they only make use of the chopsticks on either side of them. This philosopher system illustrates many of the important aspects of inter-process communication:

*   Data communication — chopsticks may be passed directly from one philosopher to another or be held in a pool of available resources.

*   Mutual exclusion — access to each chopstick must be via a critical section as two philosophers cannot have concurrent access to the same chopstick.

*   Resource implementation — each chopstick could be implemented via a server that passes them to the philosophers, or as a protected resource (i.e. with mutual exclusion).

*   Condition synchronisation — a philosopher cannot eat until two chopsticks are free.

*   Deadlocks — a solution of the form

```
loop
   pick up left chopstick;
   pick up right chopstick;
   eat;
   put down left chopstick;
   put down right chopstick;
   think;
end loop;
```

will lead to a deadlock if all philosophers pick up their left chopstick.

*   Indefinite postponement — it is possible for two philosophers to starve (literally) the philosopher sitting between them. If they eat alternately, the middle philosopher will never have both chopsticks.

• Efficient waiting — should a philosopher who wishes to eat constantly check on the amount of food remaining on hir or her neighbour's plate? or should the philosopher sleep and rely on a neighbouring philosopher to wake him or her up when at least one chopstick is free?

• System reliability — will the death of a philosopher alarm the others unduly? (Yes if it is while eating and the chopsticks depart with the dying philosopher.)

An Ada solution to the dining philosophers problem is given later in Section 6.11.

3.6 Shared variables and protected variables

From the above analysis it is clear that the Ada tasking model should be reliable, have an efficient wait mechanism, provide for synchronisation, data communication and in particular mutual exclusion, and should enable software to be designed that is free from deadlocks and indefinite postponements. The simplest way that two Ada tasks can interact is via variables that are in scope for both tasks; however, the safe use of these shared variables is not straightforward, as was illustrated by the multiple update problem described above. It is possible to provide mutual exclusion by using only shared variables but a reliable solution that is free from deadlocks and indefinite postponements is not trivial. The following code implements Dekker's algorithm (Francez and Pnueli, 1978) for mutual exclusion:

```
procedure Dekker is
   task T1;
   task T2;
   type Flag is (Up, Down);
   Flag_1, Flag_2 : Flag := Down;
      -- flag up implies intention to enter critical section
   Turn : Integer range 1..2 := 1;
      -- used to arbitrate between tasks if they both
      -- wish to enter their critical section concurrently


   task body T1 is
   begin
      loop
         Flag_1 := Up;
         while Flag_2 = Up loop
            if Turn = 2 then
               Flag_1 := Down;
               while Turn = 2 loop
                  null;  -- busy-wait.
               end loop;
               Flag_1 := Up;
```

```
          end if;
        end loop;
        -- critical section.
        Turn := 2;
        Flag_1 := Down;
        -- rest of task.
      end loop;
    end T1;


    task body T2 is
    begin
      loop
        Flag_2 := Up;
        while Flag_1 = Up loop
          if Turn = 1 then
            Flag_2 := Down;
            while Turn = 1 loop
              null;  -- busy-wait.
            end loop;
            Flag_2 := Up;
          end if;
        end loop;
        -- critical section.
        Turn := 1;
        Flag_2 := Down;
        -- rest of task.
      end loop;
    end T2;

  begin
    null;
  end Dekker;
```

In order to protect the critical section three extra shared variables are necessary. [1] When T1 wishes to enter its critical section it first announces this to T2 by raising its flag (Flag_1); if T2 is executing the 'rest of task' then Flag_2 will be down and T1 can proceed safely into its critical section. However, if an interleaving of T1 and T2 leads to both flags being raised concurrently, then the shared variable Turn will arbitrate; if Turn has the value 2 then T1 will relinquish its request to enter its critical section by lowering its flag. Only when Turn takes the value 1 (i.e. when T2 has left its critical section) will T2 reset its flag. The switching of the value of Turn eliminates indefinite postponement.

This solution can be extended to more then two tasks but the protocols become even more complex. Hopefully, the above program illustrates the

---

[1]Note, that this solution assumes that the compiler does not attempt to optimise the code by keeping variables in a task-specific register whilst a task is manipulating them. See Section 7.11 to show how a pragma can be used to prohibit this optimisation.

difficulties of using shared variables as the basis for inter-process communication. The criticism can be summarised as follows:

- An unreliable (rogue) task that misuses shared variables will corrupt the entire system: hence the solution is unreliable.

- Only busy-waiting is possible.

- Programming synchronisations and communications is non-trivial and error-prone.

- Testing programs may not examine rare interleavings that break mutual exclusion or lead to livelocks — a livelock is similar to a deadlock except that the processes involved are busy-waiting.

- With large programs, readability, and hence understanding, is poor.

- Analysis of code, that is, proving the non-existence of dead-locks/livelocks, is almost impossible with large programs.

- No concurrent programming language relies entirely upon shared variables.

- There may be no shared physical memory between the processes!

The above shows that shared variables on their own are clearly inappropriate. They are passive entities and cannot easily be used to construct protected resources. Hence other methods have been derived. Semaphores and monitors attempt to ease the production of such resources. The alternative approach is to make all resources active (i.e. servers) and use message passing.

As semaphores and monitors are important historically, and have influenced the development of Ada, they will be described briefly in the following sections.

3.7 Semaphores

Semaphores were originally designed by Dijkstra (1968) to provide simple primitives for the programming of mutual exclusion and condition synchronisation. A semaphore is a non-negative integer variable that, apart from initialisation, can only be acted upon by two procedures: Wait and Send (called P and V by Dijkstra and Sait and Signal in other descriptions). An Ada package could define an abstract type for all semaphores that have the same initial value:

```
package Semaphore_Package is
   type Semaphore is limited private;
   procedure Wait(S : in out Semaphore);
   procedure Send(S : in out Semaphore);

private
```

```
type Semaphore is
  record
    Sem : Natural := 1;
    ...
  end record;
end Semaphore_Package;
```

The actions of Wait and Send can be described as follows:

```
Send(S) executes    S.Sem := S.Sem + 1;

Wait(S) executes    if S.Sem = 0 then
                       suspend until S.Sem > 0;
                    end if;
                    S.Sem := S.Sem - 1;
```

The suspension implies, on implementation, a queue mechanism; a process executing a Wait on a zero semaphore will be suspended until the semaphore becomes non-zero. This will occur only when some other process executes a Send on that semaphore. The additional important property of Send and Wait is that they are *indivisible operators*. Because of this property, the mutual update of a semaphore (by the concurrent executions of Wait and Send) is guaranteed to be reliable. Mutual exclusion can now be coded quite easily:

```
with Semaphore_Package; use Semaphore_Package;
procedure Mutual_Exclusion is
  Mutex : Semaphore;
  task T1;
  task T2;

  task body T1 is
  begin
    loop
      Wait(Mutex);
      -- critical section.
      Send(Mutex);
      -- rest of task.
    end loop;
  end T1;


  task body T2 is
  begin
    loop
      Wait(Mutex);
      -- critical section.
      Send(Mutex);
      -- rest of task.
    end loop;
```

```
        end T2;

        begin
           null;
        end Mutual_Exclusion;
```

The semaphore is initially set to the value one, so the first process (task T1, say) to execute Wait will not be delayed but will change the value of the semaphore to zero. If the other task now executes Wait it will be suspended; only when T1 executes Send (i.e. when it has left the critical section) will T2 be allowed to continue. The generalisation of this program to any number of tasks presents no further difficulties. If N tasks are suspended on a zero semaphore, then a Send will unblock exactly one of them. Send will increment the semaphore, one blocked task will proceed and in doing so it will decrement the semaphore back to zero (on implementation these pointless assignments to the semaphore can be eliminated in cases where a Send unblocks a waiting process).

The initial value of the semaphore sets the maximum concurrency through the critical section. If the value is one, then mutual exclusion is assured; alternatively if it has a value of, say, six, then up to six processes may have concurrent access. For condition synchronisation a value of zero is often employed; the condition for which some process is waiting, can be announced by executing a Send. By executing a Wait on a semaphore initialised to zero, the waiting process will be suspended until the condition has occurred.

Although semaphores give appropriate synchronisations that will allow, for example, safe data communication using shared variables, they can be criticised as being too low level and not sufficiently structured for reliable use. Just as with shared variables, a simple misuse of a semaphore, although less likely, will still corrupt the whole program. What is more, it cannot be assumed that all processes will make reference to the appropriate semaphore before entering their critical sections. If mutual exclusion is used to protect a resource, then reliability requires all calling processes to use the appropriate access protocols. A different approach would have the resource itself protecting usage — this is essentially the solution adopted with monitors. Finally, a semaphore solution is only partially reliable when faced with process failure. If a process terminates, or is aborted, while executing a critical section, then it will never Send; no other process will gain access and deadlock is almost certain to ensue. The main advantage of semaphores is that they can be implemented efficiently.

3.8 Monitors

A monitor is an encapsulation of a resource definition and all operators that manipulate the resource. In Ada terms, a monitor can be viewed as a package in which only procedures are defined in the specification; the resource is hidden in the monitor body and can only be accessed via these procedures. However, unlike a package, a monitor exercises control over calls to its external subprograms. Specifically, execution of monitor procedures is guaranteed, by definition, to be mutually exclusive. This ensures that variables declared in a monitor body can never be subject to concurrent access (this is not the case with ordinary packages). Monitors are found in numerous programming languages such as Mesa, Pascal Plus and Modula; the protected type in Ada bears some resemblance to the monitor (see Chapter 7).

If one considers a syntax for a monitor similar to that of an Ada package, then a simple resource control monitor would have the form

```
-- NOT Ada
monitor SIMPLE_RESOURCE is
   -- this monitor controls access to 8 identical
   -- resources by providing acquire and release operators.
   procedure ACQUIRE;
   procedure RELEASE;
end SIMPLE_RESOURCE;

monitor body SIMPLE_RESOURCE is
   RESOURCE_MAX : constant := 8;
   R : INTEGER range 0..RESOURCE_MAX := RESOURCE_MAX;
   -- R is the number of free resources.
   procedure ACQUIRE is
   begin
     if R = 0 then
        BLOCK;
     end if;
     R := R - 1;
   end ACQUIRE;

   procedure RELEASE is
   begin
     R := R + 1;
   end RELEASE;
end SIMPLE_RESOURCE;
```

Tasks that wish to make use of this resource need use no mutual exclusion protocols for the calling of either ACQUIRE or RELEASE. Mutual exclusion is catered for by only one execution of ACQUIRE or RELEASE being allowed at any one time.

The above code recognises, but does not deal with, the call of an ACQUIRE procedure when there are no resources available. This is an example of a condition synchronisation, for the ACQUIRE cannot be successful until a call of RELEASE is made. Although it would be possible to give this synchronisation using a semaphore defined within the monitor, Hoare (1974) proposed a simpler primitive. This primitive is called a *condition variable* or *signal* and is again acted upon by two procedures, which by analogy will also be known here as WAIT and SEND. Unlike a semaphore, which has an integer value, a condition variable has no associated value. However, a simple way of understanding the properties of a condition variable is to think of it as a semaphore which always has the value zero. The actions of WAIT and SEND are therefore as follows:

```
WAIT (cond_var)
   always blocks calling process.

SEND (cond_var)
   will unblock a waiting process if there is one,
   otherwise it has no effect.
```

With condition variables, the simple monitor defined above can now be fully coded as

```
-- NOT Ada
monitor body SIMPLE_RESOURCE is
   RESOURCE_MAX : constant := 8;
   R  : INTEGER range 0..RESOURCE_MAX := RESOURCE_MAX;
   CR : CONDITION_VARIABLE;

   procedure ACQUIRE is
   begin
      if R = 0 then WAIT(CR); end if;
      R := R - 1;
   end ACQUIRE;

   procedure RELEASE is
   begin
      R := R + 1;
      SEND(CR);
   end RELEASE;
end SIMPLE_RESOURCE;
```

If a process executes ACQUIRE when R=0, then it will become blocked and in doing so will release its mutual exclusive hold on the monitor so that other processes may call RELEASE or ACQUIRE. When RELEASE is called, the execution of SEND will unblock the waiting process, which can then proceed. This action could lead to a difficulty as there are are two processes active in the monitor: the unblocked process and the process that freed it. Different methods are used to ensure the integrity of the monitor in these circumstances, the simplest being that the execution of SEND must be the last action in the procedure. In effect, therefore, the process exits the monitor and passes mutual exclusive control to the unblocked process. If no process is blocked on the condition variable, then one process delayed upon entry to the monitor is freed. Hence, internally blocked processes are given priority over those blocked outside (attempting to gain access to) the monitor.

The monitor is a flexible programming aid that provides the means of tackling, reliably, most of the problems encountered with inter-process communication. It use provides a clear distinction between synchronisation and data communication, the latter being provided by shared objects. The monitor, like a package, is a passive construction. There is no mechanism within the monitor for the dynamic control of the order of executions of incoming procedure calls. Rather, they must be handled in a predefined order and then be blocked if their complete execution is not, at that time, possible. A major criticism of monitor-based languages is that condition synchronisation outside the monitor must be provided by a further mechanism. In Modula this is achieved by allowing signals to be a general language feature. However, signals (condition variables) suffer from the same criticism as semaphores: they are too low level for reliable use.

This subsection is completed by a further example. The simple resource control monitor described above is expanded so that requests state the number of resources required. Only when all these resources are available will control pass back to the calling process. Release of resources will cause all blocked processes to check, in turn, to see if enough resources are now available for them. If there are, they proceed; if not, they cycle back and become reblocked on the same condition variable. The reason for giving this example here is that Ada's method of providing condition synchronisation (the use of *guards*) is not adequate for this problem. An extension to the model (the *requeue*) is needed. But this must wait until Chapter 8 before it can be described:

```
-- NOT Ada
monitor RESOURCE_CONTROL is
  procedure ACQUIRE (AMOUNT : NATURAL);
  procedure RELEASE (AMOUNT : NATURAL);
end MONITOR;

monitor body RESOURCE_CONTROL is
  RESOURCE_MAX : constant := 8;
  AVAILABLE : INTEGER range 0..RESOURCE_MAX := RESOURCE_MAX;
  CR : CONDITION_VARIABLE;
  BLOCKED : NATURAL := 0; -- number of blocked processes
  QUEUED  : NATURAL;      -- number of blocked processes at
                          -- the time of resource release

  procedure ACQUIRE (AMOUNT : NATURAL) is
  begin
    if AVAILABLE < AMOUNT then
      BLOCKED := BLOCKED + 1;
      loop
        WAIT(CR);
        BLOCKED := BLOCKED - 1;
```

```
                QUEUED := QUEUED - 1;
                if AVAILABLE >= AMOUNT then
                  AVAILABLE := AVAILABLE - AMOUNT;
                  if QUEUED > 0 then SEND(CR); end if;
                  return;
                else
                  BLOCKED := BLOCKED + 1;
                  if QUEUED > 0 then SEND(CR); end if;
                end if;
              end loop;
          else
            AVAILABLE := AVAILABLE - AMOUNT;
          end if;
        end ACQUIRE;

        procedure RELEASE (AMOUNT : NATURAL) is
        begin
          AVAILABLE := AVAILABLE + AMOUNT;
          QUEUED := BLOCKED;
          SEND(CR);
        end RELEASE;
      end monitor;
```

This algorithm assumes a FIFO queue on the condition variable and has
introduced unreliable elements in order to simplify the code (e.g. it assumes
that processes will only release resources that they have previously received).
The actual nature of the resource and how it is passed to the calling process
for use is similarly omitted for clarity.

3.9   Message-based communication

Semaphores were introduced for synchronisation to protect shared variables; however, a possible extension to the semaphore idea would be for
the semaphore itself to carry the data to be communicated between the
synchronised processes. This is the basis of the design of message passing
primitives and allows active entities to communicate directly. One process
will SEND a message, another process will WAIT for it to arrive. If the
process executing the SEND is delayed until the corresponding WAIT is
executed, then the message passing is said to be *synchronous*. Alternatively, if
the SEND process continues executing arbitrarily, then one has *asynchronous*
message passing. The drawback with the asynchronous structure is that the
receiving process cannot know the present state of the calling process; it only
has information on some previous state. It is even possible that the process
initiating the transfer no longer exists by the time the message is processed.
To counter this, pairs of asynchronous messages (a send followed by a reply)
can be used to simulate a synchronous message.

One of the main issues to be addressed in the design of a message-based
concurrent programming language is how destinations, and sources, are

designated. The simplest form is for the unique process name to be used; this is called direct naming:

```
send <message> to <process-name>
```

A symmetrical form for the receiving process would be

```
wait <message> from <process-name>
```

Alternatively, an asymmetric form may be used if the receiver is only interested in the existence of a message rather than from whence it came:

```
wait <message>
```

The asymmetric form is particularly useful when the nature of the inter-process communication fits the *client/server* relationship. The server process renders some utility to any number of client processes (usually one client at a time). Therefore, the client must name the server in sending it a message. By comparison, the server will cycle round receiving requests and perform the service. This may necessitate the return of a reply message, but the address for this will be contained in the original message rather than in the syntax of the way it was received.

Where direct naming is inappropriate, *mailboxes* or *channels* may be used as intermediaries between the sending and receiving processes:

```
send <message> to <mailbox>

wait <message> from <mailbox>
```

With all these message structures, the receiving process, by executing a wait, commits itself to synchronisation and will be suspended until an actual message arrives. This is, in general, too restrictive; the receiving process may have a number of channels to choose from or it may be in a state that would make it inappropriate to process particular messages. For example, a buffer control process does not wish to wait on an 'extract' message if the buffer is empty. Dijkstra (1975) proposed that commands should be "guarded and selective" in order to achieve a flexible program structure. A guarded command has the following form:

```
guard => statement
```

where guard is a boolean expression; if the guard is true then the statement may be executed. Selection is achieved through the use of an alternative statement which can be constructed as follows:

```
select
  G1 => S1;
or
  G2 => S2;
or
  .
  .
  .
or
  Gn => Sn;
end select;
```

For example,

```
select
  BUFFER_NOT_FULL => WAIT <place_message>
or
  BUFFER_NOT_EMPTY => WAIT <extract_message>
end select;
```

If more than one guard is true, a non-deterministic choice is made from the open alternatives. An important aspect of the guard statement is whether or not the boolean expression can take information contained in the message into account. The language SR (Andrews, 1981, 1993) does allow a process to 'peek' at its incoming messages; Ada, as will be shown later, does not; although, as noted earlier, it does have a requeue facility.

The combination of direct naming and synchronous communication is often called a *rendezvous*. Languages usually combine the rendezvous with guards and select statements. This structure has been used in CSP and occam. The motivations for basing inter-process communication on the rendezvous are fourfold:

1. Data communication and process synchronisation should be considered as inseparable activities.

2. The communication model should be simple and amenable to analysis.

3. Direct communication, rather than via a protected third party, is a more straightforward abstraction.

4. The use of passive, shared variables is clearly unreliable.

In CSP both communicating partners are treated equally. Assume that a variable (of type VEC) is to be passed between process A and process B; let AR and BR be of type VEC, then the transmission has the form

```
In process A
  B ! AR

In process B
  A ? BR
```

Each process names its partner; when A and B are ready to communicate
(i.e. when they execute the above statements), then a rendezvous is said to
take place with data passing from the object AR in A to BR in B. The process
that executes its command first will be delayed until the other process is
ready to rendezvous. Once the communication is complete the rendezvous
is broken and both processes continue their executions independently and
concurrently. In the CSP model, a rendezvous is restricted to unidirectional
data communication.

3.9.1   Remote invocation/extended rendezvous

Finally in this chapter a brief description must be given of another high level
message passing construct, namely, *remote invocation*. Many applications
necessitate the coupling of messages in the form of a request followed by a
reply. Process A sends a message to process B; B processes the message and
sends a reply message to A. Because this type of communication is common,
it is desirable to represent it directly in concurrent programming languages.

Procedures, in general, provide this form of processing; *in* parameters are
processed to produce *out* parameters. Therefore, a simple construct is to allow
a process to call a procedure defined in another process. However, rather than
use the term *remote procedure call*, which is an implementation technique for
allowing standard procedure calls to be made across a distributed system, a
process defines an *entry*. The call of this entry is termed a *remote invocation*
(remote as it comes from another process):

```
-- NOT VALID Ada
remote entry SERVICE (A : in SOME_TYPE;
                      B : out SOME_OTHER_TYPE) is
begin
  -- use value of A.
  -- produce value for B.
end SERVICE;
```

Unfortunately, this simple structure is not sufficient. If the entry updates any
of the variables of its process, then reentrant access will be unsafe. There is
a need to allow the owner process to exercise some control over the use of
its entries. This can be achieved by replacing the entry code by an *accept*
statement in the body of the process code:

```
if SOME_CONDITION then
  accept SERVICE (A : in SOME_TYPE;
                  B : out SOME_OTHER_TYPE) do
    .

    .

    .
  end;
end if;
```

or

```
SOME_GUARD =>
  accept SERVICE(...) do
    ...
  end;
```

The code of SERVICE is now executed by the owner process and thus only one execution of SERVICE can take place concurrently.

The language DP (Distributed Processes) was the first to make use of this type of call. It enables an active process to 'export' a collection of 'entries' in a manner that recreates the rules governing the access of monitor procedures.

Ada also supports remote invocation as one of its inter-task communication methods. It differs from the rendezvous of CSP in the following:

1. The naming is asymmetric — the calling task names (directly) the called task, but not vice versa.

2. During the rendezvous data may pass in both directions.

Nevertheless, Ada and CSP have the following features in common:

1. Tasks wishing to rendezvous are blocked until their partners also indicate a wish to rendezvous.

2. Guarded and selective commands allow flexible program structures.

The rendezvous in Ada, unlike in CSP, is not just a simple data transfer but may consist of quite complex processing in order to construct the reply parameters. Hence it is often known as an *extended rendezvous*. It takes the form of an *accept* statement as outlined above.

3.9.2 Asynchronous communication

One of the significant issues in comparing synchronous and asynchronous communication is that, given one of the abstractions, it is always possible to program the other. It has already been noted that two asynchronous messages can simulate a synchronous one. The use of a protected resource or server task between two other active tasks can also implement an asynchronous relationship. This 'duality' was exploited in Ada 83 by the language only giving direct support to synchronous communication (the rendezvous). Unfortunately, the inevitable poor efficiency of a task being used to provide asynchronous message passing is not acceptable in many applications. Indeed, some implementations of Ada attempted to give special 'efficient' support to this type of server task.

The current version of Ada directly supports asynchronous communication by the use of protected resources. A protected resource can be placed between any two active tasks wishing to communicate asynchronously. The implementation of such a protected resource can make use of guarded commands, and hence has equivalent functionality to the rendezvous. Interestingly, the 'duality' property has now been used to argue that the rendezvous could be dropped from Ada as synchronous communication can now be programmed using a protected resource. Fortunately, this view has not prevailed; both models are supported directly in Ada 95.

The following chapters deal with the syntax and semantics of the Ada tasking model. Criticisms of earlier versions of the language were considerable. The current model is more expressive and arguably easier to use, and will give more efficient program implementation. Further assessment of the model will be made once the language features have been described in detail.

3.10   Summary

Process interactions require concurrent programming languages to support synchronisation and data communication. Communication can be based on either shared variables or message passing. This chapter has been concerned with the issues involved in defining appropriate inter-process communication primitives. Examples have been used to show how difficult it is to program mutual exclusion using only shared variables. Semaphores have been introduced to simplify these algorithms and to remove busy-waiting. Error conditions, in particular deadlock, livelock and indefinite postponement, have been defined and illustrated using the dining philosophers problem. Semaphores can be criticised as being too low level and error-prone in use. Monitors, by comparison are a more structured means of providing access to shared variables.

The semantics of message-based communication have been defined by consideration of two main issues:

*   the model of synchronisation; and
*   the method of process naming.

Variations in the process synchronisation model arise from the semantics of the send operation. Three broad classifications exist:

*   Asynchronous — sender process does not wait.
*   Asynchronous — sender process waits for message to be read.
*   Remote invocation — sender process waits for message to be read, acted upon and a reply generated.

Process naming involves two distinct issues: direct or indirect, and symmetry.

In order to increase the expressive power of message-based concurrent programming languages, it is necessary to allow a process to choose between alternative communications. The language primitive that supports this facility is known as a *selective waiting* construct. Here a process can choose between different alternatives; on any particular execution some of these alternatives can be closed off by using a boolean guard.

3.11 Further reading

G.R. Andrews, *Concurrent Programming: Principles and Practice*, Benjamin/Cummings, California, 1991.

J. Bacon, *Concurrent Systems*, Addison-Wesley, Wokingham, 1993.

M. Ben-Ari, *Principles of Concurrent and Distributed Programming*, Prentice Hall, New Jersey, 1990.

A. Burns and G.L. Davies, *Concurrent Programming*, Addison-Wesley, Wokingham, 1993.

N. Carriero and D. Gelernter, Linda in context, *CACM*, **32**(4), 444-58, 1989.

C.A.R. Hoare, *Communicating Sequential Processes*, Prentice-Hall, London, 1985.

R. Milner, *Communication and Concurrency*, Prentice-Hall, London, 1989.

J. Peterson and A. Silberschatz, *Operating System Concepts*, Addison-Wesley, Massachusettes, 1985.

A. Schiper, *Concurrent Programming*, North Oxford, London, 1989.

J. Welsh, J. Elder and D. Bustard, *Concurrent Program Structures*, Prentice-Hall, London, 1988.

D. Whiddett, *Concurrent Programming for Software Engineers*, Ellis Horwood, Chichester, 1987.

Chapter 4

Ada Task Types and Objects

In Chapter 2, tasks were introduced informally in order to illustrate some of the properties of concurrent programs. The *Ada Reference Manual* (ARM 1995) defines the full syntax for a task type as follows:

```
task_type_declaration ::=
   task type defining_identifier [known_discriminant_part]
   [is task_definition];
```

```
task_definition ::=
     {task_item}
[ private
     {task_item} ]
end [task_identifier];
```

```
task_item ::= entry_declaration | representation_clause
```

The task body is declared as follows:

```
task_body ::=
   task body defining_identifier is
      declarative_part
   begin
      handled_sequence_of_statements
   end [task_identifier];
```

The full declaration of a task type consists of its specification and body; the specification contains:

* The type name.

* A discriminant part — this defines the discrete or access parameters that can be passed to instances of the task type at their creation time (*note that arbitrary parameter cannot be declared as discriminants; only parameters of discrete type or access type*).

* A visible part — this defines the task type's entries and representation clauses which are visible to the user of the task type, it also includes the discriminant part.

* A private part — this defines the task type's entries and representation clauses which are invisible to the user of the task type.

The entries define those parts of a task that can be accessed from other tasks; they indicate how other tasks can communicate directly with the task. Representation clauses are intended solely for interrupt handling, (see Section 11.2.1).

Example specifications are

```
task type Controller;
-- this task type has no entries; no other task can
-- communicate directly with tasks created from this type

task type Agent(Param : Integer);
-- this task type has no entries but task objects can be
-- passed an integer parameter at their creation time

task type Garage_Attendant(Pump : Pump_Number := 1) is
    -- objects of this task type will allow communication via
    -- two entries; the number of the pump the attendant is
    -- to serve is passed at task creation time; if no value
    -- is passed, a default of 1 will be used
  entry Serve_Leaded(G : Gallons);
  entry Serve_Unleaded(G : Gallons);
end Garage_Attendant;



task type Cashier is
    -- this task type has a single entry with two 'in'
    -- parameters and one 'out' parameter
  entry Pay(Owed : Money; Paid : Money; Change : out Money);
end Cashier;

task type Telephone_Operator is
  entry Directory_Enquiry(
      Person : in  Name;
      Addr   : in  Address;
      Num    : out Number);
end Telephone_Operator;
```

A full discussion on inter-task communication is included in Chapter 5. The remainder of this chapter focuses on task creation, activation, execution, finalisation, termination and task hierarchies.

4.1 Task creation

The value of an object of a task type is a task having the entries specified (if any), the values of the discriminants (if any) and an execution defined by the task body. This body may consist of some hidden data declarations and a sequence of statements. A task type can be regarded as a template from which actual tasks are created. Consider the following simple task type, which inputs characters from a user and counts the number of digits and alphabetic characters:

```
type User is (Andy, Alan, Neil);

task type Character_Count(Max: Integer := 100;
                         From : User := Andy);

task body Character_Count is
  use Text_IO;
  use User_IO;
  package Int_IO is new Integer_Io(integer);
  use Int_IO;
  Digit_Count, Alpha_Count, Rest : Natural := 0;
  Ch : Character;
begin
  for I in 1 .. Max loop
    Get_From_User(From, Ch);
      -- Get_From_User defined in User_IO
    case Ch is
      when '0'..'9' =>
        Digit_Count := Digit_Count + 1;
      when 'a'..'z' | 'A'..'Z' =>
        Alpha_Count := Alpha_Count + 1;
      when others =>
        Rest := Rest + 1;
    end case;
    exit when Ch = '?';
  end loop;
  Put(Digit_Count);   -- Put is defined in Int_IO.
  Put(Alpha_Count);
  Put(Rest);
end Character_Count;
```

All objects of type Character_Count will execute this sequence of statements; they will, however, all have their own separate copies of their local data (Digit_Count, Alpha_Count, etc.). The discriminants (Max, From) can be viewed as local data constants which are either initialised to the values passed at task creation time or are given default values (if no values are passed). As constants they cannot be altered in the task's body.

The following illustrate how objects of a task type can be created:

```
Main_Controller : Controller;
Attendant1 : Garage_Attendant; -- pump 1 attendant
Attendant : Garage_Attendant(2);   -- pump 2 attendant
Input_Analyser : Character_Count(30, Neil);
                --input 30 characters from Neil
Another_Analyser : Character_Count;
                --input 100 characters from Andy
```

Tasks can also be declared in structured data types as illustrated in the following array and record declarations:

```
type Garage_Forecourt is array (Pump_Number range <>)
    of Garage_Attendant;

type One_Pump_Garage is
  record
    P : Garage_Attendant;
    C : Cashier;
  end record;


type Garage (Max_No_Pumps : Pump_Number := 1) is
  record
    Pumps : Garage_Forecourt(1 .. Max_No_Pumps);
    C1, C2 : Cashier;
  end record;
```

Note that, here, task objects have yet to be declared; instances of the tasks will only be created when an instance of the array or record type is created:

```
BP_Station : Garage(12);
```

If a task has a discriminant which does not have a default value, it cannot be used in an array declaration. It can, however, be used in a record declaration if the record itself has a discriminant which is passed through to the task. For example, the following is valid:

```
type Named_Agent(Id : Integer) is
  record
    Agent_Id : Integer := Id;
    The_Agent : Agent(Id);
  end record;
```

Although arrays of tasks can be created easily, assigning values to their discriminants is awkward. For example, in the above declaration of a Garage, all tasks were created with the default Pump_Number. This is clearly not what is wanted; ideally all tasks should have been created with a different number. An early version of Ada 95 incorporated new syntax to allow this; however, during the language's scope reduction, this was removed. The same effect can be achieved by calling a function with a side effect (although this is far from elegant):

```
package Count is
    function Assign_Pump_Number return Pump_Number;
end Count;
```

```
subtype New_Garage_Attendant is Garage_Attendant
              (Pump => Count.Assign_Pump_Number);

type Forecourt is array (1..10) of New_Garage_Attendant;
```

Where the body of Count is

```
package body Count is
  Number : Pump_Number := 0;
  function Assign_Pump_Number return Pump_Number is
  begin
    Number := Number + 1;
    return Number;
  end Assign_Pump_Number;
end Count;

Pumps : Forecourt;
```

This will ensure that each task receives a different pump number, although it makes no guarantee that Pumps(1) will service Pump_Number 1 (because Ada does not define the order of initialisation of the array elements).

Note that the above example made use of a task subtype. During subtyping only the default value of the discriminant can be changed. No change can be made to the number or form of the entries, nor to the structure of the discriminant part.

Task objects and types can be declared in any declarative part, including task bodies themselves. For any task type, the specification and body must be declared together in the same unit, with the body usually being placed at the end of the declarative part. The entries are in scope immediately after the task specification that defines them.

The use of tasks normally necessitates the use of the rendezvous or calls to protected objects, discussion of which is deferred until later chapters. Some algorithmic tasks, however, require no direct communication. Consider the following procedure that will calculate both the sum and difference of two large integer arrays:

```
type Vector is array (1..10_000) of Integer;
type Vector_Prt is access all Vector;
type Vector_Const is access constant Vector;

procedure Sumdif(A, B : Vector_Const;
                 Sum : Vector_Prt;
                 Diff : Vector_Prt);
```

Although a sequential solution is quite straightforward it is possible to define a concurrent structure that may, with hardware support, be more efficient. Consider the following two concurrent structures for Sumdif:

```
procedure Sumdif(A, B : Vector_Const;     -- Method 1
                 Sum : Vector_Prt;
                 Diff : Vector_Prt) is
   task type Minus;
   M : Minus;

   task body Minus is
   begin
      for I in Vector'Range loop
         Diff(I) := A(I) - B(I);
      end loop;
   end Minus;
begin
   for I in Vector'Range loop
      Sum(I) := A(I) + B(I);
   end loop;
end Sumdif; -- method 1


procedure Sumdif(A, B : Vector_Const;     -- Method 2
                 Sum : Vector_Prt;
                 Diff : Vector_Prt) is
   task type Minus;
   task type Plus;
   M : Minus;
   P : Plus;

   task body Minus is
   begin
      for I in Vector'Range loop
         Diff(I) := A(I) - B(I);
      end loop;
   end Minus;

   task body Plus is
   begin
      for I in Vector'Range loop
         Sum(I) := A(I) + B(I);
      end loop;
   end Plus;
begin
   null;
end Sumdif; -- method 2.
```

In the first method there are two concurrent processes: the task and the
main sequence of Sumdif, whereas in the second example three processes
exist: the two tasks (M and P) and the main sequence. In the second method,
however, the procedure itself consists of only the null statement. Both
these structures are acceptable, the first involves fewer tasks, and the second
has a more symmetric form. In each case, the tasks terminate naturally
and the procedure itself terminates and returns appropriate values after the

contained tasks have finished. (A detailed discussion on task termination is included later in Section 4.2.) Finally, this simple example illustrates that the concurrency deployed is only at an implementation level. The rest of the program, which makes use of Sumdif, is unaware that tasks have been employed. The body of the procedure may indeed have been coded in this manner only after the program was moved onto a hardware system that could exploit true parallelism.

Access discriminants

A task need not only manipulate data local to its body. It can access any data which is in scope (as illustrated in the previous example); furthermore, a pointer can also be passed to the data to be manipulated. Consider, for example, a task which wishes to sort an array of integers; the array concerned being identified when the task is created. The following example illustrates how this can be done using static access discriminants:

```
type AI is array(Positive range <>) of Integer;

task type Exchange_Sorter(A : access AI);

X : aliased AI(1 .. 100) := (...);

Sorter :  Exchange_Sorter(X'Access);

task body Exchange_Sorter is
  Sorted : Boolean := False;
  Tmp : Integer;
begin
  while not Sorted loop
    Sorted := True;
    for I in A'First .. A'Last - 1 loop
      if A(I) < A(I+1) then
        Tmp := A(I);
        A(I) := A(I+1);
        A(I+1) := Tmp;
        Sorted := False;
      end if;
    end loop;
  end loop;
end Exchange_Sorter;
```

4.1.1   Anonymous task types

In the examples used above, a task type was declared followed by an instance of that type. This may appear long-winded and, indeed, Ada allows a shorthand form to be used that hides the explicit declaration of the type.

There can, therefore, be anonymous task types in an identical way to there being anonymous array types. For the direct declaration of a single task, the reserved word 'type' is omitted from the specification along with any discriminant part:

```
single_task_declaration ::=
    task defining_identifier [is task_definition];
```

For example,

```
task Controller;
```

Controller now refers to the task object, not its type. The declaration of an anonymous task type is interpreted as being equivalent to the declaration of its type, followed, immediately, by the declaration of the object:

```
task type Controller_Type;
Controller : Controller_Type;
```

As no construct in Ada allows direct reference to the task's body, this form is unambiguous.

4.1.2 Task access types

If a task object has a defined type, it is possible to provide an access type for that task type:

```
task type Cashier is
    entry Pay(Owed : Money; Paid : Money; Change : out Money);
end Cashier;

type Cashier_Ptr is access Cashier;
```

Task types with associated access variables are often used where the dynamic generation of tasks is required during program execution. The task object itself is created by the evaluation of an allocator:

```
Pointer_Cashier : Cashier_Ptr := new Cashier;
```

A Cashier task object has been created and activated at the point of creation; its 'name' is Pointer_Cashier.all and its entry is designated Pointer_Cashier.Pay.

Dynamic task creation is an important feature of the language; for dynamic environments, direct support can be given to 'unbounded' numbers of controlled objects. Obviously, there is a limit to the number of tasks a system can support (usually due to memory limitations) but there are clear advantages in not having to fix a static limit artificially on, for example, the number of trackable objects in some air traffic control applications.

As well as fully dynamic tasks, it is also possible to obtain a pointer to a task which has been created by an object declaration rather than by an allocator. If pointers to the task are required, then the task must be declared as being 'aliased' and an access attribute used. For example,

```
task type Garage_Attendant is ... -- as before
Attendant1 : aliased Garage_Attendant;
```

indicates that a pointer to `Attendant1` may be used:

```
type Ptr_Attendant is access all Garage_Attendant;
PA : Ptr_Attendant;
  ...
PA := Attendant1'Access;
```

After this assignment there are two ways of referencing the task: `PA` and `Attendant1`.

Primes by sieve example

To give a more extensive example of the use of tasks (and task access types), a program will be developed that implements the "primes by sieve" algorithm (Sieve of Eratosthenes). The structure of the algorithm is as follows. A task (`Odds`) generates a continuous stream of odd integers. These are then passed down a pipeline of (`Sieve`) tasks. Each of these tasks receives a stream of integers, the first one of which is a prime number (which it keeps in the local variable `Prime`). The task then processes the rest of the numbers. Each one is checked to see if it can be divided exactly by `Prime`; if it can it is thrown away. If it cannot, then it is passed down the pipeline to the next task.

It is possible to define a static version of this algorithm with, say, N tasks in the pipeline. This will generate the first N primes. However, a more flexible program can be formed if each task creates the next task in the pipeline (where each task has an integer to pass on to the next).

In order for the tasks to pass data between themselves they must be able to communicate with each other. As communication has not yet been directly addressed we shall assume, for now, that the `Sieve` tasks use buffer tasks as the media for communication. The buffer task will have a simple interface (the body for this type of task will be given later):

```
task type Buffer is
  entry Put(I : Integer);
  entry Get(I : out Integer);
end Buffer;
```

The Sieve task type will be defined with a parameter that is a static pointer to a buffer. New Sieve tasks will be created dynamically and hence an access type is required:

```
task type Sieve(B : access Buffer);

type Sieve_Ptr is access Sieve;

function Get_New_Sieve(B : access Buffer) return Sieve_Ptr is
begin
   return new Sieve(B);
end Get_New_Sieve;
```

There is a single Odd task:

```
task Odd;

task body Odd is
   Limit : constant Positive := ...;
   Num : Positive;
   Buf : aliased Buffer;
   S : Sieve_Ptr := Get_New_Sieve(Buf'Access);
begin
   Num := 3;
   while Num < Limit loop
     Buf.Put(Num);
     Num := Num + 2;
   end loop;
end Odd;
```

The code for the sieve tasks is as follows:

```
task body Sieve;
   New_Buff : aliased Buffer;
   Next_Sieve : Sieve_Ptr;
   Prime, Num : Natural;
begin
   B.Get(Prime);
   -- Prime is a prime number, which could be output
   loop
     B.Get(Num);
     exit when Num rem Prime /= 0;
   end loop;
   -- a number must be passed on and so a new Sieve task
   -- is created; note that it is necessary to use a
   -- function as a task type cannot be used directly
   -- within its own body to create a further task instance
   Next_Sieve := Get_New_Sieve(New_Buff'Access);
   New_Buff.Put(Num);
   loop
     B.Get(Num);
     if Num rem Prime /= 0 then
```

```
        New_Buff.Put(Num);
      end if;
    end loop;
  end Sieve;
```

Note that this program will not terminate correctly. One way of programming termination, in this example, is to pass a "close-down" token such as zero down the pipeline. Other methods will be considered in later chapters.

4.2   Task activation, execution, finalisation and termination

A task is said to be *created* by its elaboration. The execution of a task object has three main active phases:

Phase 1
> *Activation* — the elaboration of the declarative part, if any, of the task body (any local variables in the body of the task are created and initialised during activation).

Phase 2
> *Normal execution* — the execution of the statements within the body of the task.

Phase 3
> *Finalisation* — the execution of any finalisation code associated with any objects in its declarative part.

A tasks, in general, indicate its willingness to begin finalisation by executing its 'end' statement. A tasks may also begin its finalisation as a result of an unhandled exception, or by executing a select statement with a terminate alternative (see Section 6.6), or by being aborted (see Section 10.2). A finished task is called *completed* or *terminated* depending on whether it has any active dependents (see Section 4.3).

4.2.1   Task activation

For static tasks, activation starts immediately after the complete elaboration of the declarative part in which they are defined:

```
declare
  task type T_Type;
  task A;
       -- task A is created when this declaration is elaborated
  B, C : T_Type;   -- tasks B and C created when
                   -- these declarations are elaborated
  I, J : Integer;
```

```
task body A is ...
task body T_Type is ...

begin
    -- all tasks created in the above declarative region begin
    -- to activate as soon as the elaboration of their
    -- declarative regions have finished

    -- first statement executed once all tasks
    -- have finished their activation

    -- sequence of statements here
end;
```

The following points should be noted:

* All static tasks created within a single declarative region begin their activations immediately the declarative region has completed elaboration (i.e. after 'begin' but before any statement following 'begin').

* The first statement following the declarative region is not executed until all tasks have finished their activation.

* Following activation, the execution of the task object is defined by the appropriate task body.

* A task need not wait for the activation of other concurrently created tasks before executing its body.

* A task may attempt to communicate with another task which, although created, has not yet been activated. The calling task will be delayed until the communication can take place.

If a task object is declared in a package specification, then it commences its execution after the elaboration of the declarative part of the package body:

```
package Client is
    task Agent(Size : Integer);
end Client;

package body Client is
    task body Agent is separate;
begin
    -- Agent starts executing before 1st statement
    -- of this sequence begins executing.
    ...
end Client;
```

If the package does not contain initialisation code, then it acts as if there is a 'null' sequence.

Dynamic tasks are activated immediately after the evaluation of the allocator (the **new** operator) which created them.

The task which executed the statement responsible for the creation is
blocked until the tasks created have finished their activation. The following
stylised code illustrates the above points:

```
declare
   -- some declarative region executed (say) by task Parent
   task type T_Type;
   type Prt_T_Type is access T_Type;
   A1 : T_Type;   -- creation of A1
   A2 : T_Type;   -- creation of A2
   task body T_Type is ...
begin -- activation of A1, A2
   declare
      B : T_Type; -- creation of B
      C : Prt_T_Type := new T_Type;
         -- creation, activation of C.all
      D : Prt_T_Type;
   begin -- activation of B
      D := new T_Type; -- creation, activation of D.all
   end;
end;
```

In this example the tasks are created and activated by the Parent task in
the following order:

1. Task A1 is created.

2. Task A2 is created.

3. Tasks A1 and A2 are activated concurrently and the Parent waits for
    them to finish their activation.

4. Assuming a successful activation A1, A2 and Parent proceed concur-
    rently.

5. Parent creates task B.

6. Parent creates and activates task C, and waits for it to finish activation.

7. Parent activates task B, and waits for it to finish activation.

8. Parent creates and activates task C, and waits for it to finish activation.

Program errors can lead to exceptions being raised during these initial phases
of a task's existence. If an exception is raised in the elaboration of a declarative part, then any task created during that elaboration becomes terminated
and is never activated. For example, if in the following Initial_Value is
a function which returns an integer value, then there is a possibility that it
will return a value outside Data_Range. This would result in the exception
Constraint_Error being raised in a declarative part which also declares a

task. In this case the Agent task is never activated. As the exception is raised on elaboration of the declarative block, it cannot be handled within that block but must be caught at an outer level. Similarly, any exception raised during the finalisation of a block cannot be handled by that block:

```
declare  -- outer block
    ...
begin
    declare  -- inner block

        task Agent(Size : Integer);
        subtype Data_Range is Integer range 1 .. 10;
        Data_Object : Data_Range := Initial_Value;

        task body Agent is ...

    begin
        ...
    exception
        -- any exception handlers here will only catch
        -- exceptions raised during the "begin .. exception",
        -- and not those raised in the elaboration or
        -- finalisation of the declarative part
    end;

exception
    when Constraint_Error =>
        -- recovery routine for exception
        -- raised in the inner block
end;
```

If an exception is raised during a task's activation, then the task itself cannot handle the exception. The task is prevented from executing its body and hence becomes completed or terminated. If any objects have already been created, then they must be finalised (see Section 4.3). As the task itself cannot handle them, the language model requires the parent (creator) task or scope to deal with the situation: the predefined exception Tasking_Error is raised. In the case of dynamic task creation, the exception is raised after the statement which issued the allocator call. However, if the call is in a declarative part (as part of the initialisation of an object), the declarative part fails and the exception is raised in the surrounding block (or calling subprogram).

For static task creation, the exception is raised prior to the first executable statement of the declarative block. This exception is raised after all created tasks have been activated (whether successfully or not) and it is raised at most once. For tasks created statically during a declarative part, the associated exception handler must be at the outermost level of the declarative block; therefore little direct error recovery is possible. The attribute Callable can, however, be used at least to identify the rogue task (assuming the well behaved tasks have not terminated correctly before the parent executes its exception handler):

```
declare
  task Child_1;
  task Child_2;
  task body Child_1 is ...
  task body Child_2 is ...
begin
  null;
exception
  when Tasking_Error =>
    if not Child_1'Callable then
      Put("Task Child_1 failed during activation");
    end if;
    if not Child_2'Callable then
      Put("Task Child_2 failed during activation");
    end if;
    if Child_1'Callable and Child_2'Callable then
      Put("Something Strange is Happening");
    end if;
end;
```

The boolean attribute Callable is defined to yield the value True if the designated task is neither Completed, Terminated nor Abnormal. (An abnormal task is one that has been aborted; the conditions necessary for an abnormal task to become terminated are discussed in Chapter 10.) In the above example, if task Child_2 fails in its elaboration, then the declaring block will display an appropriate error message. Task Child_1 will, however, be unaffected by this and will proceed in its execution. The declarative block will only exit if, and when, Child_1 subsequently terminates.

Another task attribute is Terminated which returns True if the named task has terminated, returns False otherwise.

Figure 4.1 illustrates those task states and their transitions that have been introduced so far. The state transition diagram will be extended in this and later chapters. Note that 'activating' and 'executing' are definitions of the state of the task; they do not imply that the task is actually running on the processor. This is an implementation issue. Thus, for example, the state 'executing' means able to execute (make progress) if processing resources are made available to it.

4.3   Task hierarchies

Ada is a block structured language in which blocks may be nested within blocks. A task can be declared in any block; therefore it is possible for tasks to be declared within tasks (or blocks) which themselves are declared within other tasks (or blocks). This structure is called a task hierarchy. The creation

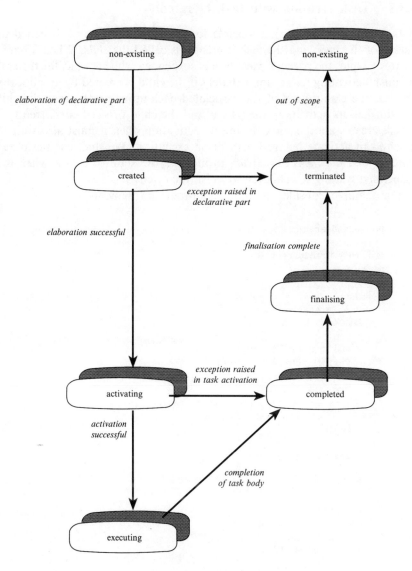

Figure 4.1: Task States.

and termination of tasks within a hierarchy affect the activation, execution, termination and finalisation of other tasks in the hierarchy.

4.3.1   Task creation with task hierarchies

A task which is directly responsible for creating another task is called the *parent* of the task, and the task it creates is called the *child*. When a parent creates a child, the parent's execution is suspended while it waits for the child to finish activating (either immediately if the child is created by an allocator, or after the elaboration of the associated declarative part). Once the child has finished its activation, the parent and the child proceed concurrently. If a task creates another task during its activation, then it must also wait for its child to activate before it can begin execution. We shall use the phrase *waiting for child tasks to activate* to indicate the state of a task when it is suspended waiting for children to finish their activation.

For example, consider the following program fragment:

```
task Grandparent;

task body Grandparent is
begin
   ...
   declare            -- inner block
      task Parent;
      task body Parent is

         task type Child;
         Child_1, Child_2 : Child;

         task body Child is
            -- declaration and initialisation
            -- of local variables etc
         begin
            ...
         end Child;

      begin
         ...
      end Parent;
   begin   -- inner block
      ...
   end;    -- inner block
   ...
end Grandparent;
```

The Grandparent task begins its execution; it enters an inner block where it is suspended waiting for its child (the Parent task) to be activated. During the Parent task's activation it creates the two child tasks Child_1 and Child_2, and therefore Parent cannot finish its activation and begin its execution until these child tasks have finished their activation. Once *both* Child_1 and Child_2 have activated, Parent finishes its activation, and the Grandparent task is free to continue. Note that if Child_1 finishes its activation before Child_2, it is not suspended but is free to execute.

The reason why parent tasks must be suspended whilst their children are activated was explained in the previous section; any problems with the creation and activation of the task must be reported to the parent. If the parent task continued to execute, it would be more difficult for it to respond to what is, in effect, an asynchronous exception. Once a child task is executing, it is considered to be independent from its parent. Any exception it raises can be handled within its own body.

4.3.2 Task termination with task hierarchies

The parent of a child task is responsible for the creation of that task. The *master* of a *dependent* task must wait for that task to terminate before it can itself terminate. In many cases the parent of a task is also the master of the task. For example, consider the following:

```
task Parent_And_Master;

task body Parent_And_Master is

    -- declaration and initialisation
    -- of local variables etc

    task Child_And_Dependent_1;
    task Child_And_Dependent_2;

    task body Child_And_Dependent_1 is
      -- declaration and initialisation
      -- of local variables etc
    begin
      ...
    end Child_And_Dependent_1;

    task body Child_And_Dependent_2 is
      -- declaration and initialisation
      -- of local variables etc
    begin
      ...
    end Child_And_Dependent_2;

  begin
    ...
  end Parent_And_Master;
```

In the above example, the Parent_And_Master task creates two child tasks called: Child_And_Dependent_1 and Child_And_Dependent_2. Once the child tasks have been activated they are free to run concurrently with the parent. When the parent finishes its execution, it must wait for its dependent tasks to finish and execute their finalisation code. This is because the dependent tasks can potentially access the local variables of their master. If the master finishes and finalises its local variables (which would then disappear), the dependents would be accessing locations in memory which may have been reused by other tasks. To avoid this situation, Ada forces the master task to wait for finalisation and termination of its dependents before it itself can finalise any variables (of which it is the master) and terminate. When a master has finished its execution but cannot terminate because its dependents are still executing, the master is said to be *completed*. Of course, any dependent tasks cannot themselves terminate until all their dependent tasks have also terminated. For example, in the Grandparent example, task Parent must wait for Child_1 and Child_2 to terminate.

The master of a task need not be another task directly, but can be a declarative block within another task (or declarative block or main program). That block cannot be exited until all its dependent tasks have terminated and any dependent variables have been finalised. For example,

```
-- code within some block, task or procedure

Master:
declare  -- internal Master block

   -- declaration and initialisation
   -- of local variables etc

   -- declaration of any finalisation routines

   task Dependent_1;
   task Dependent_2;

   task body Dependent_1 is
     -- declaration and initialisation
     -- of local variables etc
   begin
     ...
     -- potentially can access local variable
     -- in the Master block
   end Dependent_1;

   task body Dependent_2 is
     -- declaration and initialisation
     -- of local variables etc
   begin
     ...
     -- potentially can access local variable
     -- in the Master block
   end Dependent_2;
```

```
begin   -- Master block
   ...
end; -- Master  block
```

On entry to the Master block above, the executing parent task is suspended
whilst the child tasks are created and activated. Once this has occurred, the
Master block itself is free to execute. However, before the block can exit it
must wait for the dependent tasks to terminate (and any dependent variables
become finalised). When this has occurred, the task executing the block is
free to finalise its dependent variables and then continue. We shall use the
phrase *waiting for dependent task to terminate* to indicate the state of a task
when it is suspended waiting for dependents to terminate and finalise.

Task termination and dynamic tasks

With dynamic task creation the master of a task is not necessarily its
parent. The master of a task created by the evaluation of an allocator is the
declarative region which contains the access type definition. For example,

```
task type Dependent;
task body Dependent is ...;

declare  -- Outer Block,
         -- master of all tasks created using Dependent_Ptr
   type Dependent_Ptr is access Dependent;
   A : Dependent_Ptr:
begin
   ...
   declare              -- inner block
     B : Dependent;
     C : Dependent_Ptr:= new Dependent;
     D : Dependent_Ptr:= new Dependent;
   begin
     -- sequence of statements
     A := C;      -- A now points to C.all
   end;  -- must wait for B to terminate but
         -- not C.all or D.all
   ...
   -- C.all and D.all could still be active although
   -- the name C is out of scope, the task C.all can still
   -- be accessed via A.all D.all cannot be accessed
   -- directly; it is anonymous

end; -- must wait for C.all and D.all to terminate
```

Although B, C.**all** and D.**all** are created within the inner block, only B has this
block as its master; C.**all** and D.**all** are considered to be dependents of the

outer block and therefore do not affect the termination of the inner block. The inner block is, however, the parent of C.**all** and D.**all** (as well as B).

Task termination and library tasks

Tasks declared in library-level packages have the main procedure as their master. That is, the *main procedure cannot terminate until all the library-level tasks have terminated.* [1] Consider the following program:

```
package Library_Of_Useful_Tasks  is
   task type Agent(Size : Integer := 128);
   Default_Agent : Agent;
   ...
end Library_Of_Useful_Tasks;   -- a library package.

with Library_Of_Useful_Tasks; use Library_Of_Useful_Tasks;
procedure Main is
   My_Agent   : Agent;
begin
   null;
end Main;
```

In Ada, there is a conceptual task (called the *environment task*) which calls the main procedure. Before it does this, it elaborates all library units named in the 'with' clauses by the main procedure. In the above example, this elaboration will cause task Default_Agent to be created and activated. Once the task has finished activation, the environment task calls the procedure Main, which creates and activates My_Agent. This task must terminate before the procedure can exit. The Default_Agent must also terminate before the environment task terminates and the whole program finishes. A similar argument applies to tasks created by an allocator whose access type is declared in a library unit: they also have the main program as their master. Note that an exception raised during the activation of Default_Agent cannot be handled — the program fails and the main procedure is never executed.

4.4   Task identification

One of the main uses of access variables is to provide another means of naming tasks. All task types in Ada are considered to be limited private. It is therefore not possible to pass a task, by assignment, to another data structure or program unit. For example, if Robot_Arm and New_Arm are two variables of the same access type (the access type being obtained from a task type), then the following is illegal:

---

[1]In a distributed system, there can be more than one main procedure and hence the termination rules must be reinterpreted, see Section 14.2

```
Robot_Arm.all := New_Arm.all;  -- not legal Ada
```

However,

```
Robot_Arm := New_Arm;
```

is quite legal and means that Robot_Arm is now designating the same task as New_Arm. Care must be exercised here as duplicated names can cause confusion and lead to programs that are difficult to understand.

In some circumstances it is useful for a task to have a unique identifier (rather than a name). For example, a server task is not usually concerned with the type of the client tasks. Indeed, when communication and synchronisation are discussed in the next chapter it will be seen that the server has no direct knowledge of who its clients are. However, there are occasions when a server needs to know that the client task it is communicating with is the same client task that it previously communicated with. Although the core Ada language provides no such facility, the Systems Programming Annex provides a mechanism by which a task can obtain its own unique identification. This can then be passed to other tasks:

```
package Ada.Task_Identification is

  type Task_Id is private;
  Null_Task_Id : constant Task_Id;

  function "=" (Left, Right : Task_Id) return Boolean;

  function Current_Task return Task_Id;
    -- returns unique id of calling task

    -- other functions not relevant to this discussion,
    -- see Section 11.3
private
  ...
end Ada.Task_Identification;
```

As well as this package, the Annex supports two attributes:

- For any prefix T of a task type, T'Identity returns a value of type Task_Id that equals the unique identifier of the task denoted by T.

- For any prefix E that denotes an entry declaration, E'Caller returns a value of type Task_Id that equals the unique identifier of the task whose entry call is being serviced. The attribute is only allowed inside an entry body or an accept statement (see Chapters 5 and 7).

Care must be taken when using task identifiers since there is no guarantee that, at some later time, the task will still be active or even in scope.

4.5   Task creation, communication and synchronisation within task finalisation

This chapter has discussed how a 'completed' task finalises any dependent variables before becoming 'terminated' and how a master block finalises any dependent variables before exiting. This act of finalisation can itself, in theory, be complex and involve task creation, termination, communication, etc. However, this is not recommended, and issues resulting from this will not be discussed in this book. It should be noted, nevertheless, that it is a bounded error for a finalisation routine to propagate an exception.

Although task hierarchies are a powerful structuring tool they can give rise to complex initialisation and termination behaviours. Wherever possible, these complexities should be avoided. For example, task failures during activation should be prevented (by assigning initial values to all local data variables in the execution part of the task rather than on variable declaration).

4.6   Task states

In this chapter we have introduced various task states and indicated how transitions between states occur. Figure 4.2 summarises this information.

4.7   Summary

This chapter has concerned itself with the behaviour of Ada tasks. A number of states have been defined which help to distinguish between the various phases of a task's execution. These have been illustrated on *Task State* diagrams. In general, a task is created by its parent, goes through a phase of activation while its declarative part is being elaborated, and then becomes an independent executing entity. Although in some applications, tasks will be expected to run 'forever', in terminating programs each task will first complete its code, then finalise any controlled variables it has, and will then terminate when it no longer has any dependent tasks.

Tasks can be characterised as being either static (i.e. by declaring a variable of a task type) or dynamic. Dynamic tasks are created by an allocator referring to an access type. Because of different dependency relationships, the rules for activation and termination are different for these two forms of task.

When a task is created it is possible to pass initialisation data to it via a discriminant. This allows tasks of the same type to be parameterised.

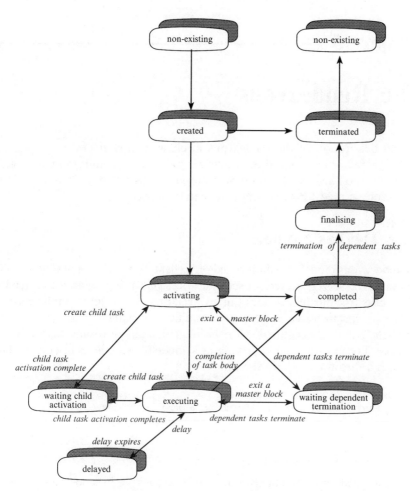

Figure 4.2: Summary of Task States and State Transmission.

Although any number of discriminants can be used, all must be of discrete or access type. Passing a positional parameter to each task in an array structure is a useful facility. Ada allows this to be done, although it requires a function with a side effect, which is not an ideal method.

Chapter 5 ───────────────────────────

The Rendezvous

A brief description of the rendezvous mechanism was given in Chapter 3. In this chapter, the standard rendezvous is explored in detail; more complex communication and synchronisation patterns are discussed in Chapter 6. The rendezvous is used for direct communication between tasks.

5.1 The basic model

The rendezvous model of Ada is based on a client/server model of interaction. One task, the server, declares a set of services that it is prepared to offer to other tasks (the clients). It does this by declaring one or more public **entries** in its task specification. Each entry identifies the name of the service, the parameters that are required with the request and the results that will be returned. For example, the following task models a telephone operator who provides a directory enquiry service:

```
task type Telephone_Operator is
  entry Directory_Enquiry(Person : in Name; Addr : in Address;
                          Num : out Number);
end Telephone_Operator;

An_Op : Telephone_Operator;
```

where Name, Address and Number are predeclared types in scope; and Person and Addr are passed to the operator (indicated by the keyword **in**) to identify the person whose telephone number is required, and Num is returned by the operator (indicated by the keyword **out**). Of course, the operator may also provide other services, such as logging faulty numbers.

A client task (also named the *calling task*) issues an 'entry call' on the server task (or *called task*) by identifying both the server and the required entry:

```
-- client task

An_Op.Directory_Enquiry("STUART JONES",
            "10 MAIN STREET, YORK", Stuarts_Number);
```

The operator indicates a willingness to provide the service at any particular time by executing an 'accept' statement:

```
-- server task

accept Directory_Enquiry(Person : in Name; Addr : in Address;
                         Num : out Number) do
   -- look up telephone number and assign
   -- the value to Num
end Directory_Enquiry;
```

For the communication to occur between the client and the server, both tasks must have issued their respective requests. When they have, the communication takes place; this is called a rendezvous because both tasks have to meet at the entry at the same time. When the rendezvous occurs, any **in** (and **in out**) parameters are passed to the server task from the client. The server task then executes the code inside the **accept** statement. When this statement finishes (by encountering its **end** statement), any **out** (and **in out**) parameters are passed back to the client and both tasks proceed independently and concurrently.

The following program fragment illustrates the client and server tasks:

```
task type Subscriber;

task type Telephone_Operator is
   entry Directory_Enquiry(Person : in Name; Addr : in Address;
                           Num : out Number);
end Telephone_Operator;

S1, S2, S3 : Subscriber; -- friends of Stuart Jones
An_Op : Telephone_Operator;

task body Subscriber is
   Stuarts_Number : Number;
begin
   ...
   An_Op.Directory_Enquiry("STUART JONES",
     "10 MAIN STREET, YORK", Stuarts_Number);
   ...
end Subscriber;

task body Telephone_Operator is
begin
   loop
      -- prepare to accept next call
      accept Directory_Enquiry(Person : in Name;
              Addr : in Address; Num : out Number) do
         -- look up telephone number and
         -- assign the value to Num
      end Directory_Enquiry;
      -- undertake housekeeping such as logging all calls
   end loop;
end Telephone_Operator;
```

It is quite possible that the client and server will not both be in a position to communicate at exactly the same time. For example, the operator may be willing to accept a service request but there may be no subscribers issuing an entry call. For the simple rendezvous case, the server is obliged to wait for a call; whilst it is waiting it frees up any processing resource (e.g. the processor) it is using; a task which is generally waiting for some event to occur is usually termed *suspended*. Similarly, if a client issues a request and the server has not indicated that it is prepared to accept the request (either because it is already servicing another request or it is doing something else), then the client must wait. [1] Clients waiting for service at a particular entry are queued. The order of the queue depends on whether the Ada implementation supports the Real-Time Systems Annex. If it does not, then the queue is first-in-first-out; if it does, then other possibilities are allowed, such as priority queuing (see Chapter 12).

Figure 5.1 illustrates the synchronisation and communication that occurs during the rendezvous.

5.2   The entry statement

A formal description of the entry statement is given below:

```
entry_declaration ::=
   entry defining_identifier [(discrete_subtype_definition)]
      parameter_profile;
```

The parameter profile is the same as for Ada procedures (**in, out, in out** — with **in** being the default). Access parameters are not permitted and default parameters are allowed.

The optional 'discrete_subtype_definition' in the entry declaration is used to declare a family of distinct entries, all of which will have the same formal part (see Section 5.4).

A task can have more than one entry with the same name if the parameters to the entries are different (the entries are said to be overloaded). For example, the following task type overloads the `Directory_Enquiry` entry, allowing a subscriber to request a number given a name and a postal or zip code instead of a name and an address:

```
task type Telephone_Operator is
   entry Directory_Enquiry(Person : in Name; Addr : in Address;
                           Num   : out Number);
   entry Directory_Enquiry(Person : in Name; Zip : in Postal_Code;
                           Num : out Number);
```

---

[1] In Chapter 6 other mechanisms will be described which allow the server and the client to withdraw their offer of communication if they cannot enter into the rendezvous immediately or within a specified time period.

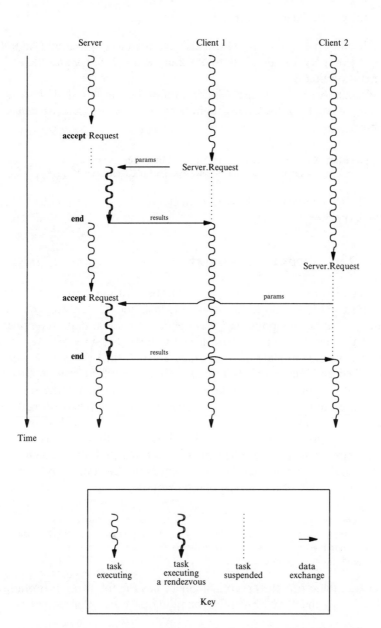

Figure 5.1: Communication and Synchronisation during a Rendezvous.

    end Telephone_Operator;

    An_Op : Telephone_Operator;

A single entry (i.e. not a family) will also overload a subprogram (Task_Name.
Entry_Name may be identical to Package_Name.Subprogram_Name) or an
enumeration literal.

    Unlike a package, a 'use' clause cannot be employed with a task to
shorten the length of the calling identifiers; however a procedure can rename
an entry:

    procedure Enquiry(Person : **in** Name; Addr : **in** Address;
            Num : **out** Number) **renames** An_Op.Directory_Enquiry;

A call to procedure Enquiry will result in an entry call to
An_Op.Directory_Enquiry.

5.3   The accept statement

For each and every entry defined in a task specification there must be at least
one accept statement in the corresponding task body. Interestingly, the ARM
is not specific on this point and it is therefore possible that a compiler may
not flag the lack of an appropriate accept statement as an error. Nevertheless,
if there is no accept statement for some entry E, then a call to E will never
be handled and the calling task may be blocked indefinitely. A task body,
however, may contain more than one accept statement for the same entry.
It should be noted that the accept statement must be placed directly in the
task body; it cannot be placed in a procedure which is called by the task
body. Such a procedure could be called from more than one task!

    An accept statement specifies the actions to be performed when an entry
is called and the formal part of the accept statement must conform exactly
to the formal part of the corresponding entry:

    accept_statement ::=
      accept entry_direct_name [(entry_index)] parameter_profile [**do**
        handled_sequence_of_statements
      end [entry_identifier]];

In general, therefore, the accept statement has the following form (although
the the family index and exception handling part are often absent):

    accept Entry_Name(Family_Index)(P : Parameters) **do**
      -- sequence of statements
    exception
      -- exception handling part
    end Entry_Name;

The sequence of statements may contain subprogram calls, entry calls, protected object calls (see Chapter 7), accept statements (but not for the same entry) and inner blocks. There are, however, good reasons for making the accept statement as simple as possible. The code it contains should be only that which is necessary for the rendezvous. If it contains extra statements, then the calling task will be held up unnecessarily. For example, if the telephone operator decided to perform its housekeeping operations inside the rendezvous, then the subscriber task would be further delayed before being allowed to continue. As a further example, consider a task that controls access to a single keyboard and VDU. Let Rec be defined by

```
type Rec is
record
   I : Integer;
   F : Float;
   S : String (1..10);
end record;
```

and the task's structure:

```
task IO_Control is
   entry Get(R : out Rec);
   entry Put(R : Rec);
        .
        .
        .
end IO_Control;
```

For Put, the accept statement might have the form

```
accept Put(R : Rec) do
   Put(R.I);   -- this procedure is constructed from Text_Io
   Put(R.F);
   Put(R.S);
end Put;
```

However, this ties up the rendezvous for the time it takes to output the three items; a better structure would be

```
accept Put(R : Rec) do
   Temp_Rec := R;
end Put;
Put(Temp_Rec.I);
Put(Temp_Rec.F);
Put(Temp_Rec.S);
```

With the Get entry some user prompts are necessary; these must be undertaken during the rendezvous:

```
accept Get(R : out Rec) do
  Put("VALUE OF I?"); Get(R.I);
  Put("VALUE OF F?"); Get(R.F);
  Put("VALUE OF S?"); Get(R.S);
end Get;
```

User errors on I/O are unavoidable and exceptions are bound to occur from time to time. A reliable accept statement for Get would therefore be

```
accept Get(R : out Rec) do
  loop
    begin
      Put("VALUE OF I?"); Get(R.I);
      Put("VALUE OF F?"); Get(R.F);
      Put("VALUE OF S?"); Get(R.S);
      return;
    exception
      when others => Put("INVALID INPUT: START AGAIN");
    end;
  end loop;
end Get;
```

Note that this example makes use of a **return** statement to exit from the **accept**.

This formulation now represents a sizeable accept statement that will hold the rendezvous for a comparatively large amount of time. An alternative structure would be for the calling task to make a request (via another entry) for the record first, and later to make a separate entry call to Get the record. The calling task would therefore make two entry calls:

```
IO_Control.Request;
    .
    .
    .
IO_Control.Get(Some_Rec);
```

The task IO_Control would then have the following code in its sequence of statements:

```
accept Request;
loop
  begin
    -- this is as before but with record variable Temp_Rec
  end;
end loop;
accept Get(R : out Rec) do
  R := Temp_Rec;
end Get;
```

This has simplified the accept statements but at the cost of a further rendezvous.

Primes by sieve example (revisited)

In the previous chapter an implementation of the "primes by sieve" algorithm was given. In that program, the tasks communicated via buffer elements. Now that the rendezvous has been defined it is possible to give an alternative structure in which the tasks call each other directly, that is, each task rendezvous with the next task in the pipeline:

```
procedure Primes_By_Sieve is
  task type Sieve is
    entry Pass_On(Int : Integer);
  end Sieve;

  task Odd;

  type Sieve_Ptr is access Sieve;

  function Get_New_Sieve return Sieve_Ptr is
  begin
    return new Sieve;
  end Get_New_Sieve;


  task body Odd is
    Limit : constant Positive := ...;
    Num : Positive;
    S : Sieve_Ptr := new Sieve;
  begin
    Num := 3;
    while Num < Limit loop
      S.Pass_On(Num);
      Num := Num + 2;
    end loop;
  end Odd;


  task body Sieve is
    New_Sieve : Sieve_Ptr;
    Prime, Num : Positive;
  begin
    accept Pass_On(Int : Integer) do
      Prime := Int;
    end Pass_On;
    -- Prime is a prime number, which could be output
    loop
      accept Pass_On(Int : Integer) do
        Num := Int;
      end Pass_On;
      exit when Num rem Prime /= 0;
    end loop;
```

```
      -- a number must be passed on and so a new Sieve task
      -- is created; note that it is necessary to use a
      -- function as a task type cannot be used directly
      -- within its own body
      New_Sieve := Get_New_Sieve;
      New_Sieve.Pass_On(Num);
      loop
        accept Pass_On(Int : Integer) do
          Num := Int;
        end Pass_On;
        if Num rem Prime /= 0 then
          New_Sieve.Pass_On(Num);
        end if;
      end loop;
    end Sieve;

  begin -- procedure
    null;
  end Primes_By_Sieve;
```

As with the example given in the previous chapter, this program still does
not terminate correctly. The next chapter (see Section 6.6.) will give the final
correctly terminating algorithm.

Synchronisation without communication

Where the sequence of statements inside an accept statement is precisely null,
then there is nothing to do within the rendezvous and the accept statement
can be terminated by a semicolon following the formal part. This might
be the case where only synchronisation is required. For example, consider
the following simple telephone home security service, which, on receiving a
specific entry call, will turn security lights on or off. Here there is no need
for data communication:

```
      task type Security_Operator (House : House_Id) is
        entry Turn_Lights_On;
        entry Turn_Lights_Off;
      end Security_Operator;

      task body Security_Operator is
      begin
        loop
          accept Turn_Lights_On;
          -- turn correct security light on
          accept Turn_Lights_Off;
          -- turn correct security light off
        end loop;
      end Security_Operator;
```

Note that the discriminant informs the task which house to access.

5.3.1 The Count attribute

Each entry queue has an attribute associated with it that allows the current length of the queue to be accessible to the owning task. E'Count returns a natural number representing the number of entry calls currently queued on the entry E, where E is either a single entry or a single entry of a family.

If E is an entry of task T, then E'Count can only be used within the body of T but not within a dependent program unit of that body.

The attribute Count would appear to be a useful one in enabling a synchronisation task to exercise specific control over outstanding requests. Care must, however, be taken when using Count as its value will not only increase with the arrival of new entry calls but may decrease as a result of a timed entry call or abort (see Chapters 6 and 10).

5.4 Entry families

Ada provides a facility which effectively allows the programmer to declare a one-dimensional array of entries. Such an array is called a *family*; it is declared by specifying a discrete range in the entry declaration before the parameter specification. For example, the following declares a multiplexer task with a family of three entries, each representing a channel on which data is to be received:

```
task Multiplexer is
   entry Channel(1..3)(X : in Data);
end Multiplexer;
```

In the body of a task declaring a family of entries, each member is treated as an individual entry and will therefore have its own accept statement. For example, a body for the multiplexer task is shown below:

```
task body Multiplexer is
begin
  loop
    accept Channel(1)(X : in Data) do
      -- consume input data on channel 1
    end Channel;
    accept Channel(2)(X : in Data) do
      -- consume input data on channel 2
    end Channel;
    accept Channel(3)(X : in Data) do
      -- consume input data on channel 3
    end Channel;
  end loop;
end Multiplexer;
```

The task simply waits for communication on the first channel, then the second channel and then the third channel. Alternatively, the task could have been written as

```
task body Multiplexer is
begin
  loop
    for I in 1..3 loop
      accept Channel(I)(X : in Data) do
        -- consume input data on channel I
      end Channel;
    end loop;
  end loop;
end Multiplexer;
```

A client task of the multiplexer must now not only specify the task and its entry but also which particular member of the family it wishes to communicate with:

```
Multiplexer.Channel(2)(My_Data);
```

As well as providing a mechanism by which several identical entries can be conveniently defined, entry families give a way of processing entry calls in a user-defined order. For example, consider a server task which wishes to give priority to certain tasks. This could be achieved by the following:

```
task Server is
  entry Request_High_Priority(...);
  entry Request_Medium_Priority(...);
  entry Request_Low_Priority(...);
end Server;
```

Within the body of this task, calls to Request_High_Priority would be processed first, then calls to Request_Medium_Priority and then finally calls to Request_Low_Priority. The entries are distinct and therefore separate queues are supplied and supported for each. A more appropriate solution to this problem is possible, however, using a family of entries:

```
type Request_Priority is (High,Medium,Low);

task Server is
  entry Request(Request_Priority)(...);
end Server;
```

An entry call would then specify the priority of the request:

```
Server.Request(Medium)(...);
```

The structure of the task Server is such that only one call to Request should be processed at a time. If concurrent execution of Request(High), Request(Medium) and Request(Low) were allowed by the requirements of the system, then an array of Server tasks would be a more appropriate structure:

```
type Request_Priority is (High, Medium, Low);
task type Server is
   entry Request(...);
end Server;
Servers : array (Request_Priority) of Server;
```

A high priority task would then call

```
Servers(High).Request(...);
```

and so on.

5.5   Three-way synchronisation

Although a rendezvous can only take place between two tasks, nested accept statements can be used to tie together more than just two tasks. Consider a program in which a task (Device) simulates the actions of an external device, and where Controller is a task acting as a device driver and User is some task that wishes to use the (input) device:

```
procedure Three_Way is
   task User;
   task Device;
   task Controller is
      entry Doio (I : out Integer);
      entry Start;
      entry Completed (K : Integer);
   end Controller;

   task body User is ...;
      -- includes calls to Controller.Doio(...)

   task body Device is
      J : Integer;
      procedure Read (I : out Integer) is ...;
   begin
      loop
         Controller.Start;
         Read(J);
         Controller.Completed(J);
      end loop;
   end Device;
```

```
task body Controller is
begin
  loop
    accept Doio (I : out Integer) do
      accept Start;
      accept Completed (K : Integer) do
        I := K;
      end Completed;
    end Doio;
  end loop;
end Controller;
begin
  null;
end Three_Way;
```

At the assignment of K to I, User is in rendezvous with Controller, and the rendezvous itself is in rendezvous with Device: three tasks are therefore synchronised.

A task can also issue an entry call to another task from within an accept statement. For example, consider the following tasks which model the customer interaction in a spare parts department for an automobile manufacturer. One task (Customer_Service) interfaces directly with the customer through an entry Request_Part. If this server task is unable to determine if the particular part is in stock, it communicates with a Warehouse task. If necessary, the requested part is placed on order:

```
task Warehouse is
  entry Enquiry(Item: Part_Number; In_Stock : Boolean);
  ...
end Warehouse;

task body Warehouse is separate; -- details not shown

task Customer_Service is
  entry Request_Part(Order : Part_Number;
                     Part : out Spare_Part;
                     Order_Id : out Order_Number);
end Customer_Service;


task body Customer_Service is
  Found : Boolean := False;
  ...
begin
  loop
    ...
    accept Request_Part(Order : Part_Number;
                        Part : out Spare_Part;
                        Order_Id : out Order_Number) do
      ...
```

```
        if Part_Found then
          Part := Found_Part;
          Order_Id := Null_Order;
        else
          Warehouse.Enquiry(Order, Found); -- entry call
          if Found then
            -- go and get part from warehouse
            Part := Found_Part;
            Order_Id := Null_Order;
          else
            -- make out order number
            Part := Null_Part;
            Order_Id := Next_Order_Number;
          end if;
        end if;
      end Request_Part;
    end loop;
end Customer_Service;
```

5.6   Private entries

So far in this chapter, all entries have been declared as public entries of the owning task. This makes them visible to all tasks for which the owning task's declaration is visible. In Ada it is also possible to declare entries as private to the owning task. There are several reasons why the programmer might wish to do this:

1. The task has several tasks declared internally; these internal tasks have access to the private entries.

2. The entry is to be used internally by the task for requeuing purposes (see Chapter 8).

3. The entry is an interrupt entry, and the programmer does not wish any software tasks to call this entry (see Chapter 11).

To illustrate the use of private entries, consider the controller program given earlier as an example of three-way communication. A possible way of rearranging this code is to have the device task contained within the controller task. This would be an appropriate decomposition for many systems, particularly when the controller has access to more than one device. With the new structure, only one of the controllers entries can be called from 'outside'. To enforce this restriction, private entries are used:

```
procedure Three_Way is
  task User;
  task Controller is
    entry Doio (I : out Integer);
```

```
private
  entry Start;
  entry Completed (K : Integer);
end Controller;

task body User is ...; -- includes calls to
                       -- Controller.Doio(...)

task body Controller is
  task Device;
  task body Device is
    J : Integer;
    procedure Read (I : out Integer) is ...;
  begin
    loop
      Controller.Start;
      Read(J);
      Controller.Completed(J);
    end loop;
  end Device;

begin
  loop
    accept Doio (I : out Integer) do
      accept Start;
      accept Completed (K : Integer) do
        I := K;
      end Completed;
    end Doio;
  end loop;
end Controller;
begin
  null;
end Three_Way;
```

5.7 Exceptions and the rendezvous

In Section 5.3, it was indicated that exceptions may be raised during the
rendezvous itself. In that discussion, all exceptions were trapped using a
'**when others**' exception handler. Clearly, it is possible for some exceptions to
propagate outside the accept statement. If this happens, then the rendezvous
is terminated and the exception is raised again in *both* the server (called) and
the client (calling) tasks.

To illustrate the flow of exceptions between tasks engaged in a rendezvous,
consider the following extension to the example given in Section 5.3:

```
accept Get(R : out Rec; Valid_Read : Boolean) do
  loop
    begin
```

```
          Put("VALUE OF I?"); Get(R.I);
          Put("VALUE OF F?"); Get(R.F);
          Put("VALUE OF S?"); Get(R.S);
          Valid_Read := True;
          return;
        exception
          when Text_Io.Data_Error =>
            Put("INVALID INPUT: START AGAIN");
        end;
      end loop;
    exception
      when Text_Io.Mode_Error =>
        Valid_Read := False;
    end Get;
```

If, during data input, the user types an inappropriate character, then Data_Error will be raised. As before, this is handled within the accept statement. Alternatively, if the file has been opened with the wrong mode, then the exception Mode_Error will be caught by the accept statement's handler and again it will not propagate.

The only other alternative is for an exception other than Data_Error or Mode_Error to be raised. For example, if the first call to Get causes Device_Error to be raised, then the exception will propagate out of the accept statement. Now the exception will be reraised in two tasks: the caller of this entry and the task owning the entry. If the caller happens not to have 'withed' Text_Io, then the exception will be anonymous in that task. It could only be handled with a "when others" handler.

The other interaction between exceptions and rendezvous occurs when a task attempts to call a task that has already terminated (completed or has become abnormal). In these situations the caller task gets the exception Tasking_Error raised at the point of call. If the called task has already terminated, then the exception is raised immediately. It can also be the case that the called task becomes terminated while the caller is queued on an entry. Again, Tasking_Error is raised.

If a task calls an entry family giving an index outside the permitted range, Constraint_Error is raised at the point of call. The called task is unaffected.

5.8 Task states

In this chapter the basic rendezvous mechanism has been described. The synchronisation required to perform a rendezvous means that a task may be suspended. This introduces further states into the state transition diagram that was introduced in Section 4.6. Figure 5.2 summarises the states of an Ada task introduced so far in this book.

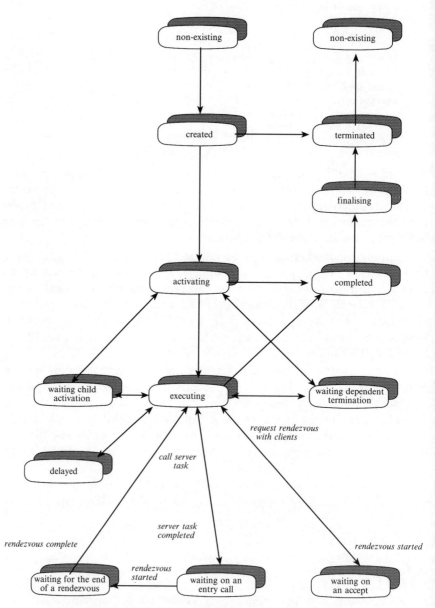

Figure 5.2: Summary of Task States and State Transitions.

5.9 Summary

The rendezvous represents a high level language abstraction for direct synchronous inter-task communication. Tasks declare entries that are called from other tasks. Within the called task an accept statement defines the statements that are executed while the two tasks are linked in the rendezvous.

Ada's model for the rendezvous is a flexible one allowing any number of parameter of any valid type to be passed. Moreover, it allows data to flow in the opposite direction to the rendezvous call.

Other issues covered in the chapter were entry families (these acts like one dimensional arrays of entries), private entries (which can help in visibility control) and exceptions. An exception raised in an accept statement can either be handled within the accept statement (in which case there are no further consequences), or it can be allowed to propagate beyond the accept statement. In this latter case the exception is raised both in the called and the calling task.

Although the basic model of the rendezvous is straightforward, some specific rules must be remembered when using this feature:

* Accept statements can only be placed in the body of a task.

* Nested accept statements for the same entry are not allowed.

* The 'Count attribute can only be accessed from within the task that owns the entry.

* Parameters to entries cannot be access parameters but can be parameters of an access type.

Chapter 6 ————————————————————

The Select Statement and the Rendezvous

The previous chapter presented the basic rendezvous model and detailed the language mechanisms by which two tasks can interact. In the basic model, a server task can only wait for a single rendezvous at any one time. Furthermore, once it has indicated that it wishes to communicate, it is committed to that communication and, if necessary, must wait indefinitely for the client to arrive at the rendezvous point. The same is true for the client task; in the basic model it can only issue a single entry call at any one time, and once issued the client is committed. In this chapter we show how some of these restrictions can be removed by using the **select** statement.

The select statement has four forms:

```
select_statement ::= selective_accept | conditional_entry_call
                   | timed_entry_call | asynchronous_select
```

This chapter will consider the first three of these forms in the context of the rendezvous mechanism. How the select statement can be applied to protected type entry calls and asynchronous transfer of control will be considered in Chapters 7 and 10 respectively.

6.1   Selective accept

The "selective accept" form of the select statement allows a server task to

* wait for more than a single rendezvous at any one time;

* time-out if no rendezvous is forthcoming within a specified period;

* withdraw its offer to communicate if no rendezvous is immediately available;

* terminate if no clients can possibly call its entries.

The syntax of the selective accept is

```
selective_accept ::=
  select
    [guard]
     selective_accept_alternative
{ or
    [guard]
     selective_accept_alternative }
[ else
    sequence_of_statement ]
  end select;

guard ::= when <condition> =>

selective_accept_alternative ::= accept_alternative
 | delay_alternative
 | terminate_alternative

accept_alternative ::=
  accept_statement [ sequence_of_statements ]

delay_alternative ::=
  delay_statement [ sequence_of_statements ]

terminate_alternative ::=
  terminate;
```

In the following sections, the various forms of the select statement will be explained and illustrated.

Waiting for more than a single rendezvous at any one time

A server task often wishes to provide more than a single service. Each service is represented by a separate entry declared in the task's specification. For example, if two services are offered, via entries S1 and S2, then the following structure is often sufficient (i.e. a loop containing a select statement which offers both services):

```
task Server is
  entry S1(...);
  entry S2(...);
end Server;

task body Server is
  ...
begin
  loop
    select
      accept S1(...) do
        -- code for this service
      end S1;
```

```
    or
        accept S2(...) do
            -- code for this service
        end S2;
    end select;
  end loop;
end Server;
```

On each execution of the loop, one of the accept statements will be executed.
To give a more illustrative example, consider the following
Telephone_Operator task type. It provides three services: an enquiry
entry requiring the name and address of a subscriber, an alternative
enquiry entry requiring the name and postal code of a subscriber and a
fault-reporting service requiring the number of the faulty line. The task also
has a private entry for use by its internal tasks:

```
task type Telephone_Operator is
  entry Directory_Enquiry(Person : in  Name; Addr : in Address;
                              Num : out Number);

  entry Directory_Enquiry(Person : in  Name;
          Zip : in Postal_Code; Num : out Number);

  entry Report_Fault(Num : Number);

private
  entry Allocate_Repair_Worker(Num : out Number);
end Telephone_Operator;
```

Without using the select statement, it is only possible to wait for one particular
entry call at any one time. Clearly, this is not sensible; the operator may
wish to wait for any one of its entries. The "select accept" form of the select
statement allows it to do just this. Consider the following, initial structure
of the Telephone_Operator task's body:

```
task body Telephone_Operator is
  Workers : constant Integer := 10;
  Failed : Number;
begin
  loop
    -- prepare to accept next request
    select
      accept Directory_Enquiry(Person : in Name;
              Addr : in Address; Num : out Number) do
        -- look up telephone number and
        -- assign the value to Num
      end Directory_Enquiry;
    or
      accept Directory_Enquiry(Person : in  Name;
              Zip : in Postal_Code; Num : out Number) do
```

```
              -- look up telephone number and
              -- assign the value to Num
          end Directory_Enquiry;
       or
          accept Report_Fault(Num : Number) do
            Failed := Num;
          end Report_Fault;
          -- log faulty line and allocate repair worker
        end select;
        -- undertake housekeeping such as
        -- logging all calls
      end loop;
  end Telephone_Operator;
```

In the above program fragment, the select statement allows the task to wait for a client task to call any one of its public entries. If none of the alternatives is immediately available (i.e. there are no entry calls waiting on the accept alternatives), then the `Telephone_Operator` task must wait (it is suspended) until a call is made, at which time a rendezvous can take place.

Clearly, it is possible that several clients may be waiting on one or more of the entries when the server task executes the select statement. In this case, the one chosen is implementation dependent. This means that the language itself does not define the order in which the requests are serviced. If the implementation is supporting the Real-Time Systems Annex, then certain orderings can be defined by the programmer (see Chapter 12). For general purpose concurrent programming, the programmer should assume that the order is arbitrary; that way the program cannot make any assumptions about the implementation of the language and thus it will be portable across different implementation approaches.

If tasks are queued on a single entry only, that entry is chosen and the rendezvous occurs with one of the client tasks; which client task is accepted again depends on whether the Real-Time Systems Annex is supported. By default, single queues are serviced on a first-come first-served basis.

It should be noted that statements can be placed after the accept statement in each arm of the select. For example, the comment "log faulty line ..." in the above code fragment can be expanded into a sequence of statements. This sequence is executed after the rendezvous has occurred. It may, of course, include another rendezvous. For example,

```
task body Telephone_Operator is
  Workers : constant Integer := 10;
  Failed : Number;
  task type Repair_Worker;
  Work_Force : array (1 .. Workers) of Repair_Worker;
  task body Repair_Worker is ...;
begin
  loop
    -- prepare to accept next request
```

```
select
   accept Directory_Enquiry(Person : in  Name;
            Addr : in Address; Num : out Number) do
      -- look up telephone number and
      -- assign the value to Num
   end Directory_Enquiry;
or
   accept Directory_Enquiry(Person : in  Name;
            Zip : in Postal_Code; Num : out Number) do
      -- look up telephone number and
      -- assign the value to Num
   end Directory_Enquiry;
or
   accept Report_Fault(Num : Number) do
      Failed := Num;
   end Report_Fault;
   -- log faulty line and allocate repair worker
   if New_Fault(Failed) then
        -- where New_Fault is a function in scope
      accept Allocate_Repair_Worker(Num : out Number) do
      Num := Failed;
      end Allocate_Repair_Worker;
   end if;
   end select;
   -- undertake housekeeping such as
   -- logging all calls
   end loop;
end Telephone_Operator;
```

Here, once a faulty number has been reported, the operator communicates the fault to a repair worker via a rendezvous on a private entry. The repair workers must indicate their availability by issuing an entry call on the operator.

The above examples should have made it clear that the execution of the select statement involves the execution of one, and only one, accept alternative. This may then be followed by an arbitrary collection of statements. If none of the accept alternatives can be taken, the task executing the select must be suspended.

6.2   Guarded alternatives

Each selective accept alternative can have a guard associated with it. This guard is a boolean expression which is evaluated when the select statement is executed. If the expression evaluates to true, the alternative is eligible for selection. If it is false, then the alternative is not eligible for selection during this execution of the select statement, even if clients are waiting on the associated entry. The general form for a guarded accept alternative is

```
select
  when Boolean_Expression =>
    accept S1(...) do
      -- code for service
    end S1;
or
  ...
end select;
```

Consider a Telephone_Operator task which will not accept a call to report a fault if all the repair workers have been allocated:

```
task body Telephone_Operator is
  ...
begin
  loop
    -- prepare to accept next request
    select
      accept Directory_Enquiry(Person : in Name;
              Addr : in Address; Num : out Number) do
        -- look up telephone number and
        -- assign the value to Num
      end Directory_Enquiry;
    or
      accept Directory_Enquiry(Person : in Name;
              Zip : in Postal_Code; Num : out Number) do
        -- look up telephone number and
        -- assign the value to Num
      end Directory_Enquiry;
    or
      when Workers_Available =>
        accept Report_Fault(Num : Number) do
          Failed := Num;
        end Report_Fault;
        ...
    end select;
    ...
  end loop;
end Telephone_Operator;
```

Note that the boolean expression is only evaluated once per execution of the select statement. If the expression accesses some shared data which might change whilst the select statement is waiting, then the change will go unnoticed until the select statement is reexecuted.

It is considered to be an error in the logic of the program if a selective accept statement has a guard on each of its alternatives and all the guards evaluate to false. When this happens, the exception Program_Error is raised. Alternatives without guards are deemed to have 'true' guards. Further discussion on guards is included in Section 6.5.

6.3   Delay alternative

Often it is the case that a server task cannot unreservedly commit itself to waiting for communication using one or more of its entries. The selective accept form of the select statement allows a server task to time-out if an entry call is not received within a certain period of time. The time-out is expressed using the delay statement and can therefore be a relative or an absolute delay. If the relative time expressed is zero or negative, or the absolute time has passed, then the delay alternative is equivalent to having an "else part" (see next section). If the expression associated with the delay statement requires evaluation, then this is done at the same time as the guards are being analysed: that is, at the beginning of the execution of the select statement. More than one delay alternative is allowed, although, for any particular execution of the select statement, only the delay with the smallest time interval will act as the time-out. Relative and absolute delay alternatives cannot be mixed (i.e. a select statement can have one or more 'delay' alternatives, or one or more "delay until" alternatives, but not both).

Generally, there are two reasons why a server task might wish to time-out waiting for an entry call; they are

1.   A task is required to execute periodically unless otherwise requested. For example, consider a periodic task which reads a sensor every ten seconds; however, it may be required to change its period during certain modes of the system's operation. This change should take effect immediately and the monitor should immediately read the sensor:

```ada
with Ada.Real_Time; use Ada.Real_Time;
   . . .
task Sensor_Monitor is
  entry New_Period(Period : Time_Span);
end Sensor_Monitor;

task body Sensor_Monitor is
  Current_Period : Time_Span := Milliseconds(10);
  Next_Cycle : Time := Clock +  Current_Period;
begin
  loop
    -- read sensor value and store in appropriate place
    select
      accept New_Period(Period : Time_Span) do
        Current_Period := Period;
      end accept;
      Next_Cycle := Clock + Current_Period;
    or
      delay until Next_Cycle;
      Next_Cycle := Next_Cycle + Current_Period;
    end select;
  end loop;
end Sensor_Monitor;
```

2.   The absence of the entry call within the specified time period indi-
     cates that an error condition has occurred (or some default action is
     required); for example consider the following task, which acts as a
     watchdog timer. The client task is meant to call the watchdog at least
     every ten seconds to indicate that all is well. If it fails to call in, the
     watchdog must raise an alarm:

```
task type Watchdog is
  entry All_Is_Well;
end Watchdog;

task body Watchdog is
begin
  loop
    select
      accept All_Is_Well;
    or
      delay 10.0;
      -- signal alarm, potentially the client has failed
      exit;
    end select;
  end loop;
  -- any further required action
end Watchdog;
```

Note that the delay time does not have to be a constant but could be a
variable.

Guards and the delay alternative

In the examples shown so far, there has only been a single unguarded
delay alternative. On occasions it may be appropriate to add a guard to a
delay branch. For example, consider the case where each repair to a faulty
telephone line is estimated to take no more than one hour:

```
task body Telephone_Operator is
  ...
begin
  loop
    -- prepare to accept next request
    select
      accept Directory_Enquiry(Person : in  Name;
              Addr : in Address; Num : out Number) do
        -- look up telephone number and
        -- assign the value to Num
      end Directory_Enquiry;
    or
      accept Directory_Enquiry(Person : in  Name;
              Zip : in Postal_Code; Num : out Number) do
```

```
        -- look up telephone number and
        -- assign the value to Num
      end Directory_Enquiry;
    or
      when Workers_Available =>
        accept Report_Fault(Num : Number) do
          Failed := Num;
        end Report_Fault;
        ...
    or
      when not Workers_Available =>
        delay 60.0;
        Workers_Available := True;
    end select;
    ...
  end loop;
end Telephone_Operator;
```

A guarded delay alternative whose guard evaluates to false on execution of the selection statement is not considered for selection. Hence, in the above example the time-out is not set if workers are available.

It may be appropriate to have more than one delay alternative in the same select statement. The same effect can be achieved by using only a single delay alternative, testing the boolean expressions just before the select statement and then setting an appropriate delay variable to the correct delay time; however, this may make the algorithm more difficult to understand.

In the general case, it could be possible that two open delay alternatives have the same delay time specified. If this is the case and the delay time expires, then either alternative may be selected depending on the queuing policy in effect.

Unnecessary use of the delay alternative

On some occasions, the use of the delay alternative might seem appropriate but can be avoided by restructuring the select statement. Consider the telephone operator example again; the operator may not wish to spend too much time waiting for a repair worker to become free, because whilst it is waiting it cannot service any directory enquiry request. It may therefore decide to wait for only a certain period of time:

```
task body Telephone_Operator is
  ...
begin
  loop
    -- prepare to accept next request
    select
      accept Directory_Enquiry(...; Addr : in Address; ...) do
        ...
```

```
            end Directory_Enquiry;
         or
            accept Directory_Enquiry(...; Zip : in Postal_Code; ...) do
               ...
            end Directory_Enquiry;
         or
            accept Report_Fault( Num : Number ) do
            -- save details of fault
            end Report_Fault;
            -- log faulty line and allocate repair worker
            while Unallocated_Faults -- Unallocated_Faults in scope
            loop
               -- get next failed number
               select
                  accept Allocate_Repair_Worker(Num : out Number) do
                     Num := Failed;
                  end Allocate_Repair_Worker;
                  -- update record of failed unallocated numbers
               or
                  delay 30.0;
                  exit;
               end select;
            end loop;
         end select;
         -- undertake housekeeping such as
         -- logging all calls
      end loop;
   end Telephone_Operator;
```

Although at first sight this seems an appropriate solution, it does cause some problems. In particular, if no workers are available, the telephone operator must keep track of the unallocated faults. With the code shown above, the operator will only attempt to find a worker to repair a line when a new request has come in. A better solution would be

```
   task body Telephone_Operator is
      ...
   begin
      loop
         -- prepare to accept next request
         select
            accept Directory_Enquiry(...) do ... end Directory_Enquiry;
         or
            accept Directory_Enquiry(...) do ... end Directory_Enquiry;
         or
            accept Report_Fault( Num : Number ) do
            -- save details of fault
            end Report_Fault;
         or
            when Unallocated_Faults =>
               accept Allocate_Repair_Worker( Num : out Number ) do
                  -- get next failed number
```

```
                Num := Next_Fault;
            end Allocate_Repair_Worker;
            -- update record of failed unallocated numbers
        end select;
        ...
    end loop;
end Telephone_Operator;
```

This algorithm is now prepared to accept a call from a worker task when there are faults still to be allocated. It is simpler and avoids the use of the delay.

6.4   The else part

As well as allowing a server task to time-out in the absence of a call, the selective accept form of the select statement also allows the server to withdraw its offer to communicate if no call is immediately available.

Consider again the Sensor_Monitor task. Suppose that the requirement is that only when the task starts its next monitoring period does it check to see if its rate is to be increased or decreased:

```
task body Sensor_Monitor is
    Current_Period : Time_Span := Milliseconds(10);
    Next_Cycle : Time := Clock + Current_Period;
begin
    loop
        select
            accept New_Period(Period : Time_Span) do
                Current_Period := Period;
            end accept;
        else
            null;
        end select;
        -- read sensor value and store in appropriate place
        Next_Cycle := Next_Cycle + Current_Period;
        delay until Next_Cycle;
    end loop;
end Sensor_Monitor;
```

In this case, as the sensor is to be read every time the task executes, the else part has a null sequence of statements. If the sensor were read only in the else part, the task would miss a reading on the changeover period.

It should be noted that an else part cannot be guarded and consequently only one else part may appear in a single select statement.

The delay alternative and the else part

If one compares the actions of the else clause and the delay alternative it is clear that to have both in the same select statement would be meaningless. The else clause defines an action to be taken, immediately, if no other alternative is executable. In contrast, the delay suspends the server task for some period of real-time. For these reasons, the language does not allow a select statement to contain a delay alternative and an else part. Interestingly, as type Duration has a range including 0.0, it is possible to delay for zero time. The following are therefore equivalent (for some sequence of statements C):

```
select                        select
   accept A;                     accept A;
or                            or
   accept B;                     accept B;
else                          or
   C;                            delay 0.0;
end select;                      C;
                              end select;
```

It can therefore be argued that the else structure is redundant. However, its use does make the programmer's intention more explicit.

Finally in this section, two code fragments will be compared in order to illustrate the distinction between the delay alternative and the else part with a delay statement:

```
select  -- S1              select  -- S2
   accept A;                  accept A;
or                         else
   delay 10.0;                delay 10.0;
end select;                end select;
```

In the above, if there is an outstanding entry call on A, then these select statements will behave identically, that is, the call to A will be accepted. The distinction arises when there is no waiting call. In S1, the delay alternative will allow a call to A to be accepted if one arrives in the next ten seconds. S2 gives no such provision. If there is no outstanding call, the else part is executed; this happens to be an ordinary delay statement and so the task is delayed for ten seconds. If a call to A did arrive after, say, four seconds, S2 would not accept it (whereas S1 would). There is also a clear distinction between the behaviours of the following program fragments:

```
select                        select
   accept A;                     accept A;
or                            or
   delay 10.0;                   delay 20.0;
```

```
        delay 10.0;
      end select;                              end select;
```

The first example will accept a call to A only during the first ten seconds (it will then delay for a further ten seconds); the second example will accept a call during the entire twenty-second interval.

This apparent dual role for the delay keyword does cause confusion to programmers learning the language; it is unfortunate that another identifier such as 'time-out' was not used. However, this would increase the number of language keywords and hence complicate the language in other ways.

6.5   The correct use of guards

The boolean expression associated with a guard has no particular properties; it is however strongly recommended that shared variables should not be used. This would be a particularly inappropriate form of synchronisation and would be likely to lead to unforeseen actions by the program; these being due to the fact that the guard is only evaluated once and is not 'retested' when an entry call is made or when the value of some component of the guard changes.

Consider the following code, which controls calls to the entries Clock_In and Clock_Out. The specification of this task requires that Clock_In is not allowed before 08.30 hours (constant Start). Let Works_Clock be some function that provides the time in the correct form:

```
loop
  select
    when Works_Clock > Start =>
      accept Clock_In(N : Staff_Number) do
          . . .
      end Clock_In;
  or
      accept Clock_Out(N : Staff_Number) do
          . . .
      end Clock_Out;
  end select;
end loop;
```

This code, though superficially correct, is wrong. Consider the following interleaving:

1.   Call to Clock_Out at 8.20.

2.   Select statement is then immediately reexecuted; the guard is False so Clock_In is deemed to be closed.

3.   Call to Clock_In at 8.45 — NOT ACCEPTED.

Indeed, no calls to Clock_In would be processed until a call to Clock_Out had terminated that particular execution of the select.

A correct but inappropriate solution to this requirement would be to use an else clause:

```
loop
  select
    when Works_Clock > Start =>
      accept Clock_In(N : Staff_Number) do
        . . .
      end Clock_In;
  or
    accept Clock_Out(N : Staff_Number) do
      . . .
    end Clock_Out;
  else
    null;
  end select;
end loop;
```

Although this is now correct, in the sense that a call to Clock_In would be accepted at 8.45, it is very inefficient. This solution is, in effect, employing a busy-wait, which is not only wasteful of processor cycles but could lead to indefinite postponement of all other tasks on a single-processor system. The correct solution to this problem must employ a reference to Works_Clock inside (or immediately after) the accept statement. Two possibilities are given below:

```
(1)    accept Clock_In(N : Staff_Number; Ok : out Boolean) do
         if Works_Clock <Start then
           Ok := False;
         else
           Ok := True;
           Start_Time(N) := Works_Clock;
         end if;
       end Clock_In;
```

```
(2)    accept Clock_In(N : Staff_Number) do
         Temp_N := N;
       end Clock_In;
       if Works_Clock < Start then
         Start_Time(Temp_N) := Start;
       else
         Start_Time(Temp_N) := Works_Clock;
       end if;
```

As the above discussion indicates, the else clause should only be used when absolutely necessary. Its existence in the language encourages the use of 'polling'. Polling is characterised by a task actively and repeatedly checking for the occurrence of some event. Unless a task can genuinely proceed with useful work in the situation where an entry call is not immediately outstanding, then the task should delay itself on a select statement without an else clause.

6.6   The terminate alternative

In general, server tasks only need to exist if there are clients which require their services. However, the very nature of the client/server model is that the server does not, in general, know the identities of its client. Consequently, it is difficult for it to know when it can terminate. Conditions for termination can clearly be expressed as part of the program's logic, for example by using a special entry:

```
task General_Server is
  entry Service1(...);
  entry Service2(...);
  ...
  entry Terminate_Now(...);
end General_Server;

task body General_Server is
  ...
begin
  ...
  loop
    select
      accept Service1(...) do ... end;
    or
      accept Service2(...) do ... end;
    or
      ...
    or
      accept Terminate_Now;
      exit;
    end select;
  end loop;
end General_Server;
```

However, as this situation is common, a special select alternative is provided: the terminate alternative consists of only the single statement 'terminate' — which can be guarded. It is not possible to include a sequence of statements after the terminate alternative that the task can execute before terminating. This same effect can be achieved, however, by use of the finalisation facility (see Section 6.6.1 for a discussion on "last wishes"). With the terminate alternative, the above example simply becomes

```
task General_Server is
  entry Service1(...);
```

```
    entry Service2(...);
    ...
end General_Server;

task body General_Server is
    ...
begin
    ...
    loop
      select
        accept Service1(...) do ... end;
      or
        accept Service2(...) do ... end;
      or
        ...
      or
        terminate;
      end select;
    end loop;
end General_Server;
```

A server task which is suspended at a select statement with an open terminate alternative will become completed when the following conditions are satisfied:

- The task depends on some master whose execution is completed.

- Each task which depends on the master considered is either already terminated or similarly blocked at a select statement with an open terminate alternative.

When both the above conditions are satisfied, not only is the task being considered completed but so also are all the tasks that depend on the master being considered. Once these tasks are completed any associated finalisation code is executed.

For the server task to be completed, all remaining tasks that can call it must be suspended on appropriate select statements or have already completed. Therefore, there can be no outstanding entry calls (no task could have made such a call). Thus the terminate alternative cannot be selected if there is a queued entry call for any entry of the task. It is therefore not necessary, in normal circumstances, to guard the terminate alternative. The only real argument for using a guard is one of efficiency. On a multi-processor system, tests for termination can be expensive. If the application knows that termination cannot be possible until at least some minimum condition holds, then there is a value in guarding the 'terminate'.

As the inclusion of a terminate alternative indicates that on the execution of this select statement the server task may have no further work to do, it would be illogical to also include a delay alternative or an else clause in the same select statement. These possible combinations are therefore prohibited.

An example of the use of the terminate alternative comes from the primes by sieve program given in the previous chapter. The version given did not terminate when the total number of primes had been calculated. The Odd task terminated but the others in the pipeline remained suspended waiting for more integers to work upon. An appropriate modification allows termination to occur:

```
procedure Primes_By_Sieve is
  task type Sieve is
    entry Pass_On(Int : Integer);
  end Sieve;

  task Odd;

  type Sieve_Ptr is access Sieve;

  function Get_New_Sieve return Sieve_Ptr is
  begin
    return new Sieve;
  end Get_New_Sieve;


  task body Odd is
    Limit : constant Positive := ...;
    Num : Positive;
    S : Sieve_Ptr := new Sieve;
  begin
    Num := 3;
    while Num < Limit loop
      S.Pass_On(Num);
      Num := Num + 2;
    end loop;
  end Odd;


  task body Sieve is
    New_Sieve : Sieve_Ptr;
    Prime, Num : Positive;
  begin
    accept Pass_On(Int : Integer) do
      Num := Int;
    end Pass_On;
    -- Prime is a prime number, which could be output
    loop
      select
        accept Pass_On(Int : Integer) do
          Num := Int;
        end Pass_On;
      or
        terminate;
      end select;
```

```
      exit when Num rem Prime /= 0;
    end loop;
    -- a number must be passed on and
    -- so a new Sieve task is created
    New_Sieve := Get_New_Sieve;
    New_Sieve.Pass_On(Num);
    loop
      select
        accept Pass_On(Int : Integer) do
          Num := Int;
        end Pass_On;
      or
        terminate;
      end select;
      if Num rem Prime /= 0 then
        New_Sieve.Pass_On(Num);
      end if;
    end loop;
  end Sieve;


begin -- procedure
  null;
end Primes_By_Sieve;
```

The issue of termination in a distributed environment is discussed in Chapter 14.

6.6.1 Last wishes

One criticism made of this automatic termination feature, in Ada 83, was that the task could not execute any "last wishes". Once the conditions were right for a task to terminate, it did so. There are, however, many situations in which it is desirable to execute some finalisation code, either to close down some external resource (such as a file), or "clean up" some data structures that are shared with some later phase of execution of the program, or to produce a final report of some kind.

Controlled types allow data objects to perform last wishes (these were described in Chapter 1). A task cannot be derived from a controlled type, and therefore it is not possible to associate user-defined finalisation code with the task itself. Of course, any controlled objects defined in the task body will be finalised anyway; therefore finalisation of the task itself can be achieved by using a dummy controlled variable. It is a dummy in the sense that its only role is to invoke finalisation when the task is ready to terminate (and hence the variable is about to go out of scope).

To give a simple illustration of the use of last wishes, consider a server task that offers two services and wishes to print out, as it terminates, the

total number of calls made upon each service. The specification of the server
task is straightforward:

```
task Server is
   entry Service1(...);
   entry Service2(...);
end Server;
```

The body of this task must have visibility of the finalisation package; to do
this it is assumed that the task body is a separately compiled library unit (of
procedure Main):

```
with Ada.Finalization; use Ada;
with Text_Io; use Text_Io;
separate (Main)
task body Server is
   Count1, Count2 : Natural := 0;
   package Int_Io is new Integer_Io(Natural);

   type Task_Last_Wishes is new Finalization.Limited_Controlled
      with null record;

   procedure Finalise(Tlw : in out Task_Last_Wishes) is
   begin
      Put("Calls on Service1:");
      Int_Io.Put(Count1);
      Put("Calls on Service2:");
      Int_Io.Put(Count2);
   end Finalise;

   Last_Wishes : Task_Last_Wishes;

begin   - of task body
   -- initial housekeeping
   loop
      select
         accept Service1(...) do
            ...
         end Service1;
         Count1 := Count1 + 1;
      or
         accept Service2(...) do
            ...
         end Service1;
         Count2 := Count2 + 1;
      or
         terminate;
      end select;
      -- housekeeping
   end loop;
end Server;
```

When the conditions are right the server task will finalise the Last_Wishes variable, the two totals will be printed out and the task will then become terminated.

6.7   The exception Program_Error

If all the accept alternatives have guards then there is the possibility that all the guards will be closed. Moreover, in this situation if the select statement does not contain an else clause, then it becomes impossible for the statement to be executed. This invidious position could be catered for in the following two ways:

1.   The situation is deemed to be an error.

2.   The select statement becomes equivalent to 'null' and the task continues execution.

As indicated earlier, the designers of Ada decided upon the first solution and the exception Program_Error is raised at the point of the select statement if no alternatives are open. In general, there will normally exist a relationship between the guards that will allow an analysis of the code to prove that the exception cannot be raised. There will, however, be situations where this is not the case. Consider the following examples:

```
1.   if A then            2.   select
         accept B;                 when A =>
     end if;                           accept B;
                              end select;
3.   select
         when A =>
             accept B;
     else
         null;
     end select;
```

These three examples involve a single accept statement B and the condition A. If A is False we do not wish to accept B, but if A is True we may wish to:

(a)   accept an entry call before proceeding; or

(b)   accept an entry call if and only if one is currently outstanding.

Example 1 caters for (a); example 3 caters for (b); example 2 is unnecessary and would cause an exception to be raised if A were False.

With two accept statements and two conditions the situation is more complex:

```
4.   if A then            5.   select
```

```
          accept B;                      when A =>
       elsif C then                        accept B;
          accept D;                     or
       end if;                             when C =>
                                             accept D;
                                          end select;


    6.  select
           when A = >
              accept B;
           or
           when C =>
              accept D;
           else
              null;
           end select;
```

The equivalent of case (b) is again easily catered for (example 6) in that an
open accept alternative will be taken if a call is outstanding. Example 4 does
not, however, deal appropriately with the first case, for if A and C are both
True then B will always be chosen in preference to D even when there is an
outstanding call to D but not B. True indeterminacy can only be provided by
the code in example 5; but this code will fail when A and C are both False.
If A and C are not related, then it is clearly not possible to prove that A =
C = False cannot occur. In these circumstances the select statement itself
must be 'guarded'; the correct solution to the above problem is therefore

```
   if A or C then
     select
       when A =>
          accept B;
     or
        when C =>
           accept D;
     end select;
   end if;
```

Note, however, that if A and C are shared variables, their values could change
between the if statement and the select statement.

6.8   Summary of the selective accept statement

The selective accept form of the select statement can be summarised as
follows:

*   A selective accept must contain at least one accept alternative (each
    possibly guarded).

*   A selective accept may contain one, and only one, of the following:

— a terminate alternative (possibly guarded); or
— one or more absolute delay alternatives (each possibly guarded); or
— one or more relative delay alternatives (each possibly guarded); or
— an else part.

A select alternative is said to be 'open' if it does not contain a guard or if the boolean condition associated with the guard evaluates to true. Otherwise the alternative is 'closed'. On execution of the select statement, the first action to be taken is for all the guards to be evaluated and for all open delay expressions and entry family expressions to be evaluated; all open alternatives are thus determined. For this execution of the select statement, closed alternatives are no longer considered. If one or more open accept alternatives has an outstanding entry call, then one of these accept alternatives is chosen (the choice depends on the implementation and whether the Real-Time Systems Annex is being supported). The accept statement is executed, the rendezvous takes place, any statements following the accept (within that branch of the select statement) are executed and the execution of the select statement is then complete.

If, however, no open accept alternative has an outstanding entry call, then if there is an else part this will be executed. Otherwise, the select statement will suspend waiting until:

• the arrival of an entry call associated with one of the open accept alternatives;

• the expiry of any open delay alternative; or

• the task becomes completed.

6.9   Conditional and timed entry calls

In the previous sections, it was shown how a server task could avoid unreservedly committing itself to accepting a single entry call by using a select statement. These facilities are not totally available to the client task, which can only issue a single entry call at any one time. However, the language does allow the client to avoid committing itself to the rendezvous by providing conditional and timed entry call facilities as part of the select statement.

6.9.1   Timed entry calls

A timed entry call issues an entry call which is cancelled if the call is not accepted within the specified period (relative or absolute). The syntax is

```
timed_entry_call ::=
  select
    entry_call_alternative
  or
    delay_alternative
  end select;

entry_call_alternative ::=
  entry_call_statement [sequence_of_statements]
```

Note that only one delay alternative and one entry call can be specified.
Consider, for example, the following client of the telephone operator task:

```
task type Subscriber;

task body Subscriber is
  Stuarts_Number : Number;
begin
  loop
    ...
    select
      An_Op.Directory_Enquiry("STUART JONES",
                              "10 MAIN STREET, YORK",
                              Stuarts_Number);
      -- log the cost of a directory enquiry call
    or
      delay 10.0;
      -- phone up his parents and ask them,
      -- log the cost of a long distance call
    end select;
    ...
  end loop;
end Subscriber;
```

Here the task waits for ten seconds for the operator to accept the call. If
the call is not accepted before the ten seconds have expired, the subscriber's
call is cancelled and (in this case) the task attempts to obtain the required
number via an alternative source.

The main point to note about the timed entry call is that it provides a
facility whereby the client can cancel the call if it is not accepted within
the specified period. *It makes no guarantee that the results from the call will
be returned in that period.* For example, consider the following telephone
operator task:

```
task body Telephone_Operator is
  ...
begin
  loop
    -- prepare to accept next request
```

```
    select
      accept Directory_Enquiry(Person : in Name;
             Addr : in Address; Num : out Number) do
        delay 60.0; -- take a lunch break
      end Directory_Enquiry;
    or
      ...
    end select;
    ...
  end loop;
end Telephone_Operator;
```

Here the operator, once it has accepted an enquiry request, delays for one hour before servicing the request. The client task is now forced to wait because the call has been accepted. To avoid this possibility, the client must use the select's asynchronous transfer of control facility (see Section 10.3).

6.9.2 Conditional entry call

The conditional entry call allows the client to withdraw the offer to communicate if the server task is not prepared to accept the call immediately. It has the same meaning as a timed entry call, where the expiry time is immediate; the syntax is

```
conditional_entry_call ::=
  select
    entry_call_alternative
  else
    sequence_of_statements
  end select;
```

For example, a very impatient client of the telephone operator task may not be prepared to wait for a connection:

```
task type Subscriber;

task body Subscriber is
  Stuarts_Number : Number;
begin
  loop
    ...
    select
      An_Op.Directory_Enquiry("STUART JONES",
                               "10 MAIN STREET, YORK",
                               Stuarts_Number);
      -- log the cost of a directory enquiry call
    else
      -- phone up his parents and ask them,
      -- log the cost of a long distance call
    end select;
```

```
   ...
   end loop;
end Subscriber;
```

Clearly, it is possible for two clients to issue simultaneous conditional entry calls, or timed entry calls with immediate expiry times. There is therefore an obligation on the Ada run-time support system to make the commit operation an indivisible action so that only one client task can see the state of the server at any one time.

A conditional entry call should only be used when the task can genuinely do other productive work if the call is not accepted. Care should be taken not to program polling, or busy-wait, solutions   unless they are explicitly required.

Note that the conditional entry call uses an 'else', the timed entry call an 'or'. Moreover, they cannot be mixed, nor can two entry call statements be included. A client task cannot therefore wait for more than one entry call to be serviced.

6.10   Mutual exclusion and deadlocks

A number of the inherent difficulties associated with concurrent programming were considered in Chapter 3. Of paramount importance is ensuring the integrity of resources that should not be accessed by more than one task at a time (non-concurrent resources). This integrity is usually assured by defining a critical section of code that must be protected by mutual exclusion. With a server task, mutual exclusion can easily be constructed:

```
task type Server is
   entry A(...);
   entry B(...);
   ...
end T;

task body Server is
   -- The resource is represented by the definition
   -- of some appropriate data structure.
begin
   loop
      select
         accept A(...) do
            ...
         end A;
         -- housekeeping
      or
         accept B(...) do
            ...
         end B;
         -- housekeeping
```

```
    or
       . . .
    end select;
    -- housekeeping
    end loop;
  end Server;
```

Each task of type `Server` will define a new resource. For each of these resources, although entries A, B, etc., may give access, the semantics of the task body (with or without a select statement) ensure that only one accept statement at a time can be executing. The accept statement is itself the critical section. As long as the resource is defined within the task body, and is not accessible to 'subtasks' defined within the same body, then mutual exclusion is provided. Mutual exclusion does not, however, extend to including the evaluations of the actual parameters to an entry call. The evaluation of such parameters in two distinct entry calls may therefore interfere with each other if shared variables are used directly or are influenced by side effects.

Deadlocks are another matter! Consider the following code:

```
task T1 is                          task T2 is
  entry A;                            entry B;
end T1;                             end T2;

task body T1 is                     task body T2 is
begin                               begin
  T2.B;                               T1.A;
  accept A;                           accept B;
end T1;                             end T2;
```

Clearly, each tasks will be placed on an entry queue for the other task. They will therefore not be in a position to accept the outstanding call. A task can even call its own entries and deadlock! Guidelines can reduce the possibility of deadlocks but inherent deadlocks should (must!) be recognised early in the design of systems and evasive action taken.

The following points are pertinent:

* Tasks should be constructed to be either active entities or servers.

* Active tasks make entry calls but do not have entries.

* Server tasks accept entry calls but make no calls themselves.

* Entry calls from within rendezvous should only be used when absolutely necessary.

Where a collection of servers is accessed by a number of tasks, then

1. Tasks should use servers one at a time if possible.

2. If (1) is not possible, then all tasks should access the servers in the same predefined order.

3. If (1) and (2) are not possible, then the server tasks must be designed to take appropriate remedial action. For example, resources could be preemptively removed from active tasks using a time-out structure.

With deadlocks, there is no substitute for proving that they cannot occur in the first place!

To ensure liveness, select statements can be constructed to force the system to examine each queue in turn:

```
loop
  select
     accept A;
  else
     null;
  end select;
  select
     accept B;
  else
     null;
  end select;
  select
     accept A;
  or
     accept B;
  end select;
end loop;
```

This structure would, of course, become very tedious if a large number of entries were involved! The final select statement is needed to delay the server task if no outstanding entry calls exist (otherwise the task would loop around and poll the entry queues).

6.11   The dining philosophers

In this section a solution to the dining philosophers program that was outlined in Section 3.5 will be given. It is assumed that the chopsticks are under the control of server tasks, as is the deadlock prevention rule that only allows N-1 philosophers to eat at a time. To obtain an array of static philosopher tasks (each with a unique discriminant) would require the side-effect initialisation function described in Section 4.1. In the following code an alternative structure is used: a static array of a task access type. Each task is then created with the correct discriminant:

```
procedure Dining_Philosophers is
   package Activities is
      procedure Think;
      procedure Eat;
```

```
end Activities;

N : constant := 5;  -- number of philosophers.
type Philosophers_Range is new Integer range 0..N-1;

task type Phil(P : Philosophers_Range);
type Philosopher is access Phil;

task type Chopstick_Control is
  entry Pick_Up;
  entry Put_Down;
end Chopstick_Control;

task Deadlock_Prevention is
  entry Enters;
  entry Leaves;
end Deadlock_Prevention;

Chopsticks : array(Philosophers_Range) of Chopstick_Control;
Philosophers : array(Philosophers_Range) of Philosopher;

package body Activities is separate;
task body Phil is separate;
task body Chopstick_Control is separate;
task body Deadlock_Prevention is separate;

begin
  for P in Philosophers_Range loop
    Philosophers(P) := new Phil(P);
  end loop;
end Dining_Philosophers;
```

The procedures Think and Eat in the package Activities will consist of
some appropriate delay statement and will be called concurrently by the
philosophers, who are structured as active tasks. Each of the chopsticks
resource is represented by a server task:

```
separate (Dining_Philosophers)
task body Chopstick_Control is
begin
  loop
    accept Pick_Up;
    accept Put_Down;
  end loop;
end Chopstick_Control;
```

Deadlocks are prevented by noting that they can only occur if all the
philosophers wish to eat at the same time. By stopping just one philosopher
from entering the eating stage, deadlocks are prevented; moreover, as only
one philosopher task is delayed (and therefore freed when a single philosopher
stops eating), liveness is preserved:

```
separate (Dining_Philosophers)
task body Deadlock_Prevention is
  Max : constant Integer := N - 1;
  People_Eating : Integer range 0..Max := 0;
begin
  loop
    select
      when People_Eating < Max =>
        accept Enters;
        People_Eating := People_Eating + 1;
    or
      accept Leaves;
      People_Eating := People_Eating - 1;
    end select;
  end loop;
end Deadlock_Prevention;
```

The philosophers themselves are necessarily programmed as tasks and have a simple life-cycle. In order to know which chopsticks to pick up, each philosopher must know its own identity. This is achieved by passing a unique array index during task creation. The process task therefore makes calls upon the server agents and is not itself called:

```
separate (Dining_Philosophers)
task body Phil (P : Philosophers_Range) is
  Chop_Stick1, Chop_Stick2 : Philosophers_Range;
begin
  Chop_Stick1 := P;
  Chop_Stick2 := (Chop_Stick1 + 1) mod N;
  loop
    Think;
    Deadlock_Prevention.Enters;
    Chopsticks(Chop_Stick1).Pick_Up;
    Chopsticks(Chop_Stick2).Pick_Up;
    Eat;
    Chopsticks(Chop_Stick1).Put_Down;
    Chopsticks(Chop_Stick2).Put_Down;
    Deadlock_Prevention.Leaves;
  end loop;
end Philosopher;
```

The structure used above ensures an indefinite execution of the program. If a limited execution is desired, then the Philosopher would need to exit from its life-cycle after a number of iterations or after some duration of time. The synchronisation tasks would all have "or terminate" alternatives on their select statements.

The reliability of this solution is typical of many concurrent Ada programs. Firstly, it can be seen that the failure of any of the server tasks would be disastrous for the program as a whole. A Philosopher could, however, terminate without affecting the system unless he or she happened to have control of a chopstick at that time. Resources can, in general, be programmed to put themselves back in the resource pool in this eventuality. Assume that there is an upper limit of Interval on the time it takes for a philosopher to eat, such that if a chopstick is not returned within that period the philosopher can be assumed to have died (of overeating!). The body for the task Chopstick_Control would then take the following form (including a termination alternative):

```
task body Chopstick_Control is
begin
  loop
    select
      accept Pick_Up;
    or
      terminate;
    end select;
    select
      accept Put_Down;
    or
      delay Interval;
      -- As the philosopher has not called Put_Down he or
      -- she is assumed to be 'dead', the chopsticks can
      -- therefore be rescued.
    end select;
  end loop;
end Chopstick_Control;
```

6.12 Task states

In this chapter the basic rendezvous mechanism has been extended. The select statement has introduced further states into the state transition diagram. Figure 6.1 summarises the states of an Ada task introduced so far in this book.

6.13 Summary

In order to increase the expressive power of rendezvous-based communications, Ada provides the select statement. This allows a task to choose between alternative actions. The fundamental use of the select statement is to allow a server task to choose to execute one of any number of possible accept statements. The server task does not need to give a fixed ordering, it can choose any of the accept statements that have outstanding entry calls.

There are a number of different variations of the select statement. Not only can a server task wait for more than one call, it can choose to limit its

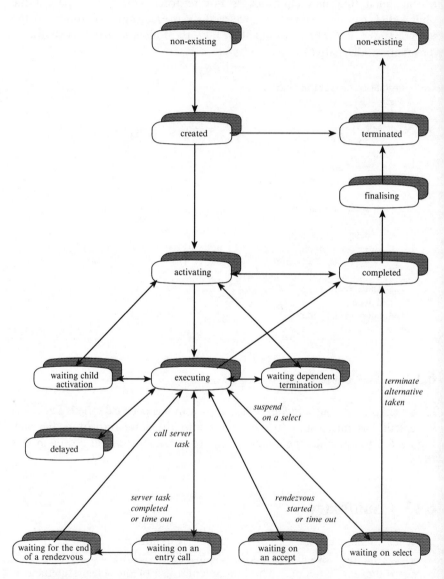

Figure 6.1: Summary of Task States and State Transitions.

wait to a period of real-time; indeed it can choose not to wait at all if there are no outstanding calls.

The select statement is also used to support a form of termination that is very useful in concurrent programs with hierarchical task structures. A task will terminate if it is suspended on a select statement, with a terminate alternative, if all tasks that could call it are either already terminated or are similarly suspended on this type of select statement. If a task wishes to perform some last rites before terminating, then it can use a controlled variable.

In addition to selecting between different incoming calls, the select statement can also allow an external outgoing call to be made conditionally (i.e. if the call cannot be accepted immediately, it is cancelled) or be 'offered' for only a limited period of time. In the latter case if the call is not accepted within the defined time interval it is cancelled.

Although flexible, the select statement does not allow a task to select between more than one entry call, or to choose between an accept statement and an entry call.

Chapter 7 ————————————————————

Protected Objects and Data-Oriented Communication

The problem of sharing resources between processes was briefly discussed in Chapter 3. Two requirements were identified as being essential: mutual exclusion and condition synchronisation. This chapter discusses various ways in which these requirements can be met in Ada without having to encapsulate the resource in a server task and using the rendezvous. Ada gives direct support to protected data by the abstraction of a *protected object*, the discussion of which is the main focus of this chapter. However, the language does also support the notions of atomic and volatile data.

7.1 Protected objects

A protected object in Ada encapsulates data items and allows access to them only via protected subprograms or protected entries. The language guarantees that these subprograms and entries will be executed in a manner that ensures that the data is updated under mutual exclusion. Consequently, they are rather like monitors (Hoare, 1974) and conditional critical regions (Brinch-Hansen, 1972) found in previous concurrent programming languages.

A protected unit may be declared as a type or as a single instance; it has a specification and a body. The specification of a protected unit has the following syntax (as with a task, there is a visible and a private part):

```
protected_type_declaration::=
    protected type defining_identifier [known_discriminant_part]
            is protected_definition;

single_protected_declaration ::= protected defining_identifier
            is protected_definition;

protected_definition ::=
        { protected_operation_declaration }
    [ private
        { protected_element_declaration } ]
    end [protected_identifier]

protected_operation_declaration ::= subprogram_declaration |
```

```
                                       entry_declaration
protected_element_declaration ::=
    protected_operation_declaration | component_declaration
```

Thus a protected type has an interface that can contain functions, procedures and entries. As with tasks and records, the discriminant can only be of a discrete or access type.

The body, which may be compiled separately from the specification, is declared using the following syntax:

```
protected_body ::=
    protected body defining_identifier is
        { protected_operation_item }
    end [protected_identifier];

protected_operation_identifier ::=
    subprogram_declaration | subprogram_body | entry_body

entry_body ::=
    entry defining_identifier entry_body_formal_part
                entry_barrier is
        declarative_part
    begin
        handled_sequence_of_statements
    end; [entry_identifier];

entry_body_formal_part ::=
    [(entry_index_specification)] parameter_profile

entry_barrier ::= when condition

entry_index_specification ::=
    for defining_identifier in discrete_subtype_definition
```

A protected type is a "limited type", and therefore there are no predefined assignment or comparison operators (the same is true for task types).

The following examples illustrate the declaration of protected types and objects, and define their full semantics.

7.2 Mutual exclusion

The following declaration illustrates how protected types can be used to provide simple mutual exclusion:

```
-- a simple integer
protected type Shared_Integer(Initial_Value : Integer) is
    function Read return Integer;
    procedure Write(New_Value : Integer);
    procedure Increment(By : Integer);
```

```
private
   The_Data : Integer := Initial_Value;
end Shared_Integer;

My_Data : Shared_Integer(42);
```

The above protected type encapsulates a shared integer. The object declaration My_Data declares an instance of the protected type and passes the initial value for the encapsulated data. The encapsulated data can now only be accessed by the three subprograms: Read, Write and Increment.

A protected procedure provides mutually exclusive read/write access to the data encapsulated. In this case, concurrent calls to the procedure Write or Increment will be executed in mutual exclusion; that is, only one can be executing at any one time. If, for example, a task attempts to call Write whilst another task is already executing the procedure (or already executing a call to Read or Increment), it is unable to enter the Write procedure until the other task has exited.

Protected functions provide concurrent read-only access to the encapsulated data. In the above example this means that many calls to Read can be executed simultaneously. However, calls to a protected function are still executed mutually exclusively with calls to a protected procedure. A Read call cannot be executed if there is a currently executing procedure call; a procedure call cannot be executed if there is one or more concurrently executing function calls.

The core language does not define the order in which tasks waiting to execute protected functions and protected procedures are executed. If, however, the Real-Time Systems Annex is being supported, certain assumptions can be made about the order of execution (see Chapter 12).

The body of the Shared_Integer is simply

```
protected body Shared_Integer is
   function Read return Integer is
   begin
      return The_Data;
   end Read;

   procedure Write(New_Value : Integer) is
   begin
      The_Data := New_Value;
   end Write;

   procedure Increment(By : Integer) is
   begin
      The_Data := The_Data + By;
   end Increment;
end Shared_Integer;
```

Without the abstraction of a protected object this shared integer would have had to be implemented as a server task with the read and write operations being coded as entries:

```
task body Shared_Integer is
   The_Data := Initial_Value;
begin
   loop
     select
       accept Read(New_Value : out Integer) do
         New_Value := The_Data;
       end Read;
     or
       accept Write(New_Value : Integer) do
         The_Data := New_Value;
       end; Write
     or
       accept Increment(By : Integer) do
         The_Data := The_Data + By;
       end Increment;
     or
       terminate;
     end select;
   end loop;
end Shared_Integer;
```

Whereas the task has an explicit select statement and loop construct, the protected object has an entirely implicit structure. It does not even need to concern itself with termination. A protected object is passive, and will thus cease to exist when its scope disappears.

Protected objects and tasks are, however, alike in that they are both limited private data types. Single protected objects can also be declared (cf. anonymous task types):

```
protected My_Data is
   function Read  return  Integer;
   procedure Write (New_Value : Integer);
private
   The_Data : Integer := Initial_Value;
end My_Data;
```

Note that `Initial_Value` is now a variable in scope rather than a discriminant.

7.3 Condition synchronisation

A protected entry is similar to a protected procedure in that it is guaranteed to execute in mutual exclusion and has read/write access to the encapsulated data. However, *a protected entry is guarded by a boolean expression (called*

a barrier) inside the body of the protected object; if this barrier evaluates to
false when the entry call is made, the calling task is suspended until the barrier
evaluates to true and no other tasks are currently active inside the protected
object.   Hence protected entry calls can be used to implement condition
synchronisation.

Consider a bounded buffer shared between several tasks. The data must
be placed in, and retrieved from, the buffer under mutual exclusion. Furthermore, condition synchronisation is required because a calling task attempting
to place data into the buffer, when the buffer is full, must be suspended until
there is space in the buffer; also a retrieving task must be suspended when
the buffer is empty. The specification of the buffer is

```
-- a bounded buffer

Buffer_Size : constant Integer := 10;
subtype Index is Natural range 0 .. Buffer_Size - 1;
subtype Count is Natural range 0 .. Buffer_Size;
type Buffer is array (Index) of Data_Item;

protected type Bounded_Buffer is
   entry Get(Item: out Data_Item);
   entry Put(Item: in Data_Item);
private
   First : Index := Index'First;
   Last : Index := Index'Last;
   Number_In_Buffer : Count := 0;
   Buf : Buffer;
end Bounded_Buffer;

My_Buffer : Bounded_Buffer;
```

Two entries have been declared; these represent the public interface of the
buffer. The data items declared in the private part are those items which
must be accessed under mutual exclusion. In this case, the buffer is an array
and is accessed via two indices; there is also a count indicating the number
of items in the buffer.

The body of this protected type is given below:

```
protected body Bounded_Buffer is

   entry Get(Item: out Data_Item)
       when Number_In_Buffer /= 0 is
   begin
     Item := Buf(First);
     First := (First + 1) mod Buffer_Size;
     Number_In_Buffer := Number_In_Buffer - 1;
   end Get;

   entry Put(Item: in Data_Item)
```

```
      when  Number_In_Buffer /= Buffer_Size is
   begin
      Last := (Last + 1) mod Buffer_Size;
      Buf(Last) := Item;
      Number_In_Buffer := Number_In_Buffer + 1;
      end Put;

   end Bounded_Buffer;
```

The Get entry is guarded by the barrier "**when** Number_In_Buffer /= 0";
only when this evaluates to true can a task execute the Get entry; similarly
with the Put entry. Barriers in protected objects have a similar function to
guards in task select statements. They define a precondition; only when they
evaluate to true can the entry be accepted.

Clearly, it is possible that more than one task may be queued on a
particular protected entry. *As with task entry queues, a protected entry queue
is, by default, ordered in a first-in-first-out fashion; however other queuing
disciplines are allowed* (see Chapter 12). In the Bounded_Buffer example,
when the buffer is empty, several tasks may queue up waiting on the Get
entry.

7.4   Entry calls and barriers

To issue a call to a protected object, a task simply names the object and
the required subprogram or entry. For example, to place some data into the
above bounded buffer requires the calling task to

```
   My_Buffer.Put(Some_Item);
```

As with task entry calls, the caller can use the select statement to issue a
timed or *conditional* entry call.

At any instant in time, a protected entry is either open or closed. It is
open if, when checked, the boolean expression evaluates to true; otherwise
it is closed. Generally, the protected entry barriers of a protected object are
evaluated when

(a)   a task calls one of its protected entries and the associated barrier
      references a variable or an attribute which might have changed since
      the barrier was last evaluated;

(b)   a task executes and leaves a protected procedure or protected entry and
      there are tasks queued on entries which have barriers which reference
      variables or attributes which might have changed since the barriers
      were last evaluated.

Note that barriers are not evaluated as a result of a protected function call.
In general, a program should not use shared variables in barriers and should

not rely on the exact circumstances in which barriers are reevaluated (i.e. an implementation may evaluate them more often than is strictly necessary).

When a task calls a protected entry or a protected subprogram, the protected object may already be locked: if one or more tasks are executing protected functions inside the protected object, the object is said to have an active **read lock**; if a task is executing a protected procedure or a protected entry, the object is said to have an active **read/write lock**. The following actions take place when a task attempts to enter a protected object (in the order given):

1. If the protected object has an active read lock and the call is a function call, the function is executed and step (14) is executed afterwards.

2. If the protected object has an active read lock and the call is an entry or a procedure call, the call is delayed while there are tasks active in the protected object. [1]

3. If the protected object has an active read/write lock, the call is delayed whilst there are tasks with conflicting access requirements active in the protected object.

4. If the protected object has no active lock and the call is a function call, the protected object read lock becomes active and step (5) is executed.

5. The function is executed; step (14) is then executed.

6. If the protected object has no active lock and the call is a procedure or entry call, the protected object read/write lock becomes active and step (7) is executed.

7. If the call is a procedure call, the procedure is executed and step (10) is then executed.

8. If the call is an entry call, its associated barrier is evaluated (if necessary) and if true the entry body is executed; step (10) is then executed.

9. If the barrier is false, the call is placed on a queue associated with the barrier (any timed or conditional entry calls are considered now) and step (10) is executed.

10. Any entry barriers with tasks queued whose barriers reference variables or attributes which might have changed since they were last evaluated are reevaluated, and step (11) is executed.

---

[1] Note that the semantics do not require the task to be queued or the run-time scheduler to be called. There is no suspended state associated with attempting to gain access to a protected object. Although this at first may seem strange, the Real-Time Systems Annex defines an implementation model which guarantees that the task can never be delayed when attempting to enter a protected object (see Section 12.1.2).

11. If there are any open entries, one is chosen (the core language does not define which one, although selection policies can be defined by the programmer if the Real-Time Systems Annex is supported, see Chapter 12), the associated entry body is executed, and step (10) is executed.

12. If no barriers with queued tasks are open, then step (13) is executed.

13. If one or more tasks are delayed awaiting access to the protected object then either a single task which requires the read/write lock is allowed to enter, or all tasks which require the read lock are allowed to enter and steps (5), (7) or (8) are executed (by the associated task); otherwise the access protocol is finished.

14. If no tasks are active in the protected object, step (13) is executed; otherwise the access protocol is finished.

The main point to note about the actions performed above is that when a protected procedure or entry is executed (or when a task queues on an entry), entry barriers are reevaluated and, potentially, entry bodies are executed. *It is not defined which tasks execute these entry bodies; it may be the task which issues the associated entry call, or the current task which caused the entry to become open.* This issue will be discussed further in Chapter 12 when the Real-Time Systems Annex is considered. Furthermore, timed and condition entry calls are not considered until the task is placed on an entry queue; any delay in accessing the protected object is not considered to be a suspension.

A task which is already active in a protected object can call a subprogram in the same protected object; this is considered to be an internal call and therefore executes immediately.

The Count **attribute**

Protected object entries, like task entries, have a count attribute defined that gives the current number of tasks queued on the specified entry. It is important to note that even if a task is destined to end up on an entry queue (due to the barrier being closed), it requires the write lock to be placed on the queue. Moreover, having been put on the queue, the count attribute will have changed (for that queue) and hence any barriers that have made reference to that attribute will need to be reevaluated. This is reflected in step (10) above. To give an example of the use of the count attribute consider a protected object that blocks calling tasks until five are queued; they are then all released:

```
protected Blocker is
   entry Proceed;
private
   Release : Boolean := False;
end Blocker;
```

```
protected body Blocker is

  entry Proceed when (Proceed'Count = 5 or Release) is
  begin
    if Proceed'Count = 0 then
      Release := False;
    else
      Release := True;
    end if;
  end Proceed;
end Blocker;
```

When the fifth task calls `Blocker.Proceed` it will find that the barrier evaluates to false and hence it will be blocked. But the barrier will then be reevaluated (as 'Count has changed). It now evaluates to true and the first task in the queue will execute the entry. The `Release` boolean variable ensures that all the other four tasks will then pass through the barrier. The last one, however, ensures that the barrier is raised again. Note that whilst releasing the five tasks, it is not possible for another task to become queued on the entry. This is because queuing a task on an entry requires the read/write lock, and this is not released until the fifth task has left the protected object.

To give a more concrete example of the use of protected objects consider the telephone example used in previous chapters. Some receiver has decided to make use of an answering phone; if a caller cannot make a direct connection (rendezvous) within a specified time interval, then a message is left on the answering phone. This phone has a finite capacity and hence may become full. The telephone is represented by a package:

```
with Message_Type; use Message_Type;
package Telephone is
  procedure Call(M : Message);
    -- for some appropriate message type
  Not_Operational : exception;
end Telephone;
```

The body of this package contains the task `Client` representing the receiver, a protected object (`Answering_Machine`) and the implementation of the procedure `Call`:

```
package body Telephone is
  Timeout_On_Client : constant Duration := 15.0;
  Timeout_On_Answering_Machine : constant Duration := 2.0;
  Max_Messages : constant : Positive := 64;
  type Message_Set is ...;

  task Client is
    entry Call(M : Message);
```

```
      end Client;

      protected Answering_Machine is
        entry Call(M : Message);
        procedure Replay(Ms : out Message_Set);
      private
        Tape : Message_Set;
        Messages_On_Tape : Natural := 0;
      end Answering_Machine;


      procedure Call(M : Message) is
      begin
        select
          Client.Call(M);
          return; -- call successful, return to caller
        or
          delay Timeout_On_Client;
        end select;
        select
          Answering_Machine.Call(M);
        or
          delay Timeout_On_Answering_Machine;
          raise Not_Operational;
        end select;
      exception
        when Tasking_Error => -- client no longer callable
          raise Not_Operational;
      end Call;


      protected body Answering_Machine is

        entry Call(M : Message)
            when Messages_On_Tape < Max_Messages is
        begin
          Messages_On_Tape := Messages_On_Tape + 1;
          -- put message on tape
        end Call;

        procedure Replay(Ms : out Message_Set) is
        begin
          Ms := Tape;
          Messages_On_Tape := 0;
        end Replay;

      end Answering_Machine;

      task body Client is ...
        -- includes calls to Answering_Machine.Replay

  end Telephone;
```

Note that this example makes use of a timed entry call on a protected entry. The semantics of this feature are identical to those of a timed entry call on a task. Conditional entry calls can also be made.

7.5   Private entries and entry families

So far this section has considered the basic protected type. As with tasks, protected objects may have private entries. These are not directly visible to users of the protected object. They may be used during requeue operations (see Chapter 8).

A protected type can also declare a family of entries by placing a discrete subtype definition in the specification of the entry declaration. Unlike task entry families, however, the programmer need not provide a separate entry body for each member of the family. The barrier associated with the entry can use the index of the family (usually to index into an array of booleans). Consider the following:

```
type Family is Integer range 1 ..3;

protected Controller is
   entry Request(Family)(...);
end Controller;

task Server is
   entry Service(Family)(...);
end Server;
```

In the case of the Server task it is necessary, inside the body of the task, to provide an accept statement for each member of the family. For example, to wait for a request from any member requires a select statement:

```
task body Server is
begin
   ...
   loop
     select
       when Some_Guard_1 =>
         accept Service(1)(...) do
           ...
         end Service;
     or
       when Some_Guard_2 =>
         accept Service(2)(...) do
           ...
         end Service;
     or
       when Some_Guard_3 =>
         accept Service(3)(...) do
```

```
         . . .
      end Service;
   end select;
   . . .
   end loop;
end Server;
```

For the protected body, it is not necessary to enumerate all the members of the family (indeed, the programmer is not allowed to do so). Instead, a shorthand notation is provided:

```
protected body Controller is
   entry Request(for I in Family )(...)
      when Some_Barrier_Using(I) is
   begin
      . . .
   end Request;
end Controller;
```

This is notionally equivalent to

```
-- Not Valid Ada
protected body Controller is
   entry Request(1)(...) when Some_Barrier_Using(1) is
   begin
      . . .
   end Request;

   entry Request(2)(...) when Some_Barrier_Using(2) is
   begin
      . . .
   end Request;

   entry Request(3)(...) when Some_Barrier_Using(3) is
   begin
      . . .
   end Request;
end Controller;
```

For example, the following defines a protected type which provides a group communication facility. The type Group defines several communications groups. The protected procedure Send_To_Group sends a Data_Item to a particular group. The family of entries Receive allows a task to wait for a Data_Item on a particular group:

```
type Group is new Integer range 1 .. 10;
type Group_Data_Arrived is array(Group) of Boolean;

protected type Group_Controller is
   procedure Send(To_Group : Group; This_Data : Data_Item);
   entry Receive(Group)(Data : out Data_Item);
```

```
private
  Arrived : Group_Data_Arrived := (others => False);
  The_Data : Data_Item;
end Group_Controller;


My_Controller : Group_Controller;


protected body Group_Controller is

  procedure Send(To_Group : Group; This_Data : Data_Item) is
  begin
    if Receive(To_Group)'Count > 0 then
      Arrived(To_Group) := True;
      The_Data := This_Data;
    end if;
  end Send;

  entry Receive(for From in Group)(Data : out Data_Item)
              when Arrived(From) is
    -- this is a family of entries
  begin
    if Receive(From)'Count = 0 then
      Arrived(From) := False;
    end if;
    Data := The_Data;
  end Receive;
end Group_Controller;
```

When a task sends data to a particular group, the Send procedure looks to see if any tasks are waiting on the Receive entry for that particular member of the family. If tasks are waiting, it sets a boolean flag associated with the member to true. [2] On exit from the procedure, the barriers associated with the Receive family entries are reevaluated. The appropriate group's boolean evaluates to true and so that entry of the family is open. The entry body is executed and, if only one task is waiting, the boolean is set to false; in either case the data is sent to the first queued task. If the guard is still open, the entry body is executed again, and so on until all tasks queued for the group are released with the multi-cast value. Note that, once a task is executing inside the protected object, no other task can join an entry queue or be removed from an entry queue.

There are other ways of manipulating the barrier on the entry family (for example saving the identifier of the group during the Send operation and comparing the family index with the group identifier). However, the given solution is easily extendable if the message is to be sent to more than one group.

It is useful to dwell on one further feature of the above code. In general, a call of Send may release blocked tasks on Receive. But it cannot just lower

---

[2]Note that the Count attribute can be applied to a specific family member.

the barrier on `Receive`: it must first check to see if any task is blocked (using the `'Count` attribute). Moreover, the last task to be released must raise the barrier again. These checks must be made, as a change to a barrier value is persistent. This can be compared to a signal on a monitor's condition variable (see Chapter 3) which either has an immediate effect or no effect at all.

An alternative way of structuring the above code is to have the sending task call in twice: once to place the data and open the barrier, and the second time to close the barrier. As the internal unblocked tasks have precedence over the second external call, the following code will have the same effect as the original:

```
protected type Group_Controller is
   procedure Send_Start(To_Group : Group; This_Data: Data_Item);
   procedure Send_Complete(To_Group : Group);
   entry Receive(Group)(Data : out Data_Item);
private
   Arrived : Group_Data_Arrived := (others => False);
   The_Data : Data_Item;
end Group_Controller;

My_Controller : Group_Controller;

procedure Send(To_Group : Group; This_Data: Data_Item) is
   -- this is the procedure that is called externally
begin
   My_Controller.Send_Start(To_Group, This_Data);
   My_Controller.Send_Complete(To_Group);
end Send;

protected body Group_Controller is

   procedure Send_Start(To_Group : Group;
                           This_Data: Data_Item) is
   begin
     Arrived(To_Group) := True;
     The_Data := This_Data;
   end Send_Start;

   procedure Send_Complete(To_Group : Group) is
   begin
     Arrived(To_Group) := False;
   end Send_Complete;

   entry Receive(for From in Group) (Data : out Data_Item)
        when Arrived(From) is
   begin
     Data := The_Data;
   end Receive;
end Group_Controller;
```

7.6   Restrictions on protected objects

In general, code executed inside a protected object should be as minimal as possible. This is because whilst the code is being executed other tasks are delayed when they try to gain access to the protected object. The Ada language clearly cannot enforce a maximum length of execution time for a protected action. However, it does try to ensure that a task cannot be blocked indefinitely waiting to gain access to a protected procedure or a protected function (as a protected entry has a barrier which must evaluate to true before the operation can be executed, the language can make no guarantees that it will ever evaluate to true). The ARM defines it to be a bounded error to call a *potentially suspending* operation from within a protected action. It defines the following operations to be potentially suspending:

* a select statement;

* an accept statement;

* an entry call statement;

* a delay statement;

* task creation or activation;

* a call on a subprogram whose body contains a potentially suspending operation.

Note that it is also a bounded error to call an external procedure, from a protected object, which in turn calls back to the protected object. This is because the procedure still holds the read/write lock and attempts to acquire it again. For example,

```
protected P is
   procedure X;
   procedure Y;
end P;

procedure External is
begin
   P.Y; -- or P.X
end External;

protected body P is
   procedure X is
   begin
      External_Call;
   end X;

   procedure Y is ...
end P;
```

Of course, there may be several levels of indirection before the call is returned to the protected object. Moreover, the ARM distinguishes between external and internal calls by the use, or not, of the full protected object name. So, for example, a call to P.Y from within X would be deemed an external call and therefore a bounded error, whilst a call of just Y from within X is an internal call and is thus legal. A similar situation applies to internal and external requeue operations (see Chapter 8). In contrast, it is always a bounded error to call an entry, either internal or external, from a protected object.

If a bounded error is detected, Program_Error is raised. If not detected, the bounded error might result in deadlock.

Note that a call to an external protected subprogram is NOT considered a potentially suspending action. This might seem strange, as a task may have to wait to gain access to an external subprogram because some other task is already active inside the protected object. However, as the other task cannot suspend inside the target protected object, the time the first task must wait will be bounded (and hopefully small).

In general, it may be difficult for the programmer to know whether subprograms in library packages are potentially suspending or not. Consequently, all subprogram declarations should contain comments to indicate whether they suspend. The ARM indicates that all language defined library units which are declared *pure* (see Chapter 14) contain no potentially suspending operations. Furthermore, package Calendar does not contain any potentially suspending operations. However, all input and output related packages are potentially suspending.

Currently, the way protected actions have been defined (in the core language), it is possible for two tasks to deadlock by one calling protected object A, which calls a protected subprogram in protected object B, and the other calling protected object B, which calls a subprogram in protected object A. Clearly, there is an order of execution whereby it is possible for the first task to execute a protected action in A and then for the other task to execute a protected action in B. Now neither task can complete its protected action until the other has completed. This problem is common to all concurrent programming languages which allow tasks to request and allocate non-sharable resources (see discussion in previous chapter). However, the problem can be avoided in Ada if the Real-Time Systems Annex is supported (see Chapter 12).

7.7 Access variables and protected types

In common with all types in Ada, it is possible to declare an access type to a protected type. This enables pointers to instances of protected types to be passed as parameters to subprograms and entries. Consider, by way of an example, a protected type which implements a broadcast of aircraft altitude data (Section 9.7 will generalise the facility to illustrate a generic broadcast facility):

```
protected type Broadcast is
   procedure Send(This_Altitude : Altitude);
   entry Receive(An_Altitude : out Altitude);
private
   Altitude_Arrived : Boolean := False;
   The_Altitude : Altitude;
end Broadcast;
```

Suppose now that there are various tasks on the aircraft which can measure the altitude by different means (barometric pressure, radar altimeter, inertial navigation, etc.). It is possible to implement the following name server:

```
package Name_Server is
   type Ptr_Broadcast is access all Broadcast;
   type Group_Name is new String(1 .. 20);

   procedure Register(G : Ptr_Broadcast; Name : Group_Name);
   function Find(Name : Group_Name) return Ptr_Broadcast;
end Name_Server;

package body Name_Server is separate;
   -- details of no importance here
```

The above package declares an access type for the Broadcast protected type and allows clients to register and retrieve names. It is now possible for the various tasks to register their names and broadcast altitude readings to those tasks who are interested. For example,

```
task Barometric_Pressure_Reader;
task body Barometric_Pressure_Reader is
   My_Group : Ptr_Broadcast := new Broadcast;
   Altitude_Reading : Altitude;
begin
   ...
   Name_Server.Register(My_Group, "Barometric_Pressure ");
   ..
   loop
      ...
      -- periodically
      My_Group.Send(Altitude_Reading);
      ...
   end loop;
end Barometric_Pressure_Reader;


task Auto_Pilot;
task body Auto_Pilot is
```

```
    Bp_Reader :  Ptr_Broadcast;
    Current_Altitude : Altitude;
begin
    ...
    Bp_Reader := Name_Server.Find("Barometric_Pressure ");
    ...
    select
      Bp_Reader.Receive(Current_Altitude);
        -- get new reading if available
    or
      delay 0.1;
    end select;
    ...
end Auto_Pilot;
```

Of course, as with task access variables, an instance of a protected type can be declared with the alaised keyword, in which case a pointer can be obtained using the 'Access attribute:

```
task Barometric_Pressure_Reader;
task body Barometric_Pressure_Reader is
    My_Group : aliased Broadcast;
    Altitude_Reading : Altitude;
begin
    ...
    Name_Server.Register(My_Group'Access,
                         "Barometric_Pressure ");
    ..
    loop
      ...
      -- periodically
      My_Group.Send(Altitude_Reading);
      ...
    end loop;
end Barometric_Pressure_Reader;
```

As well as declaring access types for protected objects, Ada also allows the programmer to declare an access type to a protected subprogram:

```
access_to_subprogram_definition ::=
    access [protected] procedure parameter_profile
  | access [protected] function parameter_and_result_profile
```

An example of this will be given in Section 9.2.

7.8   Elaboration, finalisation and exceptions

A protected object is elaborated when it comes into scope in the usual way. However, a protected object cannot simply go out of scope if there are still tasks queued on its entries. Finalisation of a protected object requires that any tasks left on entry queues have the exception Program_Error raised. Although this may seem unusual, there are two situations where this can happen:

- A protected object, created by an allocator, is subject to unchecked deallocation via the access pointer to it.

- A task calls an entry in another task which requeues the first task on a protected object which then goes out of scope (this possibility is discussed again in Section 8.3).

In an earlier discussion, it was mentioned that the exception Program_Error was raised when a protected action issued a potentially suspending operation. Other exceptions can be raised during the execution of protected operations:

- any exception raised during the evaluation of a barrier results in Program_Error being raised in all tasks currently waiting on the entry queues associated with the protected object containing the barrier;

- any exception raised whilst executing a protected subprogram or entry, and not handled by the protected subprogram or entry, is propagated to the task that issued the protected call (as if the call were a normal subprogram call).

7.9   Shared data

This discussion on protected types is concluded by returning to their most common usage — the provision of mutual exclusion over some shared data. At the beginning of the chapter a protected shared integer was used to illustrate a simple protected object. The generalisation of this structure is a generic package that defines an appropriate protected type. Note it is not possible to have a generic protected object (or generic task):

```
generic
   type Data_Item is private;
   Default_Data : Data_Item;
package Shared_Data_Template is

   protected type Shared_Data is
      function Read return  Data_Item;
      procedure Write(New_Value : in Data_Item);
   private
      The_Data : Data_Item := Default_Data;
   end Shared_Data;
end Shared_Data_Template;
```

```
package body Shared_Data_Template is
   protected body Shared_Data is
      function Read return  Data_Item is
      begin
         return The_Data;
      end Read;

      procedure Write(New_Value : in Data_Item) is
      begin
         The_Data := New_Value;
      end Write;
   end Shared_Data;
end Shared_Data_Template;
```

Note that, as a discriminant can only be of access or discrete type, the default value of the data item must be assigned from the generic parameter.

7.9.1   The readers and writers problem

One of the motivations for the notion of a protected object is that a single mechanism provides both mutual exclusion and condition synchronisation. Unfortunately, many synchronisation protocols are much more sophisticated. A commonly used example of such protocols is the readers and writers problem. Consider a (non-sharable) resource such as a file. Because of multiple update difficulties, the necessary synchronisations are such that if one process is writing to the file, then no other process should be either writing or reading. If, however, there is no writer process, then any number of processes should have read access.

As just illustrated, a standard protected object can implement the readers/writers algorithm if the read operation is encoded as a function and the write as a procedure. There are, however, two drawbacks with this simple approach:

1.   The programmer cannot easily control the order of access to the protected object; specifically, it is not possible to give preference to write operations over reads.

2.   If the read or write operations are potentially suspending, then they cannot be made from within a protected object.

To overcome these difficulties the protected object must be used to implement an access control protocol for the read and write operations (rather than encapsulate them). The following code does this whilst giving preference to writes over reads:

```
with Data_Items; use Data_Items;
package Readers_Writers is
   procedure Read (I : out Item);   -- for some type Item
```

```
   procedure Write (I : Item);
end Readers_Writers;

package body Readers_Writers is
  procedure Read_File(I : out Item) is separate;
  procedure Write_File(I : Item) is separate;

  protected Control is
    entry Start_Read;
    procedure Stop_Read;
    entry Request_Write;
    entry Start_Write;
    procedure Stop_Write;
  private
    Readers : Natural := 0; -- Number of current readers
    Writers : Boolean := False; -- Writers present
  end Control;


  procedure Read (I : out Item) is
  begin
    Control.Start_Read;
      Read_File(I);
    Control.Stop_Read;
  end Read;

  procedure Write (I : Item) is
  begin
    Control.Request_Write;
    Control.Start_Write;
      Write_File(I);
    Control.Stop_Write;
  end Write;



  protected body Control is

    entry Start_Read when not Writers is
    begin
      Readers := Readers + 1;
    end Start_Read;

    procedure Stop_Read is
    begin
      Readers := Readers - 1;
    end Stop_Read;

    entry Request_Write when not Writers is
    begin
      Writers := True;
    end Request_Write;
```

```
entry Start_Write when Readers = 0 is
begin
    null;
end Start_Write;

procedure Stop_Write is
begin
    Writers := False;
end Stop_Write;

end Control;

end Readers_Writers;
```

The entry protocol for a writer requires two steps; the first waits until there are no further writers and then sets the writers flag to true. This will stop any further readers. When all the current readers have exited (and the readers count is zero), the writer can enter. The exit protocol for both readers and writers is a non-blocking call to announce the termination of that operation.

This package has addressed both the criticisms that were apparent with the simple use of a protected object. However, a slightly simpler form is available if the Write_File procedure is non-blocking (and hence can be made from within the protected control object):

```
package body Readers_Writers is
    procedure Write_File(I : Item) is separate;
    procedure Read_File(I : out Item) is separate;

    protected Control is
        entry Start_Read;
        procedure Stop_Read;
        entry Write(I : Item);
    private
        Readers : Natural := 0;
    end Control;

    procedure Read (I : out Item) is
    begin
        Control.Start_Read;
            Read_File(I);
        Control.Stop_Read;
    end Read;

    procedure Write (I : Item) is
    begin
        Control.Write(I);
    end Write;

    protected body Control is

        entry Start_Read when Write'Count = 0 is
```

```
begin
  Readers := Readers + 1;
end Start_Read;

procedure Stop_Read is
begin
  Readers := Readers - 1;
end Stop_Read;

entry Write(I : Item) when Readers = 0 is
begin
  Write_File(I);
end Write;

end Control;

end Readers_Writers;
```

It should be noted that neither of these solutions is resilient to the readers and writers failing whilst executing their critical sections. For example, a reader process which fails in Read_File will causes all write operations to be suspended indefinitely. A more robust version of these algorithms is given in Section 10.5.

7.9.2　The specification of synchronisation agents

The readers and writers problem illustrates the use of a package, with procedure specifications, to encapsulate the necessary synchronisations for some resource usage. The package specification does not, however, give any indication as to the protocols that the package body will implement. Indeed, it is usually not clear that a task can be delayed by calling one of these apparently straightforward procedures. The use of comments can help in the readability and understanding of such packages. Moreover, they form a valuable aid in the verification of programs. The simplest property that a synchronisation package can have is that it will lead to the potential suspending of callers. It is recommended that such potential suspending should always be indicated:

```
package Readers_Writers is
  procedure Read(I : out Item);
    -- potentially suspending
  procedure Write(I : Item);
    -- potentially suspending
end Readers_Writers;
```

For more informative specifications, a more formal notation can be used in the comments. For example, path expressions can be employed to state quite explicitly the protocol that is, or should be, supported by the package body. The following comment implies mutual exclusion:

    --| path 1 : (Read, Write) end

Here one procedure is permitted at a time and it is either a Read or a Write. In general, the readers/writers algorithm allows a number of simultaneous reads, so that the associated path expression becomes

    --| path 1 : ([Read], Write) end

the square brackets imply 'de-restriction'. If a specific sequence of calls is required, then a semicolon can replace the comma:

    --| path 1 : (Write; Read) end

This now implies that there must be a strict sequence to the calls of the procedures; first Write, then Read, then Write, etc. The appropriate comment for the bounded buffer example can now be developed. Firstly, there must be a Put before a Get, so:

    --| path 1 : (Put; Get) end

But this is too restrictive for there can be up to N Puts before a Get (for buffer size N), that is, Put can get ahead of Get by up to N calls:

    --| path N : (Put; Get) end

Unfortunately, this has now removed the mutual exclusion property. For a buffer, a call to Put can be concurrent with a call to Get but not with another call to Put; therefore the Puts and Gets must be protected from themselves:

    --| path N : (1 : (Put); 1 : (Get)) end

If the construct were a stack, then mutual exclusion would have to extend to both subprograms. This is indicated by giving a second path restriction — the implication being that both must be obeyed:

    --| path N : (Put; Get), 1 : (Put, Get) end

the first path allows calls to Put to get ahead of calls to Get by N; the second part states that mutual exclusion on both procedures is necessary.

Path expressions were first defined by Campbell and Habermann (1974), since whence a number of extensions and variations have been proposed. It is recommended that if a package is hiding a synchronisation agent (a protected object or a task), then some form of formal comment should be used to describe the embedded synchronisations. This comment will be useful both for the design of the system, where the package body may later be coded to the specification described in the comment, and in the general readability and maintainability of the program.

Of course, it may also be possible to generate the synchronisation code automatically from the path expressions.

7.10   Shared variables

Passing data safely between two tasks can be achieved via the rendezvous or via protected objects. However, two tasks may often safely pass shared data between them because they are synchronised in some other way and it is not possible for the data to be read by one whilst it is being written by another. Unfortunately (in this instance), compilers usually attempt to optimise the code, and variables may be kept in registers; consequently a write to a shared variable may not result in the data being written to memory immediately. Hence there is the potential that a reader of the shared variable may not obtain the most up-to-date variable. Indeed, if the shared variable is being kept in a register, then the synchronisation implied by the program no longer holds and the variable may be written just when the data is being read, giving an internally inconsistent result.

The Ada language defines the conditions under which it is safe to read and write to shared variables outside the rendezvous or protected objects. They are

- Where one task writes/reads a variable before activating another task which reads/writes the variable, for example

```
The_Data : Shared_Variable;

task type Reader;
task Writer;

task body Reader is
   Param : Shared_Variable := The_Data;
begin
   ...
end Reader;

task body Writer is
begin
   ...
   The_Data := ...; -- pass parameter to Reader
   declare
      A_Reader : Reader;
   begin
```

```
   ...
  end;
end Writer;
```

- Where the activation of one task writes/reads the variable and the task awaiting completion of the activation reads/writes the variable, for example

```
The_Data : Shared_Variable;

task type Reader;
task Writer;

task body Reader is
  Param : Shared_Variable := The_Data;
begin
  ...
end Reader;

task body Writer is
begin
  ...
  The_Data := ...; -- pass parameter
  declare
    A_Reader : Reader;
  begin
    The_Data := ...; -- the previous value has now been read
  end;
end Writer;
```

- Where one task writes/reads the variable and another task waits for the termination of the task and then reads/writes the variable, for example

```
The_Data : Shared_Variable;

task type Writer;
task Reader;

task body Writer is
begin
  ...
  The_Data := ...; --pass back some results
  ...
end Writer;

task body Reader is
  Param : Shared_Variable;
```

```
begin
  ...
  declare
    A_Writer: Writer;
  begin
    ...
  end;
  Param := The_Data;   -- The_Data has now been written
end Reader;
```

- Where one task writes/reads the variable before making an entry call on another task, and the other task reads/writes the variable during the corresponding entry body or accept statement, for example

```
The_Data : Shared_Variable;

task Reader is
  entry Synchronise;
end Reader;

task Writer;

task body Reader is
  Param : Shared_Variable;
begin
  ...
  accept Synchronise do
    Param := The_Data;
  end;
  ...
end Reader;

task body Writer is
begin
  ...
  The_Data := ...;
  Reader.Synchronise;
  ...
end Writer;
```

- Where one task writes/reads a shared variable during an accept statement and the calling task reads/writes the variable after the corresponding entry call has returned, for example

```
The_Data : Shared_Variable;

task Updater is
  entry Synchronise;
```

```
end Updater;

task Writer;

task body Updater is
begin
   ...
   accept Synchronise do
      The_Data := The_Data + ...;
   end;
   ...
end Updater;

task body Writer is
begin
   ...
   The_Data := ...;
   Updater.Synchronise;
   if The_Data = ...;  -- The_Data has now been updated
   ...
end Writer;
```

- Where one task writes/reads a variable whilst executing a protected procedure body or entry, and the other task reads/writes the variable as part of a later execution of an entry body of the same protected body, for example

```
The_Data : Shared_Variable;

protected Updater is
   procedure Write;
   entry Read;
private
   Data_Written : Boolean := False;
end Updater;

protected body Updater is
   procedure Write is
   begin
      The_Data := ...;
      Data_Written := True;
   end Write;

   entry Read when Data_Written is
   begin
      if The_Data = ...;
   end;
end Updater;
```

Although data can be safely passed during the above operations, such mechanisms must be used with care as they are error-prone and lead to obscure programs. Their use is not recommended.

7.11   Volatile and atomic data

If the Systems Programming Annex is supported, there are extra facilities which can be used to control shared variables between *unsynchronised* tasks. They come in the form of extra pragmas which can be applied to certain objects or type declarations.

Pragma `Volatile`

The purpose of indicating that some shared data item is volatile is to ensure that the compiler does not optimise the code and keep the item in a register whilst it is manipulating it. Pragma `Volatile` ensures that all reads and writes go directly to memory.

Pragma `Volatile` can be applied to

• An object declaration, for example

```
I : Integer;
pragma Volatile(I); -- object I is volatile

J : Some_Record_Type;
pragma Volatile(J); -- object J is volatile

K: Some_Array_Type;
pragma Volatile(K); -- object K is volatile
```

• A non-inherited component declaration, for example

```
type Record_With_Volatile_Component is tagged
   record
      Component_1 : Integer;
      Component_2 : Float;
      Component_3 : Some_Enumeration_Type;
   end record;
pragma Volatile(Record_With_Volatile_Component.Component_2);
-- all Component_2 elements of all objects of
-- type Record_With_Volatile_Component will be volatile

type Inherited_Record is new Record_With_Volatile_Component with
   record
      Component_4 : Some_Type;
   end record;

-- Note, that the following is ILLEGAL
pragma Volatile(Inherited_Record.Component_2);

-- However, this is legal:
pragma Volatile(Inherited_Record.Component_4);
```

• A full type declaration (i.e. not a private type, or an incomplete type), for example

```
type Volatile_Data is range 1 .. 100;
pragma Volatile(Volatile_Data);
-- all object created from the type will be volatile

type Volatile_Record is
  record
     Component_1 : Integer;
     Component_2 : Float;
     Component_3 : Some_Enumeration_Type);
  end record;
pragma Volatile(Volatile_Record);
-- all objects created will be volatile, also all
-- components will be volatile (similarly for arrays)
```

Pragma Volatile_Components

Pragma Volatile_Components applies to components of an array, for example

```
type My_Array is array(1..10) of Integer;
pragma Volatile_Component(My_Array(3));
-- component 3 is volatile for all objects of type My_Array

type Two_D_Array is array (1..10, 1..100) of Integer;
D2: Two_D_Array;
pragma Volatile_Component(D2(3,50));
-- component (3,50) of  D2 is volatile

type Array_Of_Arrays is array (1 ..100) of My_Array;
pragma Volatile_Component(Array_Of_Arrays(10));
-- component array (10) is volatile as are all (1..100)(3)
-- for all objects of type Array_Of_Arrays
```

Pragma Atomic **and pragma** Atomic_Components

Whilst pragma Volatile indicates that all reads and writes must be directed straight to memory, pragma Atomic imposes the further restriction that they must be indivisible. That is, if two tasks attempt to read and write the shared variable at the same time, then the result must be internally consistent. Consider the following example:

```
subtype Axis is Integer range 0 .. 100;
type Point is
```

```
record
  X : Axis;
  Y : Axis;
end record;

Diagonal : Point := (0,0);
-- invariant X = Y
pragma Volatile(Diagonal);

procedure Draw(X: Point) is ...
function New_Point return Point is ...

task Plot_Point;

task Update_Point;

task body Plot_Point is
begin
  loop
    Draw(Diagonal);
    ...
  end loop;
end Plot_Point;

task body Update_Point is
begin
  loop
    ...
    Diagonal := New_Point;
  end loop;
end Update_Point;
```

In this example the two tasks both have access to the shared variable
Diagonal. Suppose the values returned from the New_Point function are
{(0,0), (1,1), (2,2), ...}. Although the shared variable has been declared as
volatile, this does not stop the read and the write operations becoming
interleaved. It is quite possible for the Plot_Point task to draw a point (0,1),
(2,1), etc.

To cure this problem, the Diagonal variable must be made atomic:

```
pragma Atomic(Diagonal);
```

This not only ensures that all reads and writes are directed to memory (i.e.
the variable is volatile), but also that reads and writes are indivisible; they
cannot be interleaved.

*It should be noted that an implementation is not required to support atomic
operations for all types of variable; however, if not supported for a particular
object, the pragma must be rejected by the compiler.*

The same classes of item as supported by the Volatile and
Volatile_Components pragmas are potentially supportable as Atomic
and Atomic_Components.

Mutual exclusion and Simpson's algorithm

Many implementations of the Systems Programming Annex will only support pragma atomic on variables which can be read or written as atomic actions at the machine assembly language level. Typically, this restricts the size of an object to a single word in length. However, using just this basic property it is possible to construct an algorithm which will guarantee that any size data item can be accessed without interference and without having to resort to busy-waiting. One such algorithm, due to Simpson (1990), is given here for two tasks:

```
generic
   type Data is private;
   Initial_Value : Data;
package Simpsons_Algorithm is
   procedure Write(Item: Data); -- non-suspending
   procedure Read (Item : out Data); -- non-suspending
end Simpsons_Algorithm;

package body Simpsons_Algorithm is

   type Slot is (First, Second);

   Four_Slot : array (Slot, Slot) of Data :=
              (First => (Initial_Value,Initial_Value),
               Second => (Initial_Value,Initial_Value));
   pragma Volatile(Four_Slot);

   Next_Slot : array(Slot) of Slot := (First, First);
   pragma Volatile(Next_Slot);

   Latest : Slot := First;
   pragma Atomic(Latest);
   Reading : Slot := First;
   pragma Atomic(Reading);

   procedure Write(Item : Data) is
     Pair, Index : Slot;
   begin
     if Reading = First then
       Pair := Second;
     else
       Pair := First;
     end if;
     if Latest = First then
       Index := Second;
     else
       Index := First;
     end if;
     Four_Slot(Pair, Index) := Item;
     Next_Slot(Pair) := Index;
```

```
      Latest := Pair;
    end Write;

    procedure Read(Item : out Data) is
      Pair, Index : Slot;
    begin
      Pair := Latest;
      Reading := Pair;
      Index := Next_Slot(Pair);
      Item := Four_Slot(Pair, Index);
    end Read;
  end Simpsons_Algorithm;
```

The algorithm works by keeping four slots for the data: two banks of two slots. The reader and the writer never access the same bank of slots at the same time. The atomic variable Latest contains the index of bank to which the last data item was written and the Next_Slot array indexed by this value indicates which slot in that bank contains the data.

Consider some arbitrary time when the latest value of the data item is in Four_Slot(Second, First). In this case Latest equals Second and Next(Second) = First. Assume also that this is the last value read. If another read request comes in and is interleaved with a write request, the write request will chose the first bank of slots and the first slot, and so on. Thus it is possible that the reader will obtain an old value but never an inconsistent one. If the write comes in again before the read has finished, it will write to the first bank and second slot, and then the first bank and first slot. When the reader next comes in, it will obtain the last value that was completely written (i.e. the value written by the last full invocation of Write). A full proof of this algorithm is given by Simpson (1990).

7.12   Task states

The task state diagram given in the previous three chapters can be extended again to include the new states that protected objects have introduced (see Figure 7.1). Note the important point made earlier in this chapter: waiting to gain access to a protected object is not a blocked state. Thus the only new state is "blocked on an entry call"; this will occur when a barrier evaluates to false.

7.13   Summary

Ada gives direct support to protected data by the abstraction of a *protected object*. A protected object encapsulates the data and allows access only via protected subprograms or protected entries. The language guarantees that

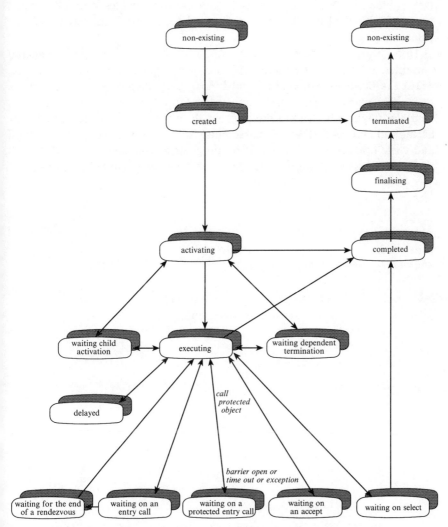

Figure 7.1: Summary of Task States and State Transitions.

these subprograms and entries will be executed in a manner that ensures the data is updated under mutual exclusion.

Protected functions allow concurrent access, as they only have a read-only impact on the protected data. Protected procedures and entries can write to the data and hence only allowed access one at a time. A procedure can always complete its execution inside a protected object (once it has the read/write lock on the data). By comparison, a protected entry first has to evaluate a boolean barrier. If the barrier evaluates to false, then the calling task is blocked. Whenever a procedure or entry completes, a check is made to see if a blocked task can now proceed (i.e. the associated barrier is now true).

In addition to protected objects, Ada also gives direct support to shared variables. It does this by the provision of a number of pragmas: Volatile, Volatile_Components, Atomic, and Atomic_Components. A volatile variable must be located in just one memory location; temporary copies that the compiler might otherwise use to improve the efficiency of the generated code are not allowed. An atomic variable must, additionally, have indivisible read and write operations. Although these pragmas are defined by the ARM it is up to any implementation to decide which types they can be applied to.

Chapter 8

Avoidance Synchronisation and the Requeue Facility

The models of synchronisation discussed in the previous four chapters have the common feature that they are based on avoidance synchronisation. Guards or barriers are used to prevent rendezvous, and task-protected object interactions, if the conditions are not appropriate for the communications event to start. Indeed, one of the key features of the tasking model is the consistent use of avoidance to control synchronisation. The use of guards and barriers represent a high level abstract means of expressing and enforcing necessary synchronisations; and as such they can be compared favourably with the use of low level primitives such as semaphores or monitor signals (see Chapter 3). This chapter starts by giving a more systematic assessment of avoidance synchronisation in order to motivate the requirement for 'requeue'. It then describes the syntax and semantics of the requeue statement and gives examples of its use.

8.1 The need for requeue

Different language features are often compared in terms of their *expressive power* and *ease of use* (*usability*). Expressive power is the more objective criterion, and is concerned with the ability of language features to allow application requirements to be programmed directly. Ease of use is more subjective, and includes the ease with which the features under investigation interact with each other and with other language primitives.

In her evaluation of synchronisation primitives, Bloom (1979) used the following criteria to evaluate and compare the expressive power and usability of different language models. She identified several issues that need to be addressed when determining the order of interaction between synchronising agents; a list of such issues is as follows:

(a)   type of service requested;

(b)   order of arrival;

(c)   internal state of the receiver (including the history of its usage);

(d)   priority of the caller;

(e)   parameters to the call.

It should be clear that the Ada model described so far deals adequately with the first three situations. The fourth will be considered in Chapter 12, when real-time issues are discussed in detail. Here, attention is focused on the fifth issue, which causes some difficulties for avoidance synchronisation mechanisms.

8.1.1   The resource allocation problem

Resource allocation is a fundamental problem in all aspects of concurrent programming. Its consideration exercises all Bloom's criteria and forms an appropriate basis for assessing the synchronisation mechanisms of concurrent languages, such as Ada.

Consider the problem of constructing a resource controller that allocates some resource to a group of client agents. There are a number of instances of the resource but the number is bounded; contention is possible and must be catered for in the design of the program. If the client tasks only require a single instance of the resource, then the problem is straightforward. For example, in the following, the resource (although not directly represented) can be encoded as a protected object:

```
protected Resource_Controller is
  entry Allocate(R : out Resource);
  procedure Release(R : Resource);
private
  Free : Natural := Max;
  ...
end Resource_Controller;
```

```
protected body Resource_Controller is
  entry Allocate(R : out Resource) when Free > 0 is
  begin
    Free := Free - 1;
    ...
  end;
  procedure Release(R : Resource) is
  begin
    Free := Free + 1;
    ...
  end;
end Resource_Controller;
```

To generalise this code requires the caller to state how many resources are required (up to some maximum). The semantics required are that either all requested resources are assigned to the caller or none are (and the caller blocks until the resources are free).

This resource allocation problem is difficult to program with avoidance synchronisation. In order to determine the size of the request, the communication must be accepted and the parameter read. But if, having read the parameter, the internal state of the resource controller is such that there are currently not enough resources available, then the communication must be terminated and the client must try again. To prevent polling, a different entry must be tried. A detailed examination of this problem (Wellings *et al.*, 1984; Burns *et al.*, 1987) has shown that an acceptable solution is not available if avoidance synchronisation only is used. Note that a solution is possible, so the issue is one of ease of use rather than expressive power. Nevertheless, the elegance of this solution is poor when compared with the monitor solution given in Section 3.8. A monitor uses condition synchronisation (not avoidance synchronisation) and it is therefore trivially easy to block the caller after the parameter has been read but before it leaves the monitor.

Using entry families

One possible solution in Ada (without requeue) to the resource allocation problem assumes that the number of distinct requests is relatively small and can be represented by a family of entries. Each entry in the family is guarded by the boolean expression F <= Free, where F is the family index:

```
type Request_Range is range 1..Max;

protected Resource_Controller is
   entry Allocate(Request_Range)(R : out Resource);
   procedure Release(R : Resource; Amount : Request_Range);
private
   Free : Request_Range := Request_Range'Last;
   ...
end Resource_Controller;


protected body Resource_Controller is
   entry Allocate(for F in Request_Range)(R : out Resource)
            when F <= Free is
   begin
      Free := Free - F;
      ...
   end Allocate;


   procedure Release(R : Resource; Amount : Request_Range) is
   begin
      ...
      Free := Free + Amount;
   end Release;
end Resource_Controller;
```

Although this solution is concise, there are two significant problems:

1.   It is not practical for a large number of resources, as there needs to be Max entry queues; these must be serviced individually, which is inefficient. Furthermore, for server tasks there is no equivalent syntactical form for families and hence an excessively long select statement must be used.

2.   It is difficult to allocate the resources selectively — when several requests can be serviced, then an arbitrary choice between them is made (note that if the Real-Time Systems Annex is supported, the request can be serviced in a priority order; if all calling tasks have the same priority, then the family is serviced from the smallest index to the largest).

The latter problem can be ameliorated by having each entry in the family guarded by its own boolean, and then selectively setting the booleans to true. For example, if on freeing new resources it is required to service the largest request first, the following algorithm can be used. Note that a request to Allocate that can be satisfied immediately is always accepted. Hence a boolean variable (Normal) is needed to distinguish between a normal allocation and a phase of allocations following a Release:

```
type Request_Range is range 1..Max;
type Bools is array(Request_Range) of Boolean;

protected Resource_Controller is
  entry Allocate(Request_Range)(R : out Resource);
  procedure Release(R : Resource; Amount : Request_Range);
private
  Free : Request_Range := Request_Range'Last;
  Barrier : Bools := (others => False);
  Normal : Boolean := True;
  ...
end Resource_Controller;
```

```
protected body Resource_Controller is
  entry Allocate(for F in Request_Range)(R : out Resource)
              when F <= Free and (Normal or Barrier(F)) is
  begin
    Free := Free - F;
    if not Normal then
      Barrier(F) := False;
      Normal := True;
      for I in reverse 1 .. F loop
        if Allocate(I)'Count /= 0 and I <= Free then
          Barrier(I) := True;
          Normal := False;
          exit;
        end if;
```

```
         end loop;
      end if;
      ...
   end Allocate;


   procedure Release(R : Resource; Amount : Request_Range) is
   begin
      Free := Free + Amount;
      for I in reverse 1 .. Free loop
         if Allocate(I)'Count /= 0 then
            Barrier(I) := True;
            Normal := False;
            exit;
         end if;
      end loop;
      ...
   end Release;
end Resource_Controller;
```

Note that the loop bound in entry Allocate is F not Free as there cannot be a task queued on Allocate requiring more than F instances of the resource.

The correctness of this algorithm relies on the property that requests already queued upon Allocate (when resources are released) are serviced before any new call to Allocate (from outside the resources controller). It also relies on tasks not removing themselves from entry queues, that is, after the count attribute has been read (and the associated barrier raised) but before the released task actually executes Allocate. Furthermore, it assumes that tasks only ever release resources that they have acquired.

The double interaction solution

One possible solution to the resource allocation problem, which does not rely on a family of entries, is for the resource controller to reject calls that cannot be satisfied. In this approach, the client must first request resources and, if refused, must try again. To avoid continuously requesting resources when no new resources are available, the client calls a different entry from the original request entry:

```
type Request_Range is range 1..Max;

protected Resource_Controller is
   entry Allocate(R : out Resource; Amount : Request_Range;
                  Ok : out Boolean);
   entry Try_Again(R : out Resource; Amount : Request_Range;
                   Ok : out Boolean);
   procedure Release(R : Resource; Amount : Request_Range);
private
```

```
      Free : Request_Range := Request_Range'Last;
      New_Resources_Released : Boolean := False;
      ...
   end Resource_Controller;


   protected body Resource_Controller is
      entry Allocate(R : out Resource; Amount : Request_Range;
                          Ok : out Boolean) when Free > 0 is
      begin
         if Amount <= Free then
            Free := Free - Amount;
            Ok := True;
            -- allocate
         else
            Ok := False;
         end if;
      end Allocate;


      entry Try_Again(R : out Resource; Amount : Request_Range;
              Ok : out Boolean) when New_Resources_Released is
      begin
         if Try_Again'Count = 0 then
            New_Resources_Released := False;
         end if;
         if Amount <= Free then
            Free := Free - Amount;
            Ok := True;
            -- allocate
         else
            Ok := False;
         end if;
      end Try_Again;


      procedure Release(R : Resource; Amount : Request_Range) is
      begin
         Free := Free + Amount;
         -- free resources
         if Try_Again'Count > 0 then
            New_Resources_Released := True;
         end if;
      end Release;
   end Resource_Controller;
```

To use this controller, each client must then make the following calls:

```
Resource_Controller.Allocate(Res,N,Done);
while not Done loop
   Resource_Controller.Try_Again(Res,N,Done);
end loop;
```

Even this code is not entirely satisfactory, for the following reasons:

1. The clients must Try_Again for their resources each time any resources are released; this is inefficient.

2. If a client is tardy in calling Try_Again, it may miss the opportunity to acquire its resources (as only those tasks queued on Try_Again, at the point when new resources become available, are considered).

3. It is difficult to allocate the resources selectively — when several requests can be serviced, then they are serviced in a FIFO order.

An alternative approach is to require the resource controller to record outstanding requests:

```
type Request_Range is range 1 .. Max;

protected Resource_Controller is
   entry Allocate(R : out Resource; Amount : Request_Range;
                  Ok : out Boolean);
   entry Try_Again(R : out Resource; Amount : Request_Range;
                   Ok : out Boolean);
   procedure Release(R : Resource; Amount : Request_Range);
private
   Free : Request_Range := Request_Range'Last;
   New_Resources_Released : Boolean := False;
   ...
end Resource_Controller;


protected body Resource_Controller is

   procedure Log_Request(Amount : Request_Range) is
   begin
      -- store details of request
   end Log_Request;

   procedure Done_Request(Amount : Request_Range) is
   begin
      -- remove details of request
   end Done_Request;

   function Outstanding_Requests return Boolean is
   begin
      -- returns True if there are outstanding requests to
      -- be serviced
   end Outstanding_Requests;

   procedure Seen_Request(Amount : Request_Range) is
   begin
      -- log details of failed request
   end Seen_Request;

   function More_Outstanding_Requests return Boolean is
```

```
begin
   -- returns True if there are outstanding requests
   -- to be serviced which have not been considered
   -- this time around
end More_Outstanding_Requests;

entry Allocate(R : out Resource; Amount : Request_Range;
               Ok : out Boolean)
      when Free > 0 and not New_Resources_Released is
begin
   if Amount <= Free then
      Free := Free - Amount;
      Ok := True;
      -- allocate
   else
      Ok := False;
      Log_Request(Amount);
   end if;
end Allocate;


entry Try_Again(R : out Resource; Amount : Request_Range;
                Ok : out Boolean) when New_Resources_Released is
begin
   if Amount <= Free then
      Free := Free - Amount;
      Ok := True;
      Done_Request(Amount);
      -- allocate
   else
      Ok := False;
      Seen_Request(Amount);
   end if;
   if not More_Outstanding_Requests  then
      New_Resources_Released := False;
   end if;
end Try_Again;


procedure Release(R : Resource; Amount : Request_Range) is
begin
   Free := Free + Amount;
   -- free resources
   if Outstanding_Requests then
      New_Resources_Released := True;
   end if;
end Release;
end Resource_Controller;
```

In order to ensure that tasks waiting on the Try_Again entry are serviced
before new requests, it is necessary to guard the Allocate entry. Unfortunately, this algorithm then breaks down if the client does not make the
call to Try_Again (due, for example, to being aborted or suffering an asyn-

chronous transfer of control — see Chapter 10). To solve this problem, it is necessary to encapsulate the double interaction in a procedure and provide a dummy controlled variable (as was done in Section 6.6.1) which, during finalisations, informs the resource controller (via a new protected procedure Done_Waiting) that it is no longer interested:

```
type Resource_Recovery is new Finalization.Limited_Controlled
    with null record;

procedure Finalize(Rr : in out Resource_Recovery) is
begin
    Resource_Controller.Done_Waiting;
end Finalize;

procedure Allocate(R : out Resource; Amount : Request_Range) is
    Got : Boolean;
    Protection : Resource_Recovery;
begin
    Resource_Controller.Allocate(R, Amount, Got);
    while not Got loop
        Resource_Controller.Try_Again(R, Amount, Got);
    end loop;
end Allocate;
```

Note that with this solution, the Done_Waiting routine will be called *every time* the procedure Allocate is left (either normally or because of task abortion). The resource controller will therefore have to keep track of the actual client tasks rather than just the requests. It can do this by using task identifiers provided by the Systems Programming Annex. The controller can then determine if a task executing Done_Waiting has an outstanding request.

Even with this solution, the controller still has difficulty in allocating resources selectively. However, the fundamental problem with this approach is that the task must make a double interaction with the resource controller even though only a single logical action is being undertaken.

8.1.2 Solutions using language support

Two methods have been proposed to increase the effectiveness of avoidance synchronisation. One of these, requeue, has been incorporated into Ada. The other approach, which is less general purpose, is to allow the guard/barrier to have access to 'in' parameters. This approach is adopted in the language SR. The resource control problem is easily coded with this approach; for example, using Ada-like syntax:

```
type Request_Range is range 1..Max;

protected Resource_Controller is
    entry Allocate(R : out Resource; Amount : Request_Range);
```

```
    procedure Release(R : Resource; Amount : Request_Range);
private
    Free : Request_Range := Request_Range'Last;
    ...
end Resource_Controller;


protected body Resource_Controller is
    entry Allocate(R : out Resource; Amount : Request_Range)
        when Amount <= Free is   -- Not Legal Ada
    begin
        Free := Free - Amount;
    end Allocate;

    procedure Release(R : Resource; Amount : Request_Range) is
    begin
        Free := Free + Amount;
    end Free;
end Resource_Controller;
```

The main drawback with this approach is implementational efficiency. It is no longer possible to evaluate a barrier once per entry; each task's placement on the entry queue will lead to a barrier evaluation. However, optimisations are possible that would allow a compiler to recognise when 'in' parameters were not being used; efficient code could then be produced.

The key notion behind requeue is to move the task (which has been through one guard or barrier — we shall use the term 'guard' in this discussion) to 'beyond' another guard. For an analogy, consider a person (task) waiting to enter a room (protected object) which has one or more doors (guarded entries) giving access to the room. Once inside, the person can be ejected (requeued) from the room and once again be placed behind a (potentially closed) door.

Ada allows requeues between task entries and protected object entries. A requeue can be to the same entry, to another entry in the same unit, or to another unit altogether. Requeues from task entries to protected object entries (and vice versa) are allowed. However, the main use of requeue is to send the calling task to a different entry of the same unit from which the requeue was executed.

The resource control problem provides illustrative examples of the application of requeue. One solution is given now; some variations are considered later in this chapter (Section 8.4).

Requeue example — concurrent solution to the resource control problem

One of the problems with the double interaction solution was that a task could be delayed (say, due to preemption) before it could requeue on the Try_Again entry. Consequently, when new resources became available it was not in a position to have them allocated. Requeue allows a task to be ejected from a protected object and placed back on an entry queue as an atomic operation. It is therefore not possible for the task to miss the newly available resources.

In the following algorithm, an unsuccessful request is now requeued on to a private entry (called `Assign`) of the protected object. The caller of this protected object now makes a single call on `Allocate`. Whenever resources are released, a note is taken of how many tasks are on the `Assign` entry. This number of tasks can then retry and either obtain their allocations or be requeued back onto the same `Assign` entry. The last task to retry lowers the barrier:

```
type Request_Range is range 1..Max;

protected Resource_Controller is
   entry Allocate(R : out Resource; Amount : Request_Range);
   procedure Release(R : Resource; Amount : Request_Range);
private
   entry Assign(R : out Resource; Amount : Request_Range);
   Free : Request_Range := Request_Range'Last;
   New_Resources_Released : Boolean := False;
   To_Try : Natural := 0;
   ...
end Resource_Controller;


protected body Resource_Controller is
   entry Allocate(R : out Resource; Amount : Request_Range)
         when Free > 0 is
   begin
     if Amount <= Free then
       Free := Free - Amount;
       -- allocate
     else
       requeue Assign;
     end if;
   end Allocate;


   entry Assign(R : out Resource; Amount : Request_Range)
      when New_Resources_Released is
   begin
     To_Try := To_Try - 1;
     if To_Try = 0 then
       New_Resources_Released := False;
     end if;
     if Amount <= Free then
       Free := Free - Amount;
       -- allocate
     else
```

```
      requeue Assign;
    end if;
  end Assign;


  procedure Release(R : Resource; Amount : Request_Range) is
  begin
    Free := Free + Amount;
    -- free resources
    if Assign'Count > 0 then
      To_Try := Assign'Count;
      New_Resources_Released := True;
    end if;
  end Release;
end Resource_Controller;
```

Note that this will only work if the Assign entry queuing discipline is FIFO. When priorities are used, two entry queues are needed. Tasks must requeue from one entry to the other (and back again after the next release). This is illustrated in the example given in Section 8.4.

Finally, it should be observed that a more efficient algorithm can be derived if the protected object records the smallest outstanding request. The barrier should then only be lowered in Release (or remain lowered in Assign) if Free >= Smallest.

Even with this style of solution, however, it is difficult to give priority to certain requests other than in FIFO or task priority order. As indicated earlier, to program this level of control requires a family of entries. However, with requeue, a more straightforward solution can be given (as compared with the earlier code that did not use requeue):

```
  type Request_Range is range 1..Max;
  type Bools is array(Request_Range) of Boolean;

  protected Resource_Controller is
    entry Allocate(Request_Range)(R : out Resource);
    procedure Release(R : Resource; Amount : Request_Range);
  private
    entry Assign(Request_Range)(R : out Resource);
    Free : Request_Range := Request_Range'Last;
    Barrier : Bools := (others => False);
    ...
  end Resource_Controller;


  protected body Resource_Controller is
    entry Allocate(for F in Request_Range)(R : out Resource)
                  when True is
    begin
      if F <= Free then
```

```
      Free := Free - F;
      ...
   else
      requeue Assign(F);
   end if;
end Allocate;


   entry Assign(for F in Request_Range)(R : out Resource)
                  when Barrier(F) is
   begin
      Free := Free - F;
      Barrier(F) := False;
      for I in reverse 1 .. F loop
         if Allocate(I)'Count /= 0 and I <= Free then
            Barrier(I) := True;
            exit;
         end if;
      end loop;
      ...
   end Assign;


   procedure Release(R : Resource; Amount : Request_Range) is
   begin
      Free := Free + Amount;
      for I in reverse 1 .. Free loop
         if Assign(I)'Count /= 0 then
            Barrier(I) := True;
            exit;
         end if;
      end loop;
      ...
   end Release;
end Resource_Controller;
```

This algorithm is not only more straightforward than the one given earlier, but it also has the advantage that it is resilient to a task removing itself from an entry queue (after the count attribute has acknowledged its presence). Once a task has been requeued it cannot be aborted or subject to a time-out on the entry call — see following discussion.

8.2 Semantics of requeue

It is important to appreciate that requeue is not a simple call. If procedure P calls procedure Q, then, after Q has finished, control is passed back to P. But if entry X requeues on entry Y, then control is not passed back to X. After Y has completed, control passes back to the object that called X. Hence, when an entry or accept body executes a requeue, that body is "completed, finalised and left" (ARM, Section 9.5.4).

One consequence of this is that when a requeue is from one protected object to another then mutual exclusion on the original object is given up once the task is queued. Other tasks waiting to enter the first object will be able to do so. However, a requeue to the same protected object will retain the mutual exclusion lock (if the target entry is open).

The entry named in a requeue statement (called the *target* entry) must either have no parameters or have a parameter profile that is equivalent (i.e. type conformant) with that of the entry (or accept) statement from which the requeue is made. For example, in the resource control program the parameters of `Assign` are identical to those of `Allocate`. Because of this rule, it is not necessary to give the actual parameters with the call; indeed it is forbidden to do so (in case the programmer tries to change them). Hence if the target entry has no parameters, then no information is passed; if it has parameters, then the corresponding parameters in the entity that is executing the requeue are mapped across.

The syntax for requeue is defined as

```
requeue_statement  ::= requeue entry_name [with abort]
```

The optional "with abort" clause has two uses. When a task is on an entry queue it will remain there until serviced unless it made a timed entry call or is aborted (see next chapter). Once the task has been accepted (or starts to execute the entry of a protected object), then the time-out is cancelled and the effect of any abort attempt is postponed until the task comes out of the entry. There is, however, a question as to what should happen with requeue. Consider the time-out issue; clearly two views can be taken:

1.   As the first call has been accepted, the time-out should now be cancelled (i.e. it cannot have an effect).

2.   If the requeue puts the calling task back onto an entry queue, then time-out expiry should again be possible.

A similar argument can be made with abort; if the task is again on an entry queue it should be abortable. The requeue statement allows both views to be programmed; the default does not allow further time-outs or aborts, the addition of the "with abort" clause enables the task to be removed from the second entry.

The real issue (in deciding whether to use "with abort" or not) is whether the protected object (or client task) having requeued the task expects it to be there when the guard/barrier is lowered. If the correct behaviour of the object requires the task's presence, then "with abort" should not be used.

The combination of time-outs and requeue can give rise to somewhat unanticipated behaviour. For example, a call of

```
select
   T.E1;
or
   delay 10.0;
end select;
```

on a task that does a requeue:

```
select -- in task T
   accept E1 do
      -- lots of computing taking 2 seconds
      requeue E2 with abort;
   end E1;
or
   ...
end select;
```

will fail if E1 is not accepted in 10.0 seconds, will not timeout between 10.0 and 12.0 seconds (if the call is accepted just before 10.0 seconds has elapsed) but will time-out after 12.0 seconds. Hence, the selective entry call may take the delay alternative some time after the value given in the delay alternative.

Now consider the following program fragment:

```
task Server is
   entry Service(Param : Parameter; Res : out Result);
private
   entry Service_Done(Param : Parameter; Res : out Result);
end Server;

task body Server is
   P : Param;
begin
   ...
   accept Service(Param : Parameter; Res : out Result) do
      P := Param;
      requeue Service_Done with abort;
   end Service;
   -- perform required service
   -- which potentially may take a long time
   select
      accept Service_Done(Param : Parameter; Res : out Result) do
         Res := ...;
      end Service_Done;
   else
      -- client has not waited
      -- throw away the result
   end select;
   ...
end Server;
```

Requeuing a request inside a rendezvous "with abort" allows a client effectively to time-out on the results being returned from the rendezvous, rather than on the start of the rendezvous.

This section concludes with a further example. In a real-time system it may be necessary to restrict the number of interrupts that can be raised from any particular source. An excessive amount of interrupt handling may undermine the schedulability of some application task. One way to do this is to use a protected object as the interrupt handler but to turn on interrupts only when a calling task (the second-level interrupt handler) indicates that it is acceptable to do so. This calling task must therefore turn on interrupts and then be suspended until an interrupt actually occurs. The use of requeue makes this straightforward:

```
protected Interface is
  pragma Interrupt_Priority(Interrupt_Level);
  entry Wait_For_Interrupt;
private
  procedure Interrupt_Handler; -- mapped onto interrupt source
  pragma Attach_Interrupt(Interrupt_Handler, ...);
  entry Private_Wait;
  Open : Boolean := False;
end Interface;
```

```
protected body Interface is
  procedure Interrupt_Handler is
  begin
    Open := True;
  end Interrupt_Handler;

  entry Wait_For_Interrupt when True is
  begin
    -- turn on interrupts
    requeue Private_Wait;
  end Wait_For_Interrupt;

  entry Private_Wait when Open is
  begin
    -- handle interrupt
    Open := False;
    -- turn off interrupts
  end Private_Wait;
end Interface;
```

A similar structure could be used to record the time at which an entry call on a protected object is made:

```
entry Call(...) when True is
begin
  Time := Clock;
  requeue Private_Call;
end Call;
```

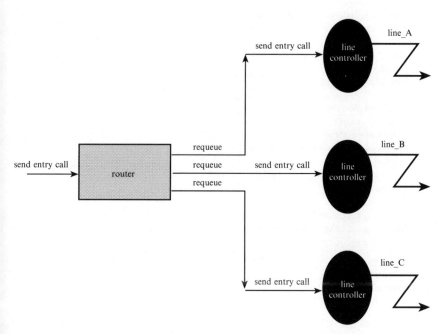

Figure 8.1: A Network Router.

Note that this example uses an entry with a "when true" barrier. All protected entries must have a barrier but when requeue is used it may be necessary to have this null barrier.

8.3 Requeuing to other entries

Although requeuing to the same entity represents the normal use of requeue, there are situations in which the full generality of this language feature is useful.

Consider the situation in which resources are controlled by a hierarchy of objects. For example, a network router might have a choice of three communication lines on which to forward messages: Line_A is the preferred route, but if it becomes overloaded Line_B can be used; if this also becomes overloaded Line_C can be used. Each line is controlled by a server task; it is an active entity as it has housekeeping operations to perform. A protected unit acts as an interface to the router; it decides which of the three channels should be used and then uses requeue to pass the request to the appropriate server. The structure of the solution is illustrated in Figure 8.1, and the program fragment is given below:

```
type Line_Id is (Line_A, Line_B, Line_C);
type Line_Status is array (Line_Id) of Boolean;

task type Line_Controller(Id : Line_Id) is
  entry Request(...);
end Line_Controller;

protected Router is
  entry Send(...);
  procedure Overloaded(Line : Line_Id);
  procedure Clear(Line : Line_Id);
private
  Ok : Line_Status := (others => True);
end Router;

La : Line_Controller(Line_A);
Lb : Line_Controller(Line_B);
Lc : Line_Controller(Line_C);


task body Line_Controller is
  ...
begin
  loop
    select
      accept Request(...) do
        -- service request
      end Request;
    or
      terminate;
    end select;
    -- housekeeping including possibly
    Router.Overloaded(Id);
    -- or
    Router.Clear(Id);
  end loop;
end Line_Controller;


protected body Router is

  entry Send(...) when Ok(Line_A) or Ok(Line_B) or Ok(Line_C) is
  begin
    if Ok(Line_A) then
      requeue La.Request with abort;
    elsif Ok(Line_B) then
      requeue Lb.Request with abort;
    else
      requeue Lc.Request with abort;
    end if;
  end Send;
```

```
      procedure Overloaded(Line : Line_Id) is
      begin
        Ok(Line) := False;
      end Overloaded;

      procedure Clear(Line : Line_Id) is
      begin
        Ok(Line) := True;
      end Clear;
    end Router;
```

When requeuing from one protected object to another it is important to understand that while the call is being evaluated a mutual exclusive lock is held on both protected objects. It is therefore a bounded error to execute an external requeue request back to the requesting object (it would inevitably lead to deadlock):

```
protected P is
   entry X;
   entry Y;
end P;

protected body P is
   entry X when ... is
   begin
      requeue Y;   -- valid internal requeue
      requeue P.Y; -- invalid external requeue
   end X;

   entry Y when ...
end P;
```

Moreover, the programmer cannot assume, when a requeue has taken place from one protected object to another, that any tasks released in the original object will execute before the entry in the destination object. Indeed, an implementation is most likely to behave as follows:

```
protected P is
   entry X;
   entry Y;
private
   Barrier_Down : Boolean := False;
end P;

protected Q is
   entry Z;
end Q;

protected body P is
   entry X when Barrier_Down is
   begin
```

```
   . . .
end X;

entry Y when True is
begin
   Barrier_Down := True;
   requeue Q.Z;
end Y;
end P;
```

Assume that a task first calls P.X and is blocked. Next, another task calls P.Y. If the entry Z in Q is open, then Z will be executed before the original call of X is completed.

Finally in this section, we show another form of interaction to be aware of. This involves the requeuing from a task to a protected object declared within the task body:

```
task T is
   entry E;
   . . .
end T;

task body T is
   protected P is
      entry E;
      procedure L;
   end P;
   protected body P is ...
begin
   loop
      select
         accept E do
            requeue P.E;
         end E;
      or
         . . .
      or
         terminate;
      end select;
      . . .
      exit when ...;
   end loop;
end T;
```

With this code a call on T.E is requeued on to a protected object where it may be blocked (to be freed again by a call of L from some other entry of T). Task T cannot terminate (with the terminate alternative) while there is a task blocked on the protected object as there must be a non-terminated task remaining that can call T (i.e. the blocked task when it is next freed). However, if T terminates for some other reason, then P must go out of scope and hence the task on its entry queue will have `Program_Error` raised at its point of call of `T.E`. Of course, if `P` were declared outside `T`, then this would not happen.

8.4 Real-time solutions to the resource control problem

Consider again the resource control problem and the use of a priority queue on the `Assign` entry. The top priority task will now be put back at the front of the queue and other tasks will not be able to proceed. To control this, two queues are needed. Whenever resources are released, unsuccessful tasks are moved from one queue to the other. A family of two is used in the following code:

```
type Family is range 1..2;
type Bools is array(Family) of Boolean;

protected Resource_Controller is
   entry Allocate(R : out Resource; Amount : Request_Range);
   procedure Release(R : Resource; Amount : Request_Range);
private
   entry Assign(Family)
               (R : out Resource; Amount : Request_Range);
   Free : Request_Range := Request_Range'Last;
   New_Resources_Released : Bools := (others => False);
   Queue_At : Family := 1;
   ...
end Resource_Controller;


protected body Resource_Controller is
   entry Allocate(R : out Resource; Amount : Request_Range)
         when Free > 0 is
   begin
     if Amount <= Free then
       Free := Free - Amount;
       -- allocate resources
     else
       requeue Assign(Queue_At);
     end if;
   end Allocate;


   entry Assign(for F in Family)
               (R : out Resource; Amount : Request_Range)
         when New_Resources_Released(F) is
   begin
     -- for this code to execute F must not equal Queue_At
```

```
  if Assign(F)'Count = 0 then
    New_Resources_Released(F) := False;
  end if;
  if Amount <= Free then
    Free := Free - Amount;
    -- allocate resources
  else
    requeue Assign(Queue_At);
  end if;
end Assign;


procedure Release(R : Resource; Amount : Request_Range) is
begin
  Free := Free + Amount;
  -- free resources
  if Assign(Queue_At)'Count > 0 then
    New_Resources_Released(Queue_At) := True;
    if Queue_At = 1 then
      Queue_At := 2;
    else
      Queue_At := 1;
    end if;
  end if;
end;
end Resource_Controller;
```

In addition to these structures, in a real-time solution we usually want to ensure that the highest priority process receives the resource as soon as possible and is blocked for a bounded minimum time. Consequently, resources are not given to lower priority waiting tasks, even though there are a sufficient number of resources to satisfy their request. The solution to this problem is not immediately obvious. Consider first a flawed attempt; it assumes that the entry queues are ordered according to the priority of the queued tasks:

```
Max : constant Positive :=10;
type Resource is new Integer;
type Request_Range is range 1..Max;

protected Resource_Controller is
  entry Allocate(R : out Resource; Amount : Request_Range);
  procedure Release(R : Resource; Amount : Request_Range);
private
  entry Assign(R : out Resource; Amount : Request_Range);
  Free : Request_Range := Request_Range 'Last;
  New_Resources_Released : Boolean := False;
end Resource_Controller;
```

```
protected body Resource_Controller is
  entry Allocate(R : out Resource; Amount : Request_Range)
                 when Free > 0 is
  begin
    if Amount <= Free then
      Free := Free - Amount;
      -- allocate
    else
      New_Resources_Released := False;
      requeue Assign;
    end if;
  end Allocate;



  entry Assign(R : out Resource; Amount : Request_Range)
               when New_Resources_Released is
  begin
    if Amount <= Free then
      Free := Free - Amount;
      -- allocate
    else
      New_Resources_Released := False;
      requeue Assign;
    end if;
  end Assign;



  procedure Release(R : Resource; Amount : Request_Range) is
  begin
    Free := Free + Amount;
    -- free resources
    New_Resources_Released := True;
  end Release;
end Resource_Controller;
```

The problem with this 'solution' is that a low priority task could be given some free resources (when it calls `Allocate`) when a higher priority task is queued on `Assign` (because there are not enough resources to satisfy its request). This breaks our requirement that the highest priority task must be serviced first. An alternative approach would be to have only a single entry for `Allocate` and `Assign`; unfortunately this fails when a new highest priority task calls in for resources that are available. The barrier would be closed until `Free` is called again.

Unless priorities can be manipulated directly the only solution is for all new calls to `Allocate` to 'open' the `Assign` barrier and then requeue onto that entry. They can then compete with any existing queued calls. The following implements this algorithm:

```
Max : constant Positive :=10;
```

```
type Resource is new Integer;
type Request_Range is range 1..Max;

protected Resource_Controller is
   entry Allocate(R : out Resource; Amount : Request_Range);
   procedure Release(R : Resource; Amount : Request_Range);
private
   entry Assign(R : out Resource; Amount : Request_Range);
   Free : Request_Range := Request_Range 'Last;
   Open_Barrier : Boolean   :=  False;
end Resource_Controller;


protected body Resource_Controller is
   entry Allocate(R : out Resource; Amount : Request_Range)
         when True is
   begin
     if Amount <= Free then
       if Assign'Count = 0 then
         Free := Free - Amount;
       else
         Open_Barrier := True;
         requeue Assign;
       end if;
     else
       Open_Barrier := False;
       requeue Assign;
     end if;
   end Allocate;


   entry Assign(R : out Resources) when Open_Barrier is
   begin
     if Amount <= Free then
       Free := Free - Amount;
       -- allocate
     else
       Open_Barrier := False;
       requeue Assign;
     end if;
   end Assign;


   procedure Release(R : Resource; Amount : Request_Range) is
   begin
     Free := Free + Amount;
     -- free resources
     Open_Barrier := True;
   end Release;
end Resource_Controller;
```

Arguably, this is not an elegant algorithm, but it works and is not too inefficient.

8.5 Entry families and server tasks

Earlier in this chapter a family of entries was used with a protected object. With server tasks, families are not as easy to use. This difficulty will be illustrated with a simple server that wishes to give priority to certain classes of user task:

```
type A_Priority is (High, Medium, Low);
task Server is
  entry Request(A_Priority)(...);
end Server;
```

a typical call would be

```
Server.Request(Low)(...);
```

Within the body of the task, a select statement is constructed so that priority is given to calls coming in on the High family entry:

```
task body Server is
  Empty : Boolean;
begin
  loop
    select
      accept Request(High)(...) do
        ...
      end Request;
    or
      when Request(High)'Count = 0 =>
        accept Request(Medium)(...) do
          ...
        end Request;
    or
      when Request(High)'Count   = 0  and
           Request(Medium)'Count = 0  =>
        accept Request(Low)(...) do
          ...
        end Request;
    or
      terminate;
    end select;
  end loop;
end Server;
```

One criticism of the above code is that for a large family the necessary guards become somewhat excessive (for a 1000 member family, the guard on the lowest value would need to contain 999 boolean evaluations!). If the Real-Time Systems Annex is being supported, then it is possible to define a queuing discipline that will use the textual ordering of the select statement to give priority to those accept statements that appear first:

```
select   -- with priority queuing and all callers having
         -- the same priority, see Chapter 12
  accept Request(High)(...) do
    ...
  end Request;
or
  ...
or
  accept Request(Low)(...) do
    ...
  end Request;
or
  terminate;
end select;
```

However, each member of the family still has to be written out individually. Ideally, a syntactical form equivalent to that available to protected objects could be used:

```
select (for P in A_Priority)   -- Not Vaid Ada
  accept Request(P)(...) do
    ...
  end Request;
or
  terminate;
end select;
```

Unfortunately, no such syntax is available. An alternative structure involves looping through all the possible values of the family:

```
task body Server is
  ...
begin
  loop
    for P in A_Priority loop
      select
        accept Request(P)(...) do
          ...
        end Request;
        exit;
      else
        null;
      end select;
    end loop;
  end loop;
end Server;
```

The task loops through the values of A_Priority in the order required until it finds an outstanding entry call. Having accepted this call it exits from the inner loop and tries to find a high priority entry again. If no entries are outstanding, then it returns via the outer loop to try again.

This last point immediately raises a question about this 'solution', for it uses a busy-wait loop which is polling for requests. A reliable and efficient algorithm must separate the acceptance of outstanding entry calls from waiting for the first new entry call to arrive. If there are no outstanding calls, then the server task must be suspended on a select statement that will accept the first incoming call, whatever its priority:

```
task body Server is
  Empty : Boolean ;   -- no outstanding calls.
begin
  loop
    loop
      Empty := True;
      for P in A_Priority loop
        select
          accept Request(P)(...) do
            ...
          end Request;
          Empty := False;
          exit;
        else
          null;
        end select;
      end loop;
      exit when Empty; -- will only exit when no requests
                       -- have been found.
    end loop;

    select
      accept Request(High)(...) do
        ...
      end Request;
    or
      accept Request(Medium)(...) do
        ...
      end Request;
    or
      accept Request(Low)(...) do
        ...
      end Request;
    or
      terminate;
    end select;
  end loop;
end Server;
```

The second half of this task body, which will accept any incoming call (or terminate), must, of necessity, name each family entry explicitly and will be lengthy for large families as a consequence. If the family size is such that this length is a problem, then a structure using requeue is possible:

```
task Server is
  entry Request(Pri : A_Priority; ...);
private
  entry Waiting(A_Priority)(Pri : A_Priority; ...);
end Server;


task body Server is
  Empty : Boolean;
  ...
begin
  loop
    select
      accept Request(Pri : A_Priority; ...) do
        requeue Waiting(Pri);
      end Request;
    or
      terminate;
    end select;
    loop
      Empty := True;
      for P in A_Priority loop
        select
          accept Request(Pri : A_Priority; ...)  do
            requeue Waiting(Pri);
          end Request;
          Empty := False;
          exit;
        or
          when Request'Count = 0 =>
            accept Waiting(P)(...) do
              ...
            end Waiting;
          Empty := False;
          exit;
        else
          null;
        end select;
      end loop;
      exit when Empty;
    end loop;
  end loop;
end Server;
```

Note that the parameter lists for Waiting and Request have to be identical so that a requeue with parameters between them can take place.

8.6 Extended example

This chapter concludes with a further example that illustrates the power of requeue as a concurrent programming primitive. The problem is one of simulating/representing the behaviour of travellers on a circular railway (metro). There are N stations on the circular track and one train (with a small finite capacity). Travellers arrive at one station and are transported to their requested destination. A full trip back to the original station is allowed.

The design of the concurrent representation of this situation consists of active entities for each traveller and an active entity for the train itself. Stations represent resources. Travellers are blocked at the station until the train arrives. The program will then requeue the passengers (if there are seats on the train) to the destination station of choice. When the train subsequently arrives at that station, the travellers disembark and continue on their way (which in the following program means taking another trip). The system is illustrated in Figure 8.2.

Each station will be represented by a protected object. This object will have a number of procedure/entry interfaces:

1. `Arrive` — entry called by passengers when they arrive at the station (they are blocked until the train arrives).

2. `Stopping` — procedure called by the train when it stops at the station.

3. `Alight` — entry requeued by passengers wishing to alight at that station.

4. `Boarding` — procedure called by the train to allow passengers onto the train.

5. `Closedoors` — procedure called by the train to indicate that it is about to leave the station.

The code for the station definition is thus

```
type Station_Address is new Natural range 1..N;
type Passengers is new Natural range 0..Max;
Capacity : constant Passengers := 10;
   -- capacity of the small train

protected type Station is
   entry Arrive(Destination : Station_Address);
   procedure Stopping(P : Passengers);
   entry Alight(Destination : Station_Address);
   procedure Boarding;
   procedure Closedoors(P : out Passengers);
private
   On_Train : Passengers;
   Trainboarding : Boolean := False;
   Trainstopped : Boolean := False;
end Station;
```

The set of stations is represented as an array:

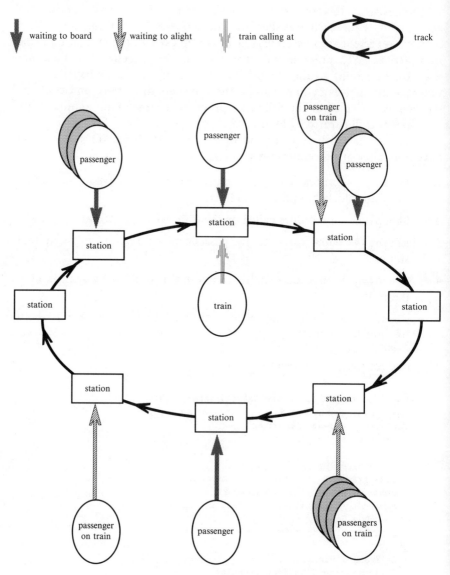

Figure 8.2: The Requeue Metro.

```
Stations : array(Station_Address) of Station;
```

The code for the body of Station can now be given:

```
protected body Station is
  entry Arrive(Destination : Station_Address)
      when Trainboarding and then On_Train < Capacity is
  begin
    On_Train := On_Train + 1;
    requeue Stations(Destination).Alight;
  end Arrive;

  procedure Stopping(P : Passengers) is
  begin
    On_Train := P;
    Trainstopped := True;
  end Stopping;

  entry Alight(Destination : Station_Address)
        when Trainstopped is
  begin
    On_Train := On_Train - 1;
    -- passenger has arrived
  end Alight;

  procedure Boarding is
  begin
    Trainstopped := False;
    Trainboarding := True;
  end Boarding;

  procedure Closedoors(P : out Passengers) is
  begin
    P := On_Train;
    Trainboarding := False;
  end Closedoors;
end Station;
```

Passengers just call on the stations and take trips:

```
task type Clients;

Travellers : array(Passengers) of Clients;

task body Clients is
  Home, Away : Station_Address;
begin
  -- choose home
  loop
    -- choose away
    Stations(Home).Arrive(Away);
    Home := Away;
```

```
    end loop;
  end Clients;
```

The train must repeat a fixed set of operations for each station:

```
  task Train;

  task body Train is
    Volume : Passengers := 0;
    Travel_Times : array(Station_Address) of Duration := ...;
  begin
    loop -- forever or until privatised
      for S in Station_Address loop
        Stations(S).Stopping(Volume);
        Stations(S).Boarding;
        Stations(S).Closedoors(Volume);
        delay Travel_Times(S);
      end loop;
    end loop;
  end Train;
```

Note that the train interacts with each station in three distinct phases. First the train stops at the station with a current passenger load of Volume; this number is copied and held internally, to the station, in On_Train. People are released at this stage and thus On_Train is decreased. Only when all such alighting passengers have left the train (and the station) can the call of Boarding be accepted. This second action of the train closes the barrier for passengers getting off, and opens the barrier for passengers getting on (up to the capacity of the train). Again, only when all boarding passengers are on the train can the train task call Closedoors; this returns the new value of Volume and closes the barrier for boarding passengers.

The key to this solution is that the train task cannot reenter the protected object until all passenger tasks released by the lowering of barriers have themselves left the protected object. It would be possible for the station object to export only a single procedure for the train, and to requeue the train call internally through the three phases. This is left as an exercise for the reader.

8.7   Task states

The requeue feature has only introduced a minor change to the state transition diagram given in previous chapters. It is now possible to move from executable to waiting on a protected (or task) entry call by a requeue operation.

8.8 Summary

The ability to program various forms of synchronisation is a fundamental requirement in any concurrent programming language. Ada's basic mechanism for programming inter-task synchronisation is the *guard*. If it is necessary for a task to prevent itself from proceeding, until some required system state is achieved, then it must call an entry in either another task or a protected object. In this called entity a guard (or barrier) is evaluated, and if found to be false the calling task is suspended. The use of guards supports avoidance synchronisation; progress is prevented if conditions are not favourable.

Unfortunately, the simple use of guards does not deal with all necessary synchronisations. There are situations in which some level of interaction is needed before the decision can be made as to whether a task should be suspended. A simple example of this is the need to evaluate incoming parameters before the suspension decision can be made. Ada has extended the expressive power of avoidance synchronisation by introducing the requeue facility. This allows a task to be returned to an entry so that it must again pass though a guard before proceeding.

The requeue facility is a general one, it allows a task to be requeued back to the same entry as before, to a different entry in the same server task or protected object, or to a different entity altogether. It is possible to requeue from a protected object to a task and visa versa. Guards plus requeue represents a powerful, but structured, means of programming all forms of task synchronisation.

Chapter 9 ————————————————

Using Protected Objects as Building Blocks

The main purpose of protected objects is to provide a mechanism within which to encapsulate data-oriented/asynchronous communication. This chapter illustrates their expressive power by showing how they can be used to program some standard communication paradigms. The goal is to provide a basis for a library of reusable communication components. The chapter concludes by considering the effect of not having a multi-way selective entry call facility for protected objects.

There are many communication paradigms; this chapter will illustrate the following: [1]

*   Semaphores

    A standard counting semaphore providing wait (P) and signal (V) operations. Also binary semaphores and quantity semaphores.

*   A persistent signal

    A signal which remains set until a single task has received it.

*   A transient signal (or Pulse)

    A signal which releases one or more waiting tasks but is lost if no tasks are waiting.

*   Events

    Events are bivalued state variables (*up* or *down*). Tasks can *set* (assign to *up*), *reset* (assign to *down*), or *toggle* an event. Any tasks *waiting* for the event to become *up* (or *down*) are released by a call of *set* (or *reset*); *toggle* can also release *waiting* tasks.

*   Buffers

    Buffers support the standard bounded buffer abstraction.

*   Blackboards

---

[1]Events, pulses, buffers, blackboards, barriers have also been defined by the ARTEWG *Catalogue of Interface Features and Options (CIFO)*, Release 3.1 (ARTEWG, 1993) as being appropriate extensions to Ada 83 for use in real-time systems. The synchronisation semantics given here closely match those defined in CIFO.

Blackboards are similar to events except that they allow arbitrary data to be transmitted between the signaling and the waiting task.

- Broadcasts

  The broadcast entry supports the standard broadcast paradigm (they are pulses with data transfer).

- Barriers

  The barrier entry provides a pure synchronisation mechanism; it allows a set number of tasks to block until all are present. They are then all released.

9.1 Semaphores

It is often claimed that semaphores are among the most flexible low level synchronisation primitives. They can easily be implemented as a protected type:

```
package Semaphores is
  protected type Semaphore (Initial : Natural := 0) is
    entry Wait; -- P operation
    procedure Signal;  -- V operation
  private
    Value : Natural := Initial;
  end Semaphore;
end Semaphores;

package body Semaphores is

  protected body Semaphore is
    entry Wait when Value > 0 is
    begin
      Value := Value - 1;
    end Wait;

    procedure Signal is
    begin
      Value := Value + 1;
    end Signal;
  end Semaphore;
end Semaphores;
```

Calls to the Wait entry are blocked until the semaphore can be decremented. Calls to Signal will increment the semaphore and this will result in any blocked task being released. An example of use of the semaphore is given below:

```
package Restricted_Tunnel_Control is
```

```
-- this package allows a certain number of cars to enter
-- a tunnel

procedure Enter_Protocol; -- potentially suspending operation
procedure Exit_Protocol;

end Restricted_Tunnel_Control;

with Semaphores; use Semaphores;
package body Restricted_Tunnel_Control is
   Max_Allowed : constant Natural := 10;
   -- maximum number of cars allowed in the tunnel

   Tunnel_Control : Semaphore (Max_Allowed);

   procedure Enter_Protocol is
   begin
      Tunnel_Control.Wait;
    end Enter_Protocol;

   procedure Exit_Protocol is
   begin
      Tunnel_Control.Signal;
      end Exit_Protocol;
end Restricted_Tunnel_Control;
```

In the above example, cars wishing to enter the tunnel must first call the
Enter_Protocol procedure. This is a potentially suspending procedure as it
calls an entry in a Semaphore protected object; only ten cars are allowed in
the tunnel at any one time. The cars call Exit_Protocol as they leave the
tunnel.

Although semaphores can be programmed using protected types, it is often
more appropriate to program the actual synchronisation required directly
rather than with a semaphore. For example, consider a binary semaphore:

```
package Binary_Semaphores is
   type Binary_Value is range 0 .. 1;
   protected type Binary_Semaphore(Initial : Binary_Value := 0) is
      entry Wait; -- P operation
      procedure Signal;   -- V operation
   private
      Value : Binary_Value := Initial;
   end Binary_Semaphore;
end Binary_Semaphores;

package body Binary_Semaphores is

   protected body Binary_Semaphore is
      entry Wait when Value = 1 is
      begin
         Value := 0;
```

```
        end Wait;

        procedure Signal is
        begin
            if Value = 0 then
                Value := 1;
            end if;
        end Signal;
    end Binary_Semaphore;
end Binary_Semaphores;
```

To obtain mutual exclusion using this semaphore requires the following:

```
with Binary_Semaphores; use Binary_Semaphores;
    ...
Mutex : Binary_Semaphore(1);
-- declaration of data requiring
-- mutually exclusive access
    ...

procedure Mutual_Exclusion is
begin
    Mutex.Wait;
    -- code to be executed in mutual exclusion
    Mutex.Signal;
end Mutual_Exclusion;
```

This can, however, more efficiently, more safely and more elegantly be written as:

```
protected Mutual_Exclusion is
    procedure Operation;
private
    -- declaration of data requiring
    -- mutually exclusive access
end Mutual_Exclusion;

protected body Mutual_Exclusion is
    procedure Operation is
    begin
        -- code to be executed in mutual exclusion
    end Operation;
end Mutual_Exclusion;
```

Another variation on the normal definition of a semaphore is the *quantity semaphore*. With this primitive, the amount to be decremented by the wait operation (and incremented by the signal operation) is not fixed at one but is given as a parameter to the procedures. In essence, the implementation of a quantity semaphore is equivalent to the resource control problem discussed in the previous chapter. An efficient implementation derived from the two-queue algorithm (presented in Section 8.4) can now be given. The two

queues are represented as a family with a boolean index. The boolean
variable First_Queue indicates if the first queue is the currently active one:

```
package Quantity_Semaphores is
  protected type Quantity_Semaphore(Initial : Natural := 0) is
    entry Wait(S : Positive);
    procedure Signal(S : Positive);
  private
    entry Waiting(Boolean)(S : Positive);
    First_Queue : Boolean := True;
    Value : Natural := Initial;
  end Quantity_Semaphore;
end Quantity_Semaphores;

package body Quantity_Semaphores is

  protected body Quantity_Semaphore is
    entry Wait(S : Positive) when Value > 0 is
    begin
      if S <= Value then
        Value := Value - S;
      else
        requeue Waiting(First_Queue) with abort;
      end if;
    end Wait;

    entry Waiting(for Q in Boolean)(S : Positive)
          when Q xor First_Queue is
    begin
      if S <= Value then
        Value := Value - S;
      else
        requeue Wait(First_Queue);
      end if;
    end Waiting;

    procedure Signal(S : Positive) is
    begin
      Value := Value + S;
      First_Queue := not First_Queue;
    end Signal;
  end Quantity_Semaphore;
end Quantity_Semaphores;
```

9.2   Persistent signals

Often a task needs to wait for a signal from another task before it can
proceed. The following protected type implements such a signal:

```
package Persistent_Signals is
```

```
protected type Persistent_Signal is
  procedure Send;
  entry Wait;
private
  Signal_Arrived : Boolean := False;
  end Persistent_Signal;
end Persistent_Signals;


package body Persistent_Signals is
  protected body Persistent_Signal is
    procedure Send is
    begin
      Signal_Arrived := True;
    end Send;

    entry Wait when Signal_Arrived is
    begin
      Signal_Arrived := False;
    end Wait;
  end Persistent_Signal;
end Persistent_Signals;
```

As an example of the use of a persistent signal, consider the following package, which provides access to a disk. One of the functions that it provides for is asynchronous output. That is, the calling task is not blocked when it requests that data be written to the disk. Instead, the package returns a pointer to a persistent signal. When the output is complete, the controller sends the associated signal:

```
with Persistent_Signals;
with System;
package Disk_Controller is

  Max_No_Blocks_On_Disk : constant Positive := 10_000; -- say
  type Sync_Agent is access Persistent_Signals.Persistent_Signal;
  type Block_Number is range 0 .. Max_No_Blocks_On_Disk;

  -- various operations including

  procedure Async_Write(To_Block : Block_Number;
            From : System.Address; Size : Positive;
            Done : out Sync_Agent);

  ...
end Disk_Controller;
```

Inside this package, the output may be queued and actually not written to the disk for some time. The client of the package can proceed as soon as the procedure returns and later check to see if the output has been written

```
with Disk_Controller; use Disk_Controller;
with System;

   ...

Output_Done : Sync_Agent;
Block_Id : Block_Number;
From_Address : System.Address;
Data_Size : Positive;

   ...
-- set up data and parameters for transfer

Async_Write(Block_Id, From_Address, Data_Size, Output_Done);
   ...
-- when the time has come to check that
-- the output is complete
select
   Output_Done.Wait;
else
   -- output not complete,
   -- perhaps initiate some recovery action
end select;
```

It should be noted that care must be taken when protected objects are created dynamically from an access type; as the protected object will still exist even though the output operation has completed. This problem is common to all objects that are created dynamically and techniques such as unchecked deallocation must be used. An alternative approach in this example is to use an access to a protected subprogram. The disk controller package becomes

```
with System;
package Disk_Controller is

   Max_No_Blocks_On_Disk : constant Integer := 10_000; -- say
   type Block_Number is
        new Integer range 0 .. Max_No_Blocks_On_Disk;

   -- various operations including

   type Sync_Agent is access protected procedure;

   procedure Async_Write(To_Block : Block_Number;
            From : System.Address;Size : Integer;
            Done : in Sync_Agent);

   ...
end Disk_Controller;
```

In the above, the Disk_Controller expects the client to provide its own synchronisation agent. All that the controller requires is a pointer to a protected procedure for signaling when the required operation is complete. The client body becomes

```
with Persistent_Signals; use Persistent_Signals;
with Disk_Controller; use Disk_Controller;
with System;

   ...

   Signal: aliased Persistent_Signal;
   Output_Done : Sync_Agent := Signal.Send'Access;
   Block_Id : Block_Number;
   From_Address : System.Address;
   Data_Size : Positive;

   ...
   -- set up data and parameters for transfer

   Async_Write(Block_Id, From_Address, Data_Size, Output_Done);
   ...
   -- when the time has come to check
   -- that the output is complete
select
   Signal.Wait;
else
   -- output not complete,
   -- perhaps initiate some recovery action
end select;
```

9.3   Transient signals

A transient signal (or a pulse) is a signal which is lost if no tasks are currently waiting. Two types can be recognised: one which releases a single task, and one which releases all tasks. They may be implemented as follows:

```
package Transient_Signals is
   protected type Transient_Signal is
      procedure Send;
      procedure Send_All;
      entry Wait;
   private
      Signal_Arrived : Boolean := False;
      Release_All : Boolean;
   end Transient_Signal;
end Transient_Signals;
```

```
package body Transient_Signals is
  protected body Transient_Signal is
    procedure Send is
    begin
      if Wait'Count > 0 then
        Signal_Arrived := True;
        Release_All := False;
      end if;
    end Send;

    procedure Send_All is
    begin
      if Wait'Count > 0 then
        Signal_Arrived := True;
        Release_All := True;
      end if;
    end Send_All;


    entry Wait when Signal_Arrived is
    begin
      if Wait'Count = 0 or not Release_All then
        Signal_Arrived := False;
      end if;
    end Wait;
  end Transient_Signal;
end Transient_Signals;
```

If more than one task is waiting for the signal and Send_All is called, all
are released. The last one detects that there are no more tasks on the queue
and sets the boolean flag to false. Any tasks which queue after this point
will have to wait for the next signal.

9.4   Events

As previously mentioned, an event is a bivalued variable (Up or Down). A
task can wait for an event to be set or reset. The following package specifies
the interface:

```
package Events is

  type Event_State is (Up, Down);

  protected type Event(Initial: Event_State := Down) is
    procedure Set;
    procedure Reset;
    procedure Toggle;
    function State return Event_State;
    entry Wait(S : Event_State);
  private
```

```
      entry Wait_Up(S : Event_State);
      entry Wait_Down(S : Event_State);
      Value : Event_State := Initial;
   end Event;

  end Events;
```

Events may be created using the protected type Event. An event is, by default, initially Down. The procedure Set causes the event to go into the Up state; the procedure Reset causes it to go into the Down state. The Toggle procedure simply changes the state of the event from Up to Down, or from Down to Up. The function State returns the current state of the event.

Synchronisation with an event is achieved using the Wait entry. This will suspend the caller until the state of the event is that required by the caller. Two private entries are used to help implement the required synchronisation, as shown in the package body below:

```
package body Events is

  protected body Event is
    procedure Set is
    begin
      Value := Up;
    end Set;

    procedure Reset is
    begin
      Value := Down;
    end Reset;

    procedure Toggle is
    begin
      if Value = Down then
        Value := Up;
      else
        Value := Down;
      end if;
    end Toggle;


    function State return Event_State is
    begin
      return Value;
    end State;

    entry Wait(S : Event_State) when True is
    begin
      if S = Up then
        requeue Wait_Up with abort;
      else
        requeue Wait_Down with abort;
```

```
        end if;
     end Wait;

     entry Wait_Up(S : Event_State) when Value = Up is
     begin
        null;
     end Wait_Up;

     entry Wait_Down(S : Event_State) when Value = Down is
     begin
        null;
     end Wait_Down;

  end Event;
end Events;
```

9.5   Buffers

The basic bounded buffer has already been described in Section 7.3; a generic
version is presented here:

```
generic
   type Message is private;
   Max_Capacity : Positive := Maximum;
     --set to some appropriate value
package Buffers is

   subtype Capacity_Range is Natural range 0 .. Max_Capacity - 1;
   subtype Count is Natural range 0 .. Max_Capacity;
   type Buffer_Array is array(Capacity_Range) of Message;

   protected type Buffer is
      entry Get (Item: out Message);
      entry Put(Item: in Message);
      function Buffer_Capacity return Capacity_Range;
   private
      First : Capacity_Range := Capacity_Range'First;
      Last : Capacity_Range := Capacity_Range'Last;
      Number_In_Buffer : Count := 0;
      Store : Buffer_Array;
   end Buffer;
end Buffers;


package body Buffers is

   protected body Buffer is

      entry Get(Item: out Message) when Number_In_Buffer /= 0 is
```

```
    begin
      Item := Store(First);
      First := (First + 1) mod Max_Capacity;
      Number_In_Buffer := Number_In_Buffer - 1;
    end Get;

    entry Put(Item: in Message)
         when  Number_In_Buffer /= Max_Capacity is
    begin
      Last := (Last +1) mod Max_Capacity;
      Store(Last) := Item;
      Number_In_Buffer := Number_In_Buffer + 1;
    end Put;

    function Buffer_Capacity return Capacity_Range is
    begin
      return Max_Capacity;
    end;
  end Buffer;

end Buffers;
```

The buffer abstraction is one in which the data, once read, is destroyed. If the data is to be retained, then the blackboard abstraction is more appropriate.

9.6   Blackboards

The blackboard abstraction can be viewed either as being similar to the events abstraction with data transfer, or the buffer abstraction with a non-destructive read and the facility to invalidate the date. Each notional item of the buffer is represented as a single blackboard:

```
generic
    type Message is private;
package Blackboards is

    type Blackboard_State is (Valid, Invalid);

    protected type Blackboard is
      procedure Write(M : Message);
      procedure Clear;
      function State return Blackboard_State;
      entry Read(M : out Message);
    private
      The_Message : Message;
      Status : Blackboard_State := Invalid;
    end Blackboard;

end Blackboards;
```

Items are placed on a Blackboard by calling Write; they are deleted by
calling Clear. The entry Read will block the caller until data on the
blackboard is valid (i.e. there is data present). The function State indicates
whether the blackboard currently has data.

The body of the package follows:

```
package body Blackboards is

  protected body Blackboard is
    procedure Write(M : Message) is
    begin
      The_Message := M;
      Status := Valid;
    end Write;

    procedure Clear is
    begin
      Status := Invalid;
    end Clear;

    function State return Blackboard_State is
    begin
      return Status;
    end State;

    entry Read (M : out Message) when Status = Valid is
    begin
      M := The_Message;
    end Read;
  end Blackboard;

end Blackboards;
```

A simpler form of blackboard does not have a clear operation; all data is
preserved until overwritten. Read would then be non-blocking and hence
could be implemented as a procedure (assuming that the backboard is
initialised to some appropriate value).

9.7   Broadcasts

The use of a broadcast facility was shown in Section 7.7. Here the facility is
generalised and the implementation is shown (which is similar in structure
to a transient signal with Send_All):

```
generic
  type Message is private;
package Broadcasts  is
  protected type Broadcast is
    procedure Send(This_Message : Message);
```

```
        entry Receive(A_Message : out Message);
      private
        Message_Arrived : Boolean := False;
        The_Message : Message;
      end Broadcast;
    end Broadcasts;


    package body Broadcasts is
      protected body Broadcast is
        procedure Send(This_Message: Message) is
        begin
          if Receive'Count > 0 then
            Message_Arrived := True;
            The_Message := This_Message;
          end if;
        end Send;

        entry Receive(A_Message : out Message)
            when Message_Arrived is
        begin
          if Receive'Count = 0 then
            Message_Arrived := False;
          end if;
          A_Message := The_Message;
        end Receive;
      end Broadcast;
    end Broadcasts;
```

The generic package allows any type of message to be sent in the broadcast. Only tasks that are waiting will receive the message.

Multicast to a group

The term, broadcast, has so far been used to indicate that the data should be sent to any task that is waiting. Often the term, broadcast, (or, more correctly, 'multicast') is used to indicate that the data should be sent to a specific group of tasks. In this situation, *all* tasks in the group should receive the data, not just those that happen to be waiting when the data is sent. This is slightly more difficult to achieve; all potential recipients must be known (say via their task identifiers) and only when all have received one item of data is another item allowed to be transmitted.

The following package specification defines the multicast interface. Tasks which are interested in receiving from a group must join the group explicitly and when they are no longer interested they must leave the group:

```
with Ada.Task_Identification; use Ada.Task_Identification;
   -- task identifiers were introduced in Chapter 4 and
   -- are discussed in detail in Chapter 11
```

```
generic
  type Message is private;
package Multicasts is

  Max_Group_Size : constant Positive :=
    --set to some appropriate value
  type Group_Range is range 1 .. Max_Group_Size;
  Default_Group_Size : constant Group_Range :=
    --set to some appropriate value

  type Task_Status is private;

  type Group_Tasks is array(Group_Range range <>) of Task_Status;

  Already_Member, Not_Member, Group_Too_Large,
  Group_Empty : exception;

  protected type Multicast(Max_Size : Group_Range :=
                                      Default_Group_Size) is
    procedure Join_Group;
      -- raises Already_Member, Group_Too_Large
    procedure Leave_Group;
      -- raises Not_Member

    entry Send(This_Message : Message);
      -- raises Group_Empty or ignore if
      -- empty group is acceptable
    entry Receive(A_Message : out Message);
      -- raises Not_Member

  private
    entry Wait_Next_Message(A_Message : out Message);

    Message_Available : Boolean := False;
    New_Message_Arrived : Boolean := False;
    The_Message : Message;
    Ok_To_Send : Boolean := True;
    Group : Group_Tasks(1 .. Max_Size);
  end Multicast;
private
  type Task_Status is
    record
      Id : Task_Id := Null_Task_Id;
      Received : Boolean := False;
    end record;
end Multicasts;
```

Inside the body of the Multicasts package, there are various housekeeping
subprograms which keep track of which tasks have received which messages.
Note the use of task identifiers to identify the calling task uniquely:

```
package body Multicasts is
```

```
protected body Multicast is

  function All_Received return Boolean is
  begin
    -- check if all tasks in the
    -- Group have received the data
  end All_Received;

  function Already_Received(Id : Task_Id) return Boolean is
  begin
    -- check if task has received the data
  end Already_Received;

  procedure Log_Received(Id : Task_Id) is
  begin
    -- log that task has received the data
  end Log_Received;

  procedure Clear_Received is
  begin
    -- set all Boolean flags in Group array to False
  end Clear_Received;

  procedure Join_Group is
  begin
    -- save ID of Current_Task in Group array
    -- raise Already_Member, or Group_Full if appropriate
  end Join_Group;


  procedure Leave_Group is
  begin
    -- delete ID of Current_Task in Group array
    -- raise Not_Member if appropriate
    if Message_Available and All_Received then
      Message_Available := False;
      Ok_To_Send := True;
      Clear_Received;
    end if;
  end Leave_Group;


  entry Send(This_Message: Message) when Ok_To_Send is
  begin
    -- if empty group raise Group_Empty
    The_Message := This_Message;
    Ok_To_Send := False;
    New_Message_Arrived := True;
  end Send;


  entry Receive(A_Message : out Message) when True is
    Id :Task_Id :=  Receive'Caller;
  begin
```

```
           -- if not member raise exception
           if Message_Available then
             if Already_Received(Id) then
               requeue Wait_Next_Message with abort;
             else
               Log_Received(Id);
             end if;
             A_Message := The_Message;
             if All_Received then
               Message_Available := False;
               Ok_To_Send := True;
               Clear_Received;
             end if;
           else
             requeue Wait_Next_Message;
           end if;
         end Receive;

         entry Wait_Next_Message(A_Message : out Message)
               when New_Message_Arrived is
           Id :Task_Id :=  Wait_Next_Message'Caller;
         begin
           Log_Received(Id);
           A_Message := The_Message;
           if All_Received then
             Ok_To_Send := True;
             New_Message_Arrived := False;
             Clear_Received;
           elsif Wait_Next_Message'Count=0 then
             New_Message_Arrived := False;
             Message_Available := True;
           else
             null;
           end if;
         end Wait_Next_Message;
       end Multicast;
     end Multicasts;
```

In the above algorithm, it is not possible to send another multicast message until the previous message has been received by everyone. Compare this with the previous algorithm, where only those waiting received the message. There is clearly a solution in between these, where the message remains available for a certain period of time or where more than one message is buffered; this a left as an exercise for the reader.

A task wishing to receive a broadcast message must first join the group. Assume that a group has already been created, for example

```
       -- package to multicast the current aircraft altitude
       -- to all interested parties
       package Altitude_Multicasts is new Multicasts(Altitude);
```

Assume now that a task, which controls some aspect of an aircraft, is implemented so as to react to any new altitude setting multicast from some sensor reading routine. It might take the following form:

```
with Altitude_Multicasts; use Altitude_Multicasts;
   ...
Barometric_Pressure_Reading : Multicast;
   ...
task Surface_Controller;

task body Surface_Controller is
   -- declaration of Current_Altitude etc
begin
   ...
   Barometric_Pressure_Reading.Join_Group;
   loop
      Barometric_Pressure_Reading.Receive(Current_Altitude);
      -- use Current_Altitude
   end loop;
   Barometric_Pressure_Reading.Leave_Group;
end Surface_Controller;
```

9.8 Barriers

A barrier simply blocks several tasks, until all have arrived. In this case, no data is passed but a form of multicast could be programmed which did pass data as well. Tasks wishing to block at a barrier simply call the Wait entry; the two functions return information about the barrier:

```
package Barriers is

   Max_Capacity : constant Positive := Maximum;
      -- set to an appropriate value
   type Capacity_Range is range 1 .. Max_Capacity;

   protected type Barrier(Needed : Capacity_Range) is
      entry Wait;
      function Barrier_Capacity return Capacity_Range;
      function Value return Capacity_Range;
   private
      Release_All : Boolean := False;
   end Barrier;
end Barriers;


package body Barriers is
   protected body Barrier is
      entry Wait when Wait'Count = Needed or Release_All is
      begin
```

```
        if Wait'Count > 0 then
          Release_All := True;
        else
          Release_All := False;
        end if;
      end Wait;

      function Barrier_Capacity return Capacity_Range is
      begin
        return Needed;
      end Barrier_Capacity;

      function Value return Capacity_Range is
      begin
        return Needed - Wait'Count;
      end Value;
    end Barrier;
  end Barriers;
```

9.9 Selective entry calls

The select statement was discussed in detail in the context of the rendezvous in Chapter 6. It was explained how a server task can wait for communication on one or more accept statements using the selective accept version of the select statement. In contrast, a client task can only issue a single entry call (albeit a timed or a conditional one). Furthermore, it is not possible to mix entry calls and accept statements in the same select statement. In Chapter 7, it was noted that an entry call to a protected task can also be used in the select statement to obtain timed and conditional protected entry calls.

The introduction of data-oriented communication via protected objects allows the possibility of creating communication abstractions such as buffers, channels, etc. This in turn leads to the requirement to wait for communication with one or more protected objects; for example, a task might wish to wait for one or more messages from different channels. During the Ada 95 design process such a facility was considered and rejected. It was called a *selective entry call* (or multi-way select), and this section will discuss the motivations for its inclusions, how to program around its absence and the reasons for its rejection by the Ada designers.

9.9.1 Motivations for selective entry calls

There are three motivations for a multi-way select statement:

1.   As a means to wait for a call to be accepted from more than one entry in one or more tasks, for example

```
task A is
  entry A1;
end A;

task B is
  entry B1;
end B;

task C;
task body C is
begin
  . . .
  select -- Not Valid Ada
    A.A1;
  or
    B.B1;
  end select;
  . . .
end C;
```

2. As a means to wait for one or more entries to become open in one or more protected objects, for example

```
protected A is
  entry A1;
private
  . . .
end A;

protected B is
  entry B1;
private
  . . .
end B;

task C;
task body C is
begin
  . . .
  select -- Not Valid Ada
    A.A1;
  or
    B.B1;
  end select;
  . . .
end C;
```

3. As a means to wait for a mixture of task entries and protected record entries, for example

```
protected A is
   entry A1;
private
   . . .
end A;

task B is
   entry B1;
end task B;

task C;
task body C is
   . . .
   select -- Not Valid Ada
      A.A1;
   or
      B.B1;
   end select;
   . . .
end C;
```

Waiting for more than one entry call

For the first case it is possible to argue that Ada 83 did not have this facility
and therefore why should Ada 95? This is indeed a valid point; however, one
should recall the comments that have been made about the asymmetrical
nature of the Ada 83 select statement. In an earlier review of Ada tasking
(Burns *et al.*, 1987) some of the difficulties this caused were reported:

> It is surprisingly difficult to broadcast (or multicast) informa-
> tion to a number of tasks. One difficulty is that the broadcaster
> must know the identities of all the recipients. Furthermore, as
> Francez and Yemini (1985) have pointed out, the natural imple-
> mentation of a broadcast is to make the broadcaster issue entry
> calls which the recipients accept. Unfortunately, the broadcaster
> is unaware of how close each recipient is to accepting the broad-
> cast. The select statement does not allow the broadcaster to wait
> for any of several entry calls to be accepted, and the broadcaster
> must therefore commit itself in advance to some fixed order of
> transmission. This may cause long delays if the order chosen is
> not consistent with the actual order of readiness. An alternative
> is to make conditional entry calls to each of the recipients in turn
> until all have responded. This is essentially a polling solution
> to the problem, and is one of the illustrations that Gehani and
> Cargill (1984) use to suggest that the Ada language, in general,
> encourages polling. A third approach is for the broadcaster to

create a set of agent tasks, such that each agent is responsible for delivering the broadcast information to a single recipient. There is clearly an overhead in agent creation, and there may be an even worse one in initialising each agent with the identity of the recipient with which it is to rendezvous.

To avoid these difficulties the broadcaster and the recipient must invert their roles, with the broadcaster accepting entry calls from the recipients. Such a solution is unnatural; furthermore there is no way for the broadcaster to ensure that each recipient makes only one entry call, or that a task does not issue an entry call when it is not an intended recipient.

A problem similar to that of broadcasting arises when a client task requires a service which can be provided by any of a number of server tasks. The client must either poll the servers to find one which is free, or invert the communication roles. Further situations which may lead to polling are those (for example pipelining) in which the most natural approach would require the select statement to include both entry calls and accept statements.

Of course, Ada now has protected types which allow the programming of broadcasts to be more convenient (see Section 9.7). Hence it is possible to argue that there is still no need for a multi-way select for entry calls.

Waiting for more than one protected record entry

Protected objects can be used for many purposes and it is therefore difficult to anticipate all the occasions where it might be necessary to wait on more than one protected object entry. However, there is a clear need in the Ada community for asynchronous communication and this is achieved by the use of protected objects.

If two tasks are to communicate asynchronously, then *both* tasks must make a call on a protected object. The sender can call either a procedure (if there is unbounded buffer space or overwriting) or an entry (if there is bounded buffer space). The receiver may also call a procedure (if it does not want to block if there are no messages) or an entry (if it wishes to block). *Without selective waiting it is not possible for a task to wait for more than one message* (without resorting to using a single entry or procedure with variant records — see workaround section (9.9.2) — or using nested asynchronous select statements — see Chapter 10). In Ada 83 terms, this would be equivalent to allowing only one accept in the select statement, and forcing the programmer to use variant records!

Consider also the broadcast case mentioned above. As broadcast/multicast messages can only be sent via a protected object, without selective waiting a task could only wait for one broadcast message.

Waiting for a mixture of task entries and protected record entries

Given the argument above, then allowing a task to wait for either a task entry call to be accepted or a protected record entry to become open is a natural extension. Furthermore, treating a task entry call and a protected object entry call identically results in a conceptually simpler language.

9.9.2 Workarounds

To illustrate how the programmer can program around the absence of a multi-way select, consider a mail box capability, and the ability for a server task to wait for a message from more than one mail box. The example chosen has three mail boxes. In Ada this should ideally be written as

```
generic
   type Data is private;
package Mail_Box is

   protected type Mbox is
      entry Send(D : Data);
      entry Receive(D : out Data);
   private
      -- buffer declaration
      Buffer_Not_Full : Boolean := False;
      Buffer_Not_Empty : Boolean := False;
   end Mbox;

end Mail_Box;

package body Mail_Box is

   protected body Mbox is

      entry Send(D : Data) when Buffer_Not_Full is
      begin
         ...
      end Send;

      entry Receive(D : out Data) when Buffer_Not_Empty is
      begin
         ...
      end Receive;

   end Mbox;
end Mail_Box;
```

This facility could be used with a multi-way select as follows:

```
type Message_A is ...;
```

```
type Message_B is ...;
type Message_C is ...;

package Mail_Box_A is new Mail_Box(Message_A);
package Mail_Box_B is new Mail_Box(Message_B);
package Mail_Box_C is new Mail_Box(Message_C);

Mboxa : Mail_Box_A.Mail_Box;
Mboxb : Mail_Box_B.Mail_Box;
Mboxc : Mail_Box_C.Mail_Box;


-- client A code
  Mboxa.Send(...);

-- client B code
  Mboxb.Send(...);

-- client C code
  Mboxc.Send(...)

-- Note: client A does not have access to client B or
-- C mail boxes; similarly for B and C.

-- server code, note it can also select a subset of
-- the messages.
select    -- Not Valid Ada
  Mboxa.Receive(...);
or
  Mboxb.Receive(...);
or
  Mboxc.Receive(...);
end select;
```

To provide similar functionality without the multi-way select requires a single protected record to be used. The following illustrates one approach:

```
type Message_Type is(A_T, B_T, C_T);

type Message_Data(D : Message_Type) is
record
  case(D) is
    when A_T =>
      A_Data : Message_A;
    when B_T =>
      B_Data : Message_B;
    when C_T =>
      C_Data : Message_C;
  end case;
end record;

protected Mbox is
```

```
entry Send(D : Message_Data);
entry Receive(D : out Message_Data);
private
-- buffer for message data
end Mbox;


-- client code
Mbox.Send(...);

-- server code
Mbox.Receive(...);
```

Several points should be made concerning this approach:

1. The clients all share the same mail box and therefore the solution is less secure.

2. The server must always be expected to service each request type.

3. There is a single buffer space.

4. The solution is *ad hoc*; a different number of mailbox requires a new (but similar) solution.

In an attempt to remove some of these restrictions the following solution could be considered:

```
type Wait_List is (A, B, C, AB, AC, BC, ABC);

protected Mbox is
   entry Send_A(D : Message_A);
   entry Send_B(D : Message_B);
   entry Send_C(D : Message_C);

   entry Receive(From : Wait_List; Available : out Message_Type);

   procedure Get_A(D : out Message_A);
   procedure Get_B(D : out Message_B);
   procedure Get_C(D : out Message_C);

private

   entry Try_Again(From : Wait_List;
                   Available : out Message_Type);

   -- buffers for A, B, and C

   New_Data : Boolean := False;
   Look_At : Integer;

end Mbox;
```

In this solution, clients call their own entry; the server calls Receive with an indication of which messages are of interest. It receives back an indication of which message it can now acquire. (In this solution it is not given a choice if more than one becomes available; it would be possible to return an indication of which ones are available.)

The server task then calls Get_A (for example) to receive the actual message. The body of Mbox is given below:

```
protected body Mbox is

   entry Send_A(D : Message_A) when A_Buffer_Not_Full is
   begin
     -- place data in buffer
     if Try_Again'Count /= 0 then
       New_Data:=True;
       Look_At:=Try_Again'Count;
     end if;
   end Send_A;

   -- similarly for Send_B and Send_C

   procedure Get_A(D : out Message_A) is
   begin
     -- remove data from buffer
     -- if buffer is empty then raise
     -- an exception
   end Get_A;

   -- similarly for Get_B and Get_C

   entry Receive(From : Wait_List; Available : out Message_Type)
        when True is
   begin
     -- if A requested and A buffer not empty then
     -- Available = A
     -- else if B requested and B buffer not empty then
     -- Available = B
     -- else if C buffer not empty then
     -- Available = C
     -- else
     -- requeue Try_Again(From, Available);
   end Receive;

   entry Try_Again(From : Wait_List; Available : out Message_Type)
        when New_Data is
   begin
     Look_At := Look_At - 1;
     if Look_At = 0 then
       New_Data := False;
     end if;

     -- look to see if request can be satisfied
```

```
        -- if so return
        -- else requeue again (assumes FIFO queuing)

    end Try_Again;

  end Mbox;
```

There are several points to make concerning this solution:

1. The server must make two calls to receive the message.

2. The server may be requeued many times inside the protected record if it is waiting for a particular message (say of type A) and clients sending type B and C messages are very active.

3. Because of (1) and (2) it may be more efficient to use a task rendezvous and selective waiting.

4. If the server is servicing many mail boxes, then this solution may not scale well. In particular, the algorithms for identifying which messages are of interest may become long-winded.

More radical solutions to this problem such as those using concurrent receiving tasks, the OOP facilities or nested asynchronous select statements could be explored.

9.9.3   Reasons for rejection of multi-way selective entry calls

The primary reason that the selective entry call facility was rejected by the Ada designers was one of cost. Studies were carried out on the cost of implementing a selective entry call statement, and the cost of dealing with its interaction with other language features. The findings from these studies indicated that the cost was comparable to that of implementing the Ada 83 selective accept facility. However, the presence of the facility significantly increased the cost of implementing the asynchronous select.

Having weighed up the benefits and the costs, the designers chose to remove the facility from the language.

9.10   Summary

This chapter has illustrated the flexibility of protected objects by showing how various communication patterns can be constructed. These packages provide the basis for a set of reusable communication paradigms. The paradigms illustrated were semaphores, persistent and transient signals, events, buffers, blackboards, broadcasts and barriers.

It has been noted that the absence of a selective entry call does make some of the examples cumbersome, but workarounds do exist. Whether these workarounds scale up to the needs of large applications remains an open issue.

In Chapter 13 some of these paradigms will be considered again in terms of supporting more abstract versions. This increased flexibility comes from the use of the object-oriented technique of inheritance. However, even without these features the examples given in this chapter should be of wide applicability.

Chapter 10

Exceptions, Abort and Asynchronous Transfer of Control

This chapter considers three related topics: exceptions (and their handling), the abort statement and asynchronous transfer of control. They are related in that they all divert a task away from its current execution path and force it to execute some other section of code.

The motivation for these facilities comes from the use of concurrent programming techniques in real-time systems. Here there are often stringent timing and reliability requirements which necessitate that the language provide facilities additional those to simply to support concurrent execution and communication and synchronisation.

10.1   Exceptions

The basic model of exception handling in Ada was presented in Chapter 1. Then, in Chapters 4-8, exceptions were discussed in the context of task creation, task communication and synchronisation. This section summarises, in the one place, the complete interaction between tasking and exceptions.

10.1.1   Exceptions during elaboration of a declarative block

An exception may be raised during elaboration of a declarative part. For example, assigning an initial value to an object which falls outside the permissible range of values would result in Constraint_Error being raised. Any tasks which would have been created during the elaboration are not activated. See Section 4.2 for further details and an example.

10.1.2   Exceptions during activation of a task

An exception may be raised during the activation of a task. For example, assigning an initial value (outside the permissible range of values) to an object declared in the task body's declarative part would result in Constraint_Error being raised. The task is unable to handle this exception and therefore becomes completed. This results in the exception

Tasking_Error being raised in the parent task after all its child tasks have been activated. Even if more than one of its children become completed during activation, the exception is only raised once. See Section 4.2 for further details.

10.1.3 Exceptions in task finalisation

It is a bounded error for an exception to be raised during any finalisation routine. If one does occur during the finalisation of a task, or a master block containing tasks, then the most likely consequence will be that the exception will be lost and the finalisation of other objects continued.

10.1.4 Exceptions and the rendezvous

The consequences of exceptions being raised during the rendezvous have been discussed in Section 5.7. The model is essentially that if an exception is not handled within the rendezvous, it is propagated to both the server and the client task.

The following exceptions may also be raised when a task attempts a rendezvous:

* Tasking_Error

  Tasking_Error is raised when a client task attempts to rendezvous with a server task that has already completed, terminated or becomes abnormal (see Section 10.2), or becomes completed, terminated or abnormal before the rendezvous starts. Tasking_Error is also raised in the client if the server becomes abnormal during the rendezvous.

* Constraint_Error

  Constraint_Error may be raised when the client or the server attempts to rendezvous using an entry family and the index used falls outside the range of the family.

* Program_Error

  Program_Error is raised when the server task executes a select statement and all arms of the select statement are closed (because all are guarded and all guards evaluate to false) and there is no 'else' part. See Section 6.7.

10.1.5 Exceptions and protected objects

The Program_Error exception may be raised when a task interacts with a protected object for the following reasons:

* when the evaluation of a barrier results in an exception condition being detected;

- when a protected action issues a potentially suspending operation;

- when a task is queued on a protected entry and the protected object is finalised.

Note that if a barrier gives rise to an exception, then all tasks waiting on that protected object get Program_Error raised.

Any exception raised whilst executing a protected subprogram or entry and not handled by the protected subprogram or entry is propagated to the task that issued the protected call (as if the call were a normal subprogram call).

As with task entry families, a client task may suffer a Constraint_Error if a family index is out of range.

10.1.6 Exceptions and abort-deferred operations

Certain operations are defined by the language to be abort-deferred. These operations have restrictions placed on them which if violated may result in the exception Program_Error being raised. See Section 10.2.1.

10.1.7 Exceptions and the asynchronous select statement

Although the asynchronous select statement introduces no new exception scopes, the interactions between exceptions and the tasks involved can be quite subtle. This issue is discussed in full later in this chapter (Section 10.3.2).

10.1.8 Exceptions in interrupt handlers

If an exception is propagated from an interrupt handler that is invoked by an interrupt, the exception has no effect.

10.2 The abort statement

Raising an exception in an errant task is an appropriate response to an error condition when:

- a task itself detects the error condition and can explicitly raise (and handle) the exception; or

- the environment in which the task executes detects an error as a result of an action being performed by the task — in this case, one of the predefined standard exceptions can be raised.

However, it may be the case that the error condition has been detected by another task. In this situation, it is not appropriate for an exception to be raised in the errant task, as the task may not be in a position to handle the error. Indeed, the task may long since have executed the code which caused the original error to occur. To help program these situations, Ada provides two facilities: the abort statement and the asynchronous select statement. The abort statement is considered in this section; the asynchronous select statement is discussed in Section 10.3.

The abort statement is intended for use in response to those error conditions where recovery by the errant task is deemed to be impossible. Tasks which are aborted are said to become *abnormal*, and are thus prevented from interacting with any other task. Ideally, an abnormal task will stop executing immediately. However, some implementations may not be able to facilitate immediate shut down, and hence all the ARM requires is that the task terminate before it next interacts with other tasks. Note that the Real-Time Systems Annex does require 'immediate' to be just that (see Chapter 12) on a single processor system.

The syntax of the abort statement is simply

```
abort_statement ::= abort task_name {,task_name};
```

Any task may abort any other named task by executing this statement (tasks named in the same statement need not even be of the same type):

```
abort Operator;
abort Philosopher(1), Philosopher(3);
```

If a task is at the receiving end of this statement, then it becomes abnormal; any non-completed tasks that depend upon an aborted task also become abnormal. Once all named tasks are marked as abnormal, then the abort statement is complete, and the task executing the abort can continue. It does not wait until the named tasks have actually terminated.

After the task has been marked as abnormal, execution of the task body is aborted. This means that the execution of every construct in the task body is aborted, unless it is involved in the execution of an *abort-deferred operation*. The execution of an abort-deferred operation is allowed to complete before it is aborted. The same rules for aborting a task body also apply to aborting a sequence of statements in the asynchronous select statement discussed later, in Section 10.3.

If a construct which has been aborted is blocked outside an abort-deferred operation (other than at an entry call), the construct becomes abnormal and is immediately completed. Other constructs must complete no later than the next *abort completion point* (if any) that occurs outside an abort-deferred operation. These are:

• the end of activation of a task;

- the point where the execution initiates the activation of another task;
- the start or end of an entry call, accept statement, delay statement or abort statement;
- the start of the execution of a select statement, or of the sequence of statements of an exception handler.

A consequence of this rule is that an abnormal task which does not reach any of the above points need not be terminated! It could be abnormal but still loop round updating shared variables, calling protected procedures and using processor cycles. There is no way of ensuring that such a task is forced to complete, although on a traditional uniprocessor system it would be normal to terminate the task at once. As indicated earlier, the Real-Time Systems Annex does require an implementation to document any aspects of implementation which might delay the completion of an aborted construct.

10.2.1 Abort-deferred operations

The issue of how immediate an abort action should be is a complex one. It can be argued that when aborted, if a task is updating some shared data structure (perhaps inside a protected object), it should be shielded from the imposed abort. But if it is shielded, then the whole point of using abort is diminished. Ada favours the view that certain actions must be protected in order that the integrity of the remaining tasks and their data be assured. The following operations are defined to be abort-deferred:

- a protected action;
- waiting for an entry call to complete;
- waiting for termination of dependent tasks;
- the execution of an 'initialize' procedure, a 'finalize' procedure or an assignment operation of an object with a controlled part.

Note that there are some further restrictions on controlled objects if their controlling procedures are to be abort-deferred (see ARM, 9.8). For example, it is a bounded error for such a procedure to create a task whose master is contained within the procedure.

10.2.2 Use of the abort statement

The use of the abort statement is clearly an extreme response to an error condition and one which carries the following warning:

> An abort statement should be used only in situations requiring unconditional termination. (ARM 9.8).

It was available in Ada 83 under the assumption that it was provided for emergency use only. Its overuse could severely hinder program understanding and validation. Nevertheless, the fact that a task can abort any other task introduces an interesting circular argument to this rationale. Hoare (1979) has been particularly critical of this language feature, remarking

> The existence of this statement causes intolerable overheads in the implementation of every other feature of tasking. Its 'successful' use depends on a valid process aborting a wild one before the wild one aborts a valid process — or does any other serious damage. The probability of this is negligible. If processes can go wild, we are much safer without aborts.

Nevertheless, the ability to abort a task is considered to be a valid requirement for real-time systems. The current version of the language makes every effort to ensure that the facility can be used as safely as possible, given its inherently dangerous nature.

10.3 Asynchronous transfer of control

The presence of an asynchronous transfer of control (ATC) facility within the Ada language, like the abort statement, is controversial, as it complicates the language's semantics and increases the complexity of the run-time support system. This section thus first considers the application requirements which justify the inclusion of such a facility. Following this, the asynchronous select statement is described and then examples of its use are given.

10.3.1 The user need for ATC

The fundamental requirement for an asynchronous transfer of control facility is to enable a task to respond *quickly* to an asynchronous event. The emphasis here is on a quick response; clearly a task can always respond to an event by simply polling or waiting for that event. The notification of the event could be mapped onto a task entry call or a protected object subprogram or entry call. The handling task, when it is ready to receive the event, simply issues the corresponding accept statement or protected object entry/subprogram call.

Unfortunately there are occasions when polling for events or waiting for the event to occur is inadequate. These include the following:

- Error recovery

  A fault may have occurred which requires a task to alter its flow of control as a consequence. For example, a hardware fault may mean that the task will never finish its planned execution because the preconditions under which it started no longer hold; the task may never reach its polling point. Also, a timing fault might have occurred, which means that the task will no longer meet the deadline for the delivery of its service. In both these situations, the task must be informed that an error has been detected and the task must undertake some error recovery as quickly as possible.

• Mode changes

A real-time system often has several modes of operation. For example, a fly-by-wire civil aircraft may have a take-off mode, a cruising mode and a landing mode. On many occasions, changes between modes can be carefully managed and will occur at well defined points in the system's execution; as in a normal flight plan for a civil aircraft. Unfortunately, in some application areas, mode changes are expected but cannot be planned. For example, a fault may lead to an aircraft abandoning its take-off and entering into an emergency mode of operation; an accident in a manufacturing process may require an immediate mode change to ensure an orderly shutdown of the plant. In these situations, tasks must be quickly and safely informed that the mode in which they are operating has changed, and that they now need to undertake a different set of actions.

• Scheduling using partial/imprecise computations

There are many algorithms where the accuracy of the results depends on how much time can be allocated to their calculation. For example, numerical computations, statistical estimations and heuristic searches may all produce an initial estimation of the required result, and then refine that result to a greater accuracy. At run-time, a certain amount of time can be allocated to an algorithm, and then, when that time has been used, the tasks must be interrupted to stop further refinement of the result.

• User interrupts

In a general interactive computing environment, users often wish to stop the current processing because they have detected an error condition and wish to start again.

In all the above situations, it is possible to abort the task and recreate it, passing information as to why the task was aborted. Indeed, it can be argued that this facility is adequate and can be implemented efficiently enough for its use in time critical situations. Furthermore, many implementations of ATC will use a "two-thread model", where the code to be interrupted is contained in one thread of control and the code waiting for the interrupt notification is in another thread. On receipt of the notification, the latter thread aborts the former and recreates it. However, requiring the programmer to code these interactions directly is error-prone, and it has been decided that special language support is preferable. The programmer can use ATC to define a sequence of statements that can be aborted if a specified triggering event occurs.

10.3.2   The asynchronous select statement

The select statement was introduced in Chapter 6, as having four forms: a selective accept (to support the server side of the rendezvous), a timed entry call (to either a task or a protected entry), a conditional entry call (also to a task or a protected entry) and an asynchronous select. The first three forms have been discussed in Chapters 6 and 7. Here attention is focused on the last form, which has the following syntax definition:

```
asynchronous_select ::=
  select
     triggering_alternative
  then abort
     abortable_part
  end select;

triggering_alternative ::=
  triggering_statement [sequence_of_statements]
triggering_statement ::=
  entry_call_statement | delay_statement

abortable_part ::= sequence_of_statements
```

There is a restriction on the sequence of statements that can appear in the abortable part. It must not contain an accept statement. The reason for this is to keep the implementation as simple as possible.

The execution of the asynchronous select begins with the issuing of the triggering entry call or the issuing of the triggering delay. If the triggering statement is an entry call, the parameters are evaluated as normal and the call issued. If the call is queued (or requeued with abort), then the sequence of statements in the abortable part is executed. If the abortable part completes before the completion of the entry call, an attempt is made to cancel the entry call and, if successful, the execution of the asynchronous select statement is finished.

Similarly, if the triggering statement is a delay statement, the delay time is calculated, and if it has not passed, the abortable part is executed. If this finishes before the delay time expires, the delay is cancelled and the execution of the asynchronous select statement is finished.

If the cancellation of the triggering event fails, because the protected action or rendezvous has started, or has been requeued (without abort), then the asynchronous select statement waits for the triggering statement to complete before executing the optional sequence of statements following the triggering statement.

If the triggering statement completes (other than due to cancellation, that is, the delay time expires or the rendezvous or protected action starts and finishes) before the execution of the abortable parts completes, the abortable part is aborted (if not already completed) and any finalisation code is executed. When these activities have finished, the optional sequence of statements following the triggering statement is executed. [1]

Clearly, it is possible for the triggering event to occur even before the abortable part has started its execution. In this case the abortable part is not executed and therefore not aborted.

Consider the following example:

```
task Server is
    entry Atc_Event;
end Server;

task To_Be_Interrupted;

task body Server is
begin
    ...
    accept Atc_Event do
        Seq2;
    end Atc_Event;
    ...
end Server;


task To_Be_Interrupted is
begin
    ...
    select   -- ATC statement
        Server.Atc_Event;
        Seq3;
    then abort
        Seq1;
    end select;
    Seq4;
    ...
end To_Be_Interrupted;
```

When the above ATC statement is executed, the statements which are executed will depend on the order of events that occur:

```
if the rendezvous is available immediately then
    Server.Atc_Event is issued
    Seq2 is executed
    Seq3 is executed
```

---

[1]See Section 10.2 for details on aborting a sequence of statements.

```
          Seq4 is executed
elsif no rendezvous starts before   Seq1 finishes then
          Server.Atc_Event is issued
          Seq1 is executed
          Server.Atc_Event is cancelled
          Seq4 is executed
elsif the rendezvous finishes before   Seq1 finishes then
          Server.Atc_Event is issued
          partial execution of   Seq1 occurs concurrently with   Seq2
          Seq1 is aborted and finalised
          Seq3 is executed
          Seq4 is executed
else (the rendezvous finishes after   Seq1 finishes)
          Server.Atc_Event is issued
          Seq1 is executed concurrently with partial execution of   Seq2
          Server.Atc_Event cancellation is attempted
          execution of   Seq2 completes
          Seq3 is executed
          Seq4 is executed
end if
```

Note that there is a race condition between Seq1 finishing and the rendezvous finishing. The situation could occur where Seq1 does finish but is nevertheless aborted.

If Seq1 contains an abort-deferred operation, then its cancellation will not occur until the operation is completed.

The above discussion has concentrated on the concurrent behaviour of Seq1 and the triggering rendezvous. Indeed, on a multi-processor implementation it could be the case that Seq1 and Seq2 are executing in parallel. However, on a single processor system, the triggering event will only ever occur if the action that causes it has a higher priority than Seq1. The normal behaviour will thus be the preemption of Seq1 by Seq2. When Seq2 (the triggering rendezvous) completes, Seq1 will be aborted before it can execute again. And hence the ATC is 'immediate' (unless an abort-deferred operation is in progress).

Exceptions and ATC

With the asynchronous select statement, potentially two activities occur concurrent: the abortable part may execute concurrently with the triggering action (when the action is an entry call). In either one of these activities, exceptions may be raised and unhandled. Therefore, at first sight it may appear that potentially two exceptions can be propagated simultaneously from the select statement. However, this is not the case; one of the exceptions is deemed to be lost and hence only one exception is propagated. Consider the following example:

```
E1, E2 : exception;
```

```
task Server is
   entry Atc_Event;
end Server;

task To_Be_Interrupted;

task body Server is
begin
   ...
   accept Atc_Event do
      Seq2; -- including raise E2;
   end Atc_Event;
   ...
end Server;

task To_Be_Interrupted is
begin
   ...
   select   -- ATC statement
      Server.Atc_Event;
      Seq3;
   then abort
      Seq1; -- including raise E1;
   end select;
exception
   when E1 =>
      Seq4;
   when E2 =>
      Seq5;
   when others =>
      Seq6;
end To_Be_Interrupted;
```

When the above ATC statement is executed, the result will be

```
if the rendezvous is available immediately then
   Server.Atc_Event is issued
   Seq2 is executed
   E2 is propagated from the select statement
         (Seq3 is not executed)
   Seq5 is executed
elsif no rendezvous starts before  Seq1 finishes then
   Server.Atc_Event is issued
   Seq1 is executed
   Server.Atc_Event is cancelled
   E1 is propagated from the select statement
   Seq4 is executed
elsif the rendezvous finishes before the  Seq1 finishes then
   Server.Atc_Event is issued
   partial execution of  Seq1 occurs concurrently with  Seq2
   Seq1 is aborted and finalised
   E2 is propagated from the select statement
   E1 is lost if it was ever raised
```

```
        Seq5 is executed
    elsif the rendezvous finishes after  Seq1 finishes
        Server.Atc_Event is issued
        Seq1 executes concurrently with the partial execution of  Seq2
        Server.Atc_Event is cancelled
        partial execution of  Seq2 occurs
        E2 is propagated from the select statement
        E1 is lost
        Seq5 is executed
    else the called task terminates before the rendezvous starts
                 or before it is cancelled
        Server.Atc_Event is issued
        Seq1 is aborted (or never starts)
        Tasking_Error is propagated from the select statement
        E1 is lost if it was ever raised
        Seq6 is executed
    end if
```

Generally, if the triggering event of an asynchronous select statement is taken, then any unhandled exception raised in the abortable part is lost. Of course, any unhandled exception raised by Seq3 will always be propagated.

10.3.3 Examples of asynchronous transfer of control

The examples presented in this section are derived from the application requirements mentioned earlier in Section 10.3.1.

Error recovery

Before recovery can be initiated to handle a fault, this fault must cause a detectable error to occur in the system. Once the error has been detected, some form of damage assessment and damage confinement must be undertaken before error recovery can begin. The details of these activities are application dependent; however, typically, a set of tasks might need to be informed of the fault. The following code fragment illustrates the approach:

```
with Broadcasts; -- see Section 9.7
   ...

type Error_Id is (Err1, Err2, Err3);
   -- some appropriate identifier

package Error_Notification is new  Broadcasts(Error_Id);

Error_Occurred : Error_Notification.Broadcast;
   -- a protected object

task Error_Monitor;
```

```
-- all tasks interested in the error
-- have the following structure
task type Interested_Party;


task body Interested_Party is
  Reason : Error_Id;
begin
  loop
    . . .
    select
      Error_Occurred.Receive(Reason);
        -- a protected entry call
      case Reason is
        when Err1 =>
          -- appropriate recovery action
        when Err2 =>
          -- appropriate recovery action
        when Err3 =>
          -- appropriate recovery action
      end case;
    then abort
      loop
        -- normal operation
      end loop;
    end select;
    . . .
  end loop;
end Interested_Party;


task body Error_Monitor is
  Error : Error_Id;
begin
  . . .
  -- when error detected
  Error_Occurred.Send(Error);
  -- a protected procedure call
  . . .
end Error_Monitor;
```

The above code fragment makes use of a generic package, introduced in the previous chapter, which provides a general purpose broadcast facility (via a protected object). The Error_Monitoring task detects the error condition and sends the broadcast to all those tasks that are listening. Those tasks executing within the select statement will receive the error notification, but those outside will not (in this case). The use of a different communication abstraction for error notification (such as a persistent signal) would ensure that all interested tasks received notification eventually.

The above example illustrates an interesting compromise between demanding that a task polls for the event or explicitly waits for the event, and forcing the task to respond immediately to the event. In Ada, the task must indicate explicitly that it is prepared to have its flow of control changed by executing the *select then abort* statement; however, once it has done this, it is free to continue executing. Any race conditions that result between the triggering event being signaled and the task issuing the *select then abort* statement must be catered for by the programmer. Furthermore, any section of code that should not be aborted must be encapsulated in a protected object, thus making it an abort-deferred operation.

Deadline overrun detection

If a task has a deadline associated with part of its execution, then the *select then abort* statement can be used to detect a deadline overrun. For example, the following task must undertake some action before a certain time:

```
with Ada.Real_Time; use Ada.Real_Time;
task Critical;

task body Critical is
  Deadline : Real_Time.Time :=; -- some appropriate value
begin
  ...
  select
    delay until Deadline;
    -- recovery action
  then abort
    -- time-critical section of code
  end select;
  ...
end Critical;
```

Alternatively, the task may wish the action to be performed within a certain period of time:

```
with Ada.Calendar; use Ada.Calendar;
task Critical;

task body Critical is
  Within_Deadline : Duration :=; -- some appropriate value
begin
  ...
  select
    delay (Within_Deadline);
    -- recovery action
  then abort
    -- time-critical section of code
  end select;
  ...
end Critical;
```

Mode changes

Consider a periodic task in an embedded application which can operate in two modes. In a non-critical mode, the task wishes to read a sensor every ten seconds, perform some exact, but extensive, calculation and output some value to an actuator. However, in a critical mode it is required to read the sensor every second, undertake a simple inexact calculation and then output this value. A mode change is signaled via a persistent signal (see Section 9.2). The following program fragment illustrates how the periodic task can be structured:

```
with Persistent_Signals; use Persistent_Signals;
with Ada.Calendar; use Ada.Calendar;
  ...

type Mode is (Non_Critical, Critical);
Change_Mode : Persistent_Signal;

task Sensor_Monitor;


task body Sensor_Monitor is
  Current_Mode : Mode := Non_Critical;
  Next_Time : Time := Clock;
  Current_Period : Duration := 10.0;
  Critical_Period : constant Duration := 1.0;
  Non_Critical_Period : constant  Duration := 10.0;
begin
  loop
    select
      Change_Mode.Wait;
      if Current_Mode = Critical then
        Current_Mode := Non_Critical;
        Current_Period := Non_Critical_Period;
      else
        Current_Mode := Critical;
        Current_Period := Critical_Period;
      end if;
    then abort
      loop
        -- read sensor
        -- perform appropriate calculation and
        -- output to actuator
        Next_Time := Next_Time + Current_Period;
        delay until Next_Time;
      end loop;
    end select;
  end loop;
end Sensor_Monitor;
```

If the output to the actuator involves a number of operations (or there is more than one actuator to set), then this action could be encapsulated in a call to a protected object. This would force the action to be an abort-deferred operation.

Partial/Imprecise computations

Partial or imprecise computations are those which can produce intermediate results of varying accuracy. Moreover, the accuracy of these results does not decrease as the execution of the tasks continues. With these tasks, it is usual to define a minimum precision that is needed by the application.

A task which is to perform a partial computation can place its data into a protected object. The client task can retrieve the data from the protected object. Using a protected object to encapsulate the passing of the result ensures that no inconsistent value is returned to the client due to the task receiving an ATC in the middle of the update.

The following illustrates the approach:

```ada
with Persistent_Signals; use Persistent_Signals;
with Ada.Real_Time; use  Ada.Real_Time;
  ...

Out_Of_Time : Persistent_Signal;

protected Shared_Data is
  procedure Write(D : Data);
  entry Read(D: out Data);
private
  The_Data : Data;
  Data_Available : Boolean := False;
end Shared_Data;

task Client;
task Imprecise_Server;

protected body Shared_Data is

  procedure Write(D : Data) is
  begin
    The_Data := D;
    Data_Available := True; -- indicates that the
                            -- data is available
  end Write;

  entry Read(D : out Data) when Data_Available is
  begin
    D := The_Data;
    Data_Available := False;
```

```
    end Read;
  end Shared_Data;



  task body Client is
    ...
  begin
    loop
      ...
      Out_Of_Time.Send;
      Shared_Data.Read(Result);
      ...
    end loop;
  end Client;



  task body Imprecise_Server is
    -- declaration of Result
  begin
    loop
      ...
      -- produce result with minimum required precision
      Shared_Data.Write(Result);
      select
        Out_Of_Time.Wait;
      then abort
        -- compute refined Result
        -- potentially this may contain
        loop
          -- next interaction
          Shared_Data.Write(Result);
          exit when Best_Result_Obtained;
        end loop;
      end select;
    end loop;
  end Imprecise_Server;
```

Again, the use of a call on a protected object in the abortable sequence of statements ensures that a consistent value is written.

10.4 Understanding the asynchronous select statement

Although the asynchronous select statement is simple in its syntactic representation, it can result in complex situations arising at run-time. To illustrate these, several contrived examples are now presented and explained.

10.4.1 Interaction with the delay statement

Consider the following examples:

```
task A;                              task B;

task body A is                       task body B is
   T: Time;                             T: Time;
   D : Duration;                        D : Duration;
begin                                begin
   . . .                                . . .
   select                               select
      delay until T;                       delay D;
   then abort                           then abort
      delay D;                             delay until T;
   end select;                          end select;
end A;                               end B;
```

In the above example, two tasks have an asynchronous select statement with a very similar structure. In both cases the result will be that the task will be delayed either until a certain time (T) in the future or until a certain interval has expired (D); whichever occurs first will result in the other being cancelled or aborted. However, note that after the delay has expired in the abortable part, the task must be rescheduled before the abortable part can complete and the triggering delay can be cancelled. The triggering delay could expire before this occurs.

10.4.2 Comparison with timed entry calls

Consider the following three tasks, all of which execute a form of timed entry call:

```
task A;                 task B;                 task C;

task body A is          task body B is          task body C is
   T: Time;                T: Time;                T: Time;
begin                   begin                   begin
   . . .                   . . .                   . . .
   select                  select                  select
      delay until T;          Server.Entry1;          Server.Entry1;
      S2;                     S1;                     S1;
   then abort              then abort              or
      Server.Entry1;          delay until T;          delay until T;
      S1;                     S2;                     S2;
   end select;             end select;             end select;
end A;                  end B;                  end C;
```

The execution of the three tasks can be compared according to whether the rendezvous starts or finishes before the time-out occurs:

- Rendezvous with Server starts and finishes before the time-out

  A executes the rendezvous, and then attempts to execute S1; if S1 does not complete before the time-out it is abandoned and S2 is executed.

  B executes the rendezvous, and then S1.

  C executes the rendezvous, and then S1.

- The rendezvous starts before the time-out but finishes after the time-out

  A executes the rendezvous and S2.

  B executes the rendezvous, part of S2 and all of S1. [2]

  C executes the rendezvous and S1.

- The time-out occurs before the rendezvous is started

  A executes S2.

  B executes S2 (part or all of it depending if the rendezvous completes before it finishes) and possibly the rendezvous and S1.

  C executes S2.

Interestingly, the semantics of the timed entry call of task C can be derived exactly using an asynchronous select statement:

```
task body C is
  T: Time;
begin
  . . .
  Occurred := False;
  select
    Server.Entry1(Occurred);
  then abort
    delay until T;
  end select;
  if Occurred then
    S1;
  else
    S2;
  end if;
end C;
```

---

[2]Note that on a single processor system, S2 might not actual get to execute if the processor is busy with the rendezvous and the rendezvous is non-blocking.

10.4.3   Multiple entry calls

The following example illustrates what happens if the triggering event of an asynchronous select statement is an entry call and the abortable part is a single entry call:

```
task A;                        task B;

task body A is                 task body B is
   T: Time;                       T: Time;
begin                          begin
   ...                            ...
   select                         select
      C.Entry1;                      D.Entry1;
   then abort                     then abort
      D.Entry1;                      C.Entry1;
   end select;                    end select;
end A;                         end B;
```

In many ways the two tasks above are the same: both appear to wait on an entry call either to task D or C. Consider the following three cases:

1. C.Entry1 becomes ready first (after the asynchronous select statement has been evaluated):

    Task A will rendezvous with task C, and possibly with task D (if the rendezvous becomes available before the rendezvous with C completes).

    Task B will rendezvous with task C, and possibly with task D (if the rendezvous becomes available before the rendezvous with C completes).

2. D.Entry1 becomes ready first (after the asynchronous select statement has been evaluated):

    Task A will rendezvous with D, and possibly with C (if the rendezvous becomes available before the rendezvous with D completes).

    Task B will rendezvous with D, and possibly with C (if the rendezvous becomes available before the rendezvous with D completes).

3. C.Entry1 and D.Entry1 are both ready when the asynchronous select statement is evaluated:

    Task A will rendezvous with C only.

    Task B will rendezvous with D only.

Now consider the following:

```
task A;

task body A is
begin
```

```
   ...
   select
      B.Entry1;
      Seq2;
   then abort
      B.Entry1;
      Seq1;
   end select;
   ...
end A;
```

If B is ready when the select statement is executed, Seq2 will be executed. If the task has to wait for the same entry call both in the abortable part and as the triggering event, then in this case the entry queuing policy will dictate which arm of the select completes first. For FIFO or priority scheduling, the triggering entry will complete and Seq2 will again be executed. The following example continues this point:

```
task A;              task B;             task C is
                                            entry Entry1;
                                            entry Entry2;
                                         end C;


task body A is      task body B is      task body C is
   T: Time;            T: Time;         begin
begin               begin                  ...
   ...                 ...                 select
   select              select                 accept Entry1 do
      C.Entry1;          C.Entry2;               ...
   then abort          then abort            end Entry1;
      C.Entry2;          C.Entry1;        or
   end select;         end select;          accept Entry2 do
end A;              end B;                    ...
                                            end Entry2;
                                         end select;
                                         ...
                                      end C;
```

Here when C is waiting at the select statement, A will rendezvous with Entry1, whereas B will rendezvous with Entry2. However, if C has not executed the select statement, then it is not defined what will happen (it will depend on the implementation of the selective accept statement).

Finally, consider the case where task C has the following structure:

```
task body C is
begin
   ...
   accept Entry1 do
      accept Entry2 do
         ...
```

```
      end;
    end;
   ...
 end C;
```

Here for task A, if C is already waiting at the outer accept statement, the system will deadlock. If it is not, then the rendezvous will be completed. For task B, both rendezvous will occur.

10.4.4   Interaction with requeue

A triggering event of an asynchronous select statement can contain a requeue statement. Consider the following tasks:

```
task A;                          task B is
                                    entry Entry1;
                                    entry Entry2;
                                 end B;

task body A is                   task body B is
begin                            begin
   ...                              ...
   select                          accept Entry1 do
     B.Entry1;                       requeue Entry2;
   then abort ;                      -- potentially ''with abort"
     Seq;                          end Entry1
   end select;                     ...
end A;                             accept Entry2 do
                                     ...
                                   end Entry2;
                                 end B;
```

If when the asynchronous select statement of task A is executed:

1. Entry1 of task B is available and the task is requeued with abort, then Seq will not begin its execution until the requeue has occurred.

2. Entry1 of task B is available and the task is requeued without abort, then Seq will never be executed.

3. Entry1 of task B becomes available after A has begun its execution of Seq, then if it is requeued with abort the entry call is cancelled when Seq has finished.

4. Entry1 of task B becomes available after A has begun its execution of Seq, then if it is requeued without abort the select must wait for the rendezvous with Entry2 to complete, even when Seq has finished.

10.4.5 Nested ATC

The sequence of statements within the abortable part of an asynchronous select statement can contain an asynchronous select statement. Consider the following example:

```
task A;

task body A is
begin
   ...
   select
     B.Entry1;
   then abort
     select   -- nested ATC
       C.Entry1;
     then abort
       Seq;
     end select;
   end select;
   ...
end A;
```

Here, task A will wait for an entry call to become complete from task B or C. If none arrives before Seq has finished its execution, both will be cancelled.

Note that if the same task and entry is mentioned in a nested ATC then, with most queuing disciplines, the outer triggering call will be handled first.

10.5 A robust readers and writers algorithm

In Chapter 7, two solutions were given to the *Readers and Writers Problem.* Although a single protected object with a function for read and a procedure for write will, in some senses, solve this problem it was pointed out in Chapter 7 that such a solution would not be adequate if priority were to be given to write operations, or if the actual read and write operations of the shared resource were potentially blocking (and hence could not be made from within a protected object). We conclude this chapter by giving a robust version of the first of the two solutions given in Chapter 7.

The difficulty with this solution is that it could lead to deadlock if client tasks failed in their execution of the read or write operations on the resource. Recall that the readers and writers protocol was controlled by a protected object:

```
protected Control is
   entry Start_Read;
   procedure Stop_Read;
   entry Request_Write;
   entry Start_Write;
```

```
   procedure Stop_Write;
private
   Readers : Natural := 0; -- Number of current readers
   Writers : Boolean := False; -- Writers present
end Control;
```

Client tasks called one of the following:

```
procedure Read(I : out Item) is
begin
   Control.Start_Read;
     Read_File(I);
   Control.Stop_Read;
end Read;

procedure Write(I : Item) is
begin
   Control.Request_Write;
   Control.Start_Write;
     Write_File(I);
   Control.Stop_Write;
end Write;
```

The first difficulty with these procedures is potential exceptions being propagated from the file I/O operations. These can easily be caught. It is also possible to remove the double interaction for the write operation by using requeue. In the following, some identifiers are thus changed to retain the symmetry of the solution (e.g., Start_Read to Request_Start):

```
procedure Read(I : out Item) is
begin
   Control.Request_Read;
     Read_File(I);
   Control.Stop_Read;
exception
   when others =>
      Control.Stop_Read;
end Read;

procedure Write(I : Item) is
begin
   Control.Request_Write;
     Write_File(I);
   Control.Stop_Write;
exception
   when others =>
      Control.Stop_Write;
end Write;
```

The next problem is that of an I/O operation that does not return. To solve this, it would be possible to set a time bound of, say, ten seconds for a write operation:

```
procedure Write(I : Item; Failed : out Boolean) is
begin
  Control.Request_Write;
  select
    delay 10.0;
    Failed := True;
  then abort
    Failed := False;
    Write_File(I);
  end select;
  Control.Stop_Write;
exception
  when others =>
    Control.Stop_Write;
    Failed := True;
end Write;
```

One of the motivations behind this solution of the readers and writers problem is to give preference to write operations. In situations where reads can take some time, and writes are not frequent, it may be desirable to abort an incomplete read action in order for an update to occur as soon as possible. This can be programmed using a nested ATC (one for time-out on failure, the other to enable a read to be abandoned):

```
procedure Read(I : out Item; Failed : out Boolean) is
begin
  loop
    Control.Request_Read;
    select
      Control.Abandon_Read;
      Control.Stop_Read;
    then abort
      select
        delay 10.0;
        Failed := True;
      then abort
        Read_File(I);
        Failed := False;
      end select;
      exit;
    end select;
  end loop;
  Control.Stop_Read;
exception
  when others =>
    Control.Stop_Read;
    Failed := True;
end Read;
```

This solution is now resilent to any failure of the file I/O operations. The controlling protected object is a refinement of that given in Chapter 7:

```
protected Control is
  entry Request_Read;
  procedure Stop_Read;
  entry Abandon_Read;
  entry Request_Write;
  procedure Stop_Write;
private
  entry Start_Write;
  Readers : Natural := 0; -- Number of current readers
  Writers : Boolean := False; -- Writers present
end Control;


protected body Control is

  entry Request_Read when not Writers is
  begin
    Readers := Readers + 1;
  end Request_Read;

  procedure Stop_Read is
  begin
    Readers := Readers - 1;
  end Stop_Read;

  entry Abandon_Read when Writers is
  begin
    null;
  end;

  entry Request_Write when not Writers is
  begin
    Writers := True;
    requeue Start_Write;
  end Request_Write;

  entry Start_Write when Readers = 0 is
  begin
    null;
  end Start_Write;

  procedure Stop_Write is
  begin
    Writers := False;
  end Stop_Write;

end Control;
```

A further refinement to this code is possible if the controller must be protected against the client tasks aborting their read or write operations; for example, if a read is requested and the procedure is then aborted. To provide protection against this eventuality requires the use of an abort-deferred region. The easiest way of obtaining this is via a controlled variable (as illustrated in Section 6.6.1 and Chapter 8):

```
type Read_Protocol is new Ada.Finalization.Limited_Controlled
    with null record;

procedure Initialise(Rp : in out Read_Protocol) is
begin
   Control.Request_Read;
end;

procedure Finalize(Rp : in out Read_Protocol) is
begin
   Control.Stop_Read;
end;

procedure Read(I : out Item; Failed : out Boolean) is
begin
  loop
    declare
       Read_Pro : Read_Protocol;
    begin
      select
         Control.Abandon_Read;
      then abort
         select
            delay 10.0;
            Failed := True;
         then abort
            Read_File(I);
            Failed := False;
         end select;
         exit;
      end select;
    end;
  end loop;
exception
  when others =>
    Failed := True;
end Read;
```

Note that there is no longer any need for the exception handler to call Control.Stop_Read as the finalisation procedure will always execute on exit from the inner block.

10.6   Task states

The task state diagram given in the early chapters can be extended (see Figure 10.1) again to include the new state introduced by the abort statement: abnormal. Modelling ATC in state transition diagrams is difficult, as a task

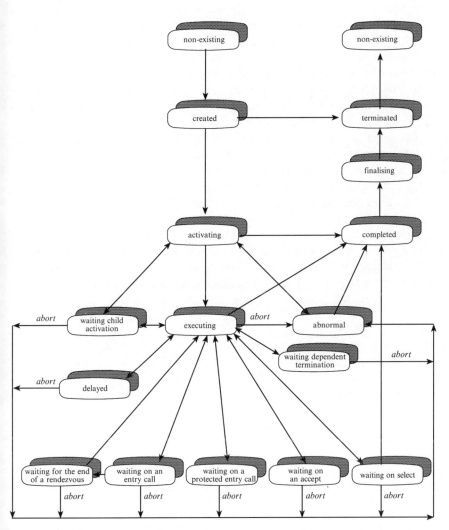

Figure 10.1: Summary of Task States and State Transitions.

can potentially be waiting for one or more triggering events and be executing at the same time (and therefore calling protected objects, creating child tasks, etc.). It is assumed that ATCs are handled as an attribute of a task and therefore not represented directly in the state transition diagrams.

10.7 Summary

The normal behaviour of a multi-tasking Ada program is for each task to make progress by following a valid execution path from activation to either termination or a repeating, indefinite sequence. This chapter has considered the ways in which this normal behaviour can be subverted.

Within a task, exceptions cause the current flow of control to be interrupted and passed to an appropriate exception handler. This is a standard feature of sequential Ada and hence it has not been explained in detail, either here or in Chapter 1. The situations in which the tasking model and the exception model interact are, however, outlined in this chapter. Many of the details of these interactions have been discussed in earlier chapters.

The most severe effect that one task can have upon another is to abort it. This is an extreme and irreversible action, and one that is not universally agreed as being appropriate in a concurrent programming language. Although a task cannot protect itself directly from an abort instruction, it will always complete correctly any protected procedures or entries that it is executing. It can also use a controlled variable to execute last rites.

A more controlled way for one task to effect another indirectly is via an asynchronous transfer of control (ATC). Here a task explicitly (via a call out to another task or protected object) indicates that is it prepared to be interrupted while executing a particular sequence of instructions. Examples of the use of ATCs were given in this chapter, as was a discussion of the interactions between ATCs and the delay statement, timed entry calls, multiple entry calls and requeue.

Chapter 11 ————————————

Tasking and Systems Programming

Ada is a high level programming language; it provides abstract constructs which allow programs in its intended application domain to be constructed easily and safely. However, it is recognised that one of the intended application areas for Ada is the production of embedded systems. Often these (and other) systems require the programmer to become more concerned with the implementation, and efficient manipulation, of these abstract program entities. Ada resolves this conflict in two ways:

(a) by allowing the programmer to specify the representation of program abstractions on the underlying hardware, for example by specifying the layout of a record or the address of a variable; and

(b) by having extra facilities in the *Systems Programming Annex* for interrupt handling, controlling access to shared variables, unique identifications of tasks and the provision of task attributes (as with all annexes, these need not be supported by all compilers).

The areas that are of concern in this book are those which relate directly to the tasking model. These are:

* device driving and interrupt handling — covered in this chapter;

* access to shared variables — covered in Section 7.10;

* task identification — motivated in Section 4.4 and covered fully in this chapter;

* task attributes — covered in this chapter.

11.1 Device driving and interrupt handling

A major difficulty in developing embedded systems is the design and implementation of device drivers. A device driver is a subsystem that has sole responsibility for controlling access to some external device. It must manipulate device registers and respond to interrupts.

A hardware device is an object which is operating in parallel with other elements of the system. It is therefore logical to consider the device as being a hardware 'task'. In Ada there are three ways in which tasks can synchronise and communicate with each other:

(a)   through the rendezvous;   .

(b)   using protected units; and

(c)   via shared variables.

In general, Ada assumes that the device and the program have access to shared memory device registers which can be specified using its representation specification techniques. In Ada 83, interrupts were represented by hardware generated task entry calls. In the current version of Ada, this facility is considered obsolete and will probably be removed from the language at the next revision. Consequently, it will not be discussed in this book.

The preferred method of device driving is to encapsulate the device operations in a protected unit. An interrupt may be handled by a protected procedure call.

This section first considers how device registers can be manipulated and specified using representation clauses, and then considers the model of interrupt handling which is supported with protected objects. Finally, an example device driver is presented.

11.1.1   Representation clauses

Representation clauses are a compromise between abstract and concrete structures. They are described in most Ada text books and are outlined below. Four distinct specifications are available:

1.   Attribute definition clause — allows various attributes of an object, task or subprogram to be set; for example, the size (in bits) of objects, the storage alignment, the maximum storage space for a task, the address of an object.

2.   Enumeration representation clause — the literals of an enumeration type may be given specific internal values.

3.   Record representation clause — record components can be assigned offsets and lengths within single storage units.

4.   At clause — this was the main Ada 83 mechanism for positioning an object at a specific address; this facility has been maintained for compatibility with Ada 83 but it is now obsolete (attributes can be used) and will therefore not be discussed further.

If an implementation cannot obey a specification request then the compiler must either reject the program or raise an exception at run-time.

As an example of the use of representation clauses, consider the control status register of a disc drive. This register is illustrated in Figure 11.1. It is assumed that all fields can be read without changing the status of the device.

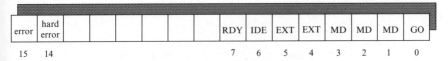

error	hard error						RDY	IDE	EXT	EXT	MD	MD	MD	GO
15	14						7	6	5	4	3	2	1	0

Figure 11.1: Control Status Register Layout.

Error, Hard-Error, RDY (Ready), IDE (interrupt enable) and GO are all two-state variables that are best thought of as flags:

```
type Flag is (Off,On);
```

with 0 representing Off and 1 giving On (this being the default representation). The "Mode of Operation"(MD) covers three bits but provides only four operations:

```
type Mode is (Reset, Write, Read, Seek);
```

The required internal codes for these four states are 0,1,2 and 4; this is specified using an enumeration clause as follows:

```
for Mode use (Reset => 0, Write => 1,Read => 2, Seek =>4);
```

As long as the sequence is still strictly increasing, any representation is allowed. The "Memory Extension Bits" (EXT) can be mapped onto a type which is restricted to two bits by an attribute definition clause:

```
type MEB is range 0..3;
for MEB'Size use 2;
```

Having constructed each individual component, the register itself can be represented as a record:

```
type Control_Status is
  record
    GO   : Flag;
    MD   : Mode;
    EXT  : MEB;
    IDE  : Flag;
    RDY  : Flag;
    Hard_Error : Flag;
    Error : Flag;
  end record;
```

The representation of the record type can then be specified:

```
Word : constant := 2; -- 2 bytes in a word
Bits_in_Word : constant := 16; -- bits in a word

for Control_Status use
  record
    GO   at 0*Word range 0..0;-- field GO at word 0 position 0
    MD   at 0*Word range 1..3;
    EXT at 0*Word range 4..5;
    IDE at 0*Word range 6..6;
    RDY at 0*Word range 7..7;
    Hard_Error at 0*Word range 14..14;
    Error at 0*Word range 15..15;
  end record;

for Control_Status'Size use Bits_In_Word;
for Control_Status'Alignment use Word;
for Control_Status'Bit_Order use Low_Order_First;
```

Each implementation has the notion of a "storage unit" to control layout. The value of this unit is contained within the predefined library package System. Each component of the record is given a position within one or more storage units; for example, Md is to be placed at storage unit 0 using bits 1,2 and 3. In this example the storage unit is deemed to have the value 8, and hence Error is to be found in the storage unit 1 at bit 7 (i.e. at word 0 bit 15).

To constrain the system to using only 16 bits in total for an object of type Control_Status, an attribute definition clause is used. The alignment clause ensures that the record is placed at an even byte boundary, and the Bit_Order attribute indicates that bit 0 is the least significant bit.

Finally, a data object to represent the control register must be defined and placed at the correct memory location; this is the physical address of the register:

```
Control_Register : Control_Status;
for Control_Register'Address use 8#777404#;
```

Having now constructed the abstract data representation of the register, and placed an appropriately defined variable at the correct address, the hardware register can be manipulated by assignments to this variable:

```
Control_Register := (GO   => On,
                     MD   => Read,
                     EXT => 0,
                     IDE => On,
                     RDY => Off,
                     Hard_Error => Off,
                     Error => Off);
```

The use of this record aggregate assumes that the entire register will be assigned values at the same time. To ensure that Go is not set before the other fields of the record it may be necessary to use a temporary (shadow) control register:

```
Temp_Cr : Control_Status;
```

This temporary register is then assigned control values and copied into the real register variable:

```
Control_Register := Temp_Cr;
```

The code for this assignment will in most cases ensure that the entire control register is updated in a single action. If any doubt still remains, then the pragma Atomic can be used (see Section 7.11).

After the completion of the I/O operation, the device itself may alter the values on the register; this is recognised in the program as changes in the values of the record components:

```
if Control_Register.Error = On then
   raise Disk_Error;
end if;
```

The object Control_Register is therefore a collection of shared variables, which are shared between the device control task and the device itself. Mutual exclusion between these two concurrent (and parallel) processes is necessary to give reliability and performance. This is achieved in Ada by using a protected object. Condition synchronisations must ensure that the correct sequence of events takes place between the hardware and its driver. The two most common are:

(a)   polling;

(b)   interrupt driven.

Whichever is used on any particular device is a property of the hardware as well as the system software. Polling cannot, therefore, be eliminated if it is the only method available for examining the condition of the device. If polling is used, then the busy-wait loop must incorporate a delay statement so that the device task does not monopolise the processor. Alternatively, the whole device driver task can be periodic.

11.2   Model of interrupts

The ARM defines the following model of an interrupt:

- An interrupt represents a class of events that are detected by the hardware or the system software.

- The *occurrence* of an interrupt consists of its *generation* and its *delivery*.

- The generation of an interrupt is the event in the underlying hardware or system which makes the interrupt available to the program.

- Delivery is the action which invokes a part of the program (called the interrupt handler) in response to the interrupt occurrence. In between the generation of the interrupt and its delivery, the interrupt is said to be *blocked*. The handler is invoked once for each delivery of the interrupt.

- When an interrupt is blocked, all future occurrences of the interrupt are prevented from being generated. It is usually device dependent as to whether a blocked interrupt remains pending or is lost. When an interrupt is being handled, further interrupts from the same source are blocked.

- Certain interrupts are *reserved*. The programmer is not allowed to provide a handler for a reserved interrupt. Usually, a reserved interrupt is handled directly by the run-time support system of Ada (for example, a clock interrupt used to implement the delay statement).

- Each non-reserved interrupt has a default handler that is assigned by the run-time support system.

11.2.1   Handling interrupts using protected procedures

The main representation of an interrupt handler in Ada is a parameterless protected procedure. Each interrupt has a unique discrete identifier which is supported by the system. How this unique identifier is represented is implementation defined; it might, for example, be the address of the hardware interrupt vector associated with the interrupt.

Identifying interrupt handling protected procedures is done using one of two pragmas:

```
pragma Attach_Handler(Handler_Name, Expression);
   -- This can appear in the specification or body of a
   -- library-level protected object and allows the
   -- static association of a named handler with the
   -- interrupt identified by the expression; the handler
   -- becomes attached when the protected object is created.
   -- Raises Program_Error:
   --   a) when the protected object is created and
```

```
--        the interrupt is reserved,
--     b) if the interrupt already has a
--        user-defined handler, or
--     c) if any ceiling priority defined is
--        not in the range Ada.Interrupt_Priority.
```

pragma Interrupt_Handler(Handler_Name);
```
-- This can appear in the specification of a library-level
-- protected object and allows the dynamic association of
-- the named parameterless procedure as an interrupt
-- handler for one or more interrupts. Objects created
-- from such a protected type must be library level.
```

The following package defines the Systems Programming Annex's support for interrupt identification and the dynamic attachment of handlers:

package Ada.Interrupts **is**
   type Interrupt_Id **is** *implementation_defined*; -- must be discrete
   type Parameterless_Handler **is access protected procedure**;

   function Is_Reserved(Interrupt : Interrupt_Id) **return** Boolean;
      -- Returns True if the interrupt is reserved,
      -- returns False otherwise.

   function Is_Attached(Interrupt : Interrupt_Id) **return** Boolean;
      -- Returns True if the interrupt is attached to a
      -- handler, returns False otherwise.
      -- Raises Program_Error if the interrupt is reserved.

   function Current_Handler(Interrupt : Interrupt_Id)
                              return Parameterless_Handler;
      -- Returns an access variable to the current handler for
      -- the interrupt. If no user handler has been attached, a
      -- value is returned which represents the default handler.
      -- Raises Program_Error if the interrupt is reserved.

   procedure Attach_Handler(New_Handler : Parameterless_Handler;
                              Interrupt : Interrupt_Id);
      -- Assigns New_Handler as the current handler
      -- for the Interrupt.
      -- If New_Handler is **null**, the default handler is restored.
      -- Raises Program_Error:
      --   a) if the protected object associated with the
      --   New_Handler has not been identified with a
      --   **pragma** Interrupt_Handler,
      --   b) if the interrupt is reserved,
      --   c) if the current handler was attached statically
      --   using pragma Attach_Handler.

   procedure Exchange_Handler(
              Old_Handler : **out** Parameterless_Handler;
              New_Handler : Parameterless_Handler;
              Interrupt : Interrupt_Id);
```
```

```
                    -- Assigns New_Handler as the current handler for the
                    -- Interrupt and returns the previous handler in
                    -- Old_Handler.
                    -- If New_Handler is null, the default handler is restored.
                    -- Raises Program_Error:
                    --      a) if the protected object associated with the
                    --         New_Handler has not been identified with a
                    --         pragma Interrupt_Handler,
                    --      b) if the interrupt is reserved,
                    --      c) if the current handler was attached statically
                    --         using pragma Attach_Handler.

                procedure Detach_Handler(Interrupt : Interrupt_Id);
                    -- Restores the default handler for the
                    -- specified interrupt.
                    -- Raises Program_Error:
                    --      a) if the interrupt is reserved,
                    --      b) if the current handler was attached statically
                    --         using pragma Attach_Handler.

                function Reference(Interrupt : Interrupt_Id)
                        return System.Address;
                    -- Returns an Address which can be used to attach
                    -- a task entry to an interrupt via an address
                    -- clause on an entry.
                    -- Raises Program_Error if the interrupt cannot be
                    -- attached in this way.

            private
                ... -- not specified by the language
            end Ada.Interrupts;
```

In all cases where Program_Error is raised, the currently attached handler is not changed.

It should be noted that the Reference function provides the mechanisms by which interrupt task entries are supported. As mentioned earlier, this model of interrupt handling is considered obsolete and should therefore not be used.

It is possible that an implementation will also allow the association of names with interrupts via the following package:

```
            package Ada.Interrupts.Names is
                implementation_defined : constant Interrupt_Id := implementation_defined;
                ...
                implementation_defined : constant Interrupt_Id := implementation_defined;
            private
                ... -- not specified by the language
            end Ada.Interrupts.Names;
```

This will be used in the following examples.

11.2.2 A simple driver example

A common class of equipment to be attached to an embedded computer system is the analogue to digital converter (ADC). The converter samples some environmental factors such as temperature or pressure; it translates the measurements it receives, which are usually in millivolts, and provides scaled integer values on a hardware register. Consider a single converter that has a 16 bit result register at hardware address 8#150000# and a control register at 8#150002#. The computer is a 16 bit machine and the control register is structured as follows:

Bit	Name	Meaning
0	A/D Start	Set to 1 to start a conversion.
6	Interrupt Enable/Disable	Set to 1 to enable interrupts
7	Done	Set to 1 when conversion is complete.
8-13	Channel	The converter has 64 analogue inputs, the particular one required is indicated by the value of the channel.
15	Error	Set to 1 by the converter if device malfunctions.

The driver for this ADC will be structured as a protected type within a package, so that the interrupt it generates can be processed as a protected procedure call, and so that more than one ADC can be catered for:

```
package Adc_Device_Driver is
   Max_Measure : constant := (2**16)-1;
   type Channel is range 0..63;
   subtype Measurement is Integer range 0..Max_Measure;
   procedure Read(Ch: Channel; M : out Measurement);
      -- potentially blocking
   Conversion_Error : exception;

private
   for Channel'Size use 6;
   -- indicates that six bits only must be used
end Adc_Device_Driver;
```

For any request, the driver will make three attempts before raising the exception. The package body follows:

```
with Ada.Interrupts.Names; use Ada.Interrupts;
with System; use System;
package body Adc_Device_Driver is
   Bits_In_Word : constant := 16;
   Word : constant := 2; -- bytes in word
   type Flag is (Down, Set);

   type Control_Register is
```

```
record
  Ad_Start : Flag;
  Ie       : Flag;
  Done     : Flag;
  Ch       : Channel;
  Error    : Flag;
end record;

for Control_Register use
  -- specifies the layout of the control register
  record
    Ad_Start at 0*Word range 0..0;
    Ie        at 0*Word range 6..6;
    Done      at 0*Word range 7..7;
    Ch        at 0*Word range 8..13;
    Error     at 0*Word range 15..15;
  end record;

for Control_Register'Size use Bits_In_Word;
  -- the register is 16 bits long
for Control_Register'Alignment use Word;
  -- on a word boundary

type Data_Register is range 0 .. Max_Measure;
for Data_Register'Size use Bits_In_Word;
  -- the register is 16 bits long


Contr_Reg_Addr : constant Address := 8#150002#;
Data_Reg_Addr  : constant Address  := 8#150000#;
Adc_Priority : constant Interrupt_Priority := 63;
Control_Reg : aliased Control_Register;
for Control_Reg'Address use Contr_Reg_Addr;
    -- specifies the address of the control register
Data_Reg : aliased Data_Register;
for Data_Reg'Address use Data_Reg_Addr;
    -- specifies the address of the data register


protected type Interrupt_Interface(Int_Id : Interrupt_Id;
                  Cr : access Control_Register;
                  Dr : access Data_Register) is
  entry Read(Chan : Channel; M : out Measurement);
private
  entry Done(Chan : Channel; M : out Measurement);
  procedure Handler;
  pragma Attach_Handler(Handler, Int_Id);
  pragma Interrupt_Priority(Adc_Priority);
    -- see next chapter for discussion on priorities
  Interrupt_Occurred : Boolean := False;
  Next_Request : Boolean := True;
end Interrupt_Interface;
```

```
Adc_Interface : Interrupt_Interface(Names.Adc,
              Control_Reg'Access, Data_Reg'Access);
   -- this assumes that 'Adc' is registered as an
   -- Interrupt_Id in Ada.Interrupts.Names


protected body Interrupt_Interface is

   entry Read(Chan : Channel; M : out Measurement)
        when Next_Request is
     Shadow_Register : Control_Reg;
   begin
     Shadow_Register := (Ad_Start => Set, Ie => Set,
          Done => Down, Ch   => Chan, Error => Down);
     Cr.all := Shadow_Register;
     Interrupt_Occurred := False;
     Next_Request := False;
     requeue Done;
   end Read;

   procedure Handler is
   begin
     Interrupt_Occurred := True;
   end Handler;

   entry Done(Chan : Channel; M : out Measurement)
                           when Interrupt_Occurred is
   begin
     Next_Request := True;
     if Cr.Done = Set and Cr. Error = Down then
          M := Measurement(Dr.all);
     else
        raise Conversion_Error;
     end if;
   end Done;
 end Interrupt_Interface;


procedure Read(Ch : Channel; M : out Measurement) is
begin
   for I in 1..3 loop
     begin
        Adc_Interface.Read(Ch,M);
        return;
     exception
        when Conversion_Error => null;
     end;
   end loop;
   raise Conversion_Error;
end Read;

end Adc_Device_Driver;
```

The client tasks simply call the Read procedure indicating the channel number from which to read, and an output variable for the actual value read. Inside the procedure, an inner loop attempts three conversions by calling the Read entry in the protected object associated with the converter. Inside this entry, the control register, Cr, is set up with appropriate values. Once the control register has been assigned, the client task is requeued on a private entry to await the interrupt.

Once the interrupt has arrived (as a parameterless protected procedure call), the barrier on the Done entry is set to true; this results in the Done entry being executed (as part of the interrupt handler), which ensures that Cr.Done has been set and that the error flag has not been raised. If this is the case, the out parameter M is constructed, again using a type conversion, from the value on the buffer register. (Note that this value cannot be out of range for the subtype Measurement.) If conversion has not been successful, the exception Conversion_Error is raised; this is trapped by the Read procedure, which makes three attempts in total at a conversion before allowing the error to propagate.

The above example illustrates that it is often necessary when writing device drivers to convert objects from one type to another. In these circumstances the strong typing features of Ada can be an irritant. It is, however, possible to circumvent this difficulty by using a generic function that is provided as a predefined library unit:

```
generic
   type Source (<>) is limited private;
   type Target (<>) is limited private;
function Ada.Unchecked_Conversion(S : Source) return Target;
pragma Convention(Intrinsic, Ada.Unchecked_Conversion);
pragma Pure(Ada.Unchecked_Conversion);
```

The effect of unchecked conversion is to copy the bit pattern of the source over to the target. The programmer must make sure that the conversion is sensible and that all possible patterns are acceptable to the target.

11.2.3   Dynamic attachment of interrupt handlers

In the previous section, the Adc_Device_Driver interrupt interface was established when the associated protected object was created. It is possible, using the Ada.Interrupts package, to attach and detach handlers to interrupts dynamically. Suppose, for example, that a programmer under certain conditions wishes to change the interrupt handler for the ADC device. The original protected type is no longer suitable, and should be replaced with the following:

```
protected type New_Interrupt_Interface(
            Cr : access Control_Register;
```

```
                        Dr : access Data_Register) is
       entry Read(Ch : Channel; M : out Measurement);
       procedure Handler;
       pragma Interrupt_Handler(Handler);
    private
       entry Done(Ch : Channel; M : out Measurement);
       pragma Interrupt_Priority(Adc_Priority);
       -- register declarations etc
    end New_Interrupt_Interface;

    New_Adc_Interface : New_Interrupt_Interface(Control_Reg'Access,
                          Data_Reg'Access);
```

Here the pragma Interrupt_Handler indicates that the procedure Handler
will be used as an interrupt handler. Now, to switch over to (and back from)
the new handler requires

```
    Old : Parameterless_Handler := null;
      ...
    -- attach new handler
    if Is_Attached(Names.Adc) then
       -- handler attached
       Exchange_Handler(Old,New_Adc_Interface.Handler'Access,
                     Names.Adc);
    else
       -- no user handler attached
       Attach_Handler(New_Adc_Interface.Handler'Access,
                     Names.Adc);
    end if;
      ...
    -- change back handlers
    if Old = null then
       Detach_Handler(Names.Adc);
    else
       Attach_Handler(Old, Names.Adc);
    end if;
```

Initially, of course the default handler will be attached. Note that, strictly
speaking, changing back could be accomplished simply by

```
    Attach_Handler(Old,Names.Adc);
```

as a null handler is taken to mean the default handler.

11.2.4 User implemented timers

As a further example of interrupt handling, consider the implementation of
a user-defined delay statement. The motivation for such a facility is to allow
the programmer to access a particular interval timer which has a granularity
different from that supplied with the standard implementation of Ada.

Tasks wishing to be delayed call the procedure Set_Alarm given below. The first parameter indicates the interval and the second is a reference to a protected object which implements a persistent signal (see Chapter 9):

```
with Persistent_Signals; use Persistent_Signals;
package User_Timers is

   type Fine_Duration is delta 0.000004 range 0.0 .. 17179.0;
        -- 32 bit timer with a resolution of 4 microseconds
   Max_Alarm_Events : constant Integer := ...;
        -- some appropriate value
   procedure Set_Alarm(For_Time : Fine_Duration;
                       Sync : access Persistent_Signal);
   -- potentially suspending

   Capacity_Exceeded : exception;
   -- raised by Set_Alarm if the number of currently
   -- delayed tasks exceeds some maximum

end User_Timers;
```

The body of the package keeps an ordered list of intervals and alarms. The first item in the list indicates the time to the next alarm, the second item indicates the time after that to the following alarm. So, for example, if there are three tasks delayed with values D1, D2, D3 where D1 < D2 < D3, then the list will be ordered with values (D1, D2 - D1, D3 - D2). Every time the clock interrupts, the first item in the list is decremented (the other values remain the same). When the first item reaches 0, it is removed from the list and its associated alarm is sent. When a task issues a Set_Alarm call, the list is searched and the task is inserted in the appropriate place.

The algorithm is implemented using a static array and a list of array elements ordered according to release position:

```
with System; use System;
with Ada.Interrupts.Names; use Ada.Interrupts;
with Ada.Interrupts; use Ada.Interrupts;
package body User_Timers is

   subtype Index is Integer range 1 .. Max_Alarm_Events;
   subtype Next_Range is Integer range 0 .. Max_Alarm_Events;
   type Signal is access all Persistent_Signal;
   type Alarm_Event is
     record
       Interval : Fine_Duration;
       Tell : Signal;
       Next_Event : Next_Range; -- Index of next Alarm_Event,
                                 -- 0 is terminator
     end record;

   type Waiting_Array is array(Index) of Alarm_Event;
```

```
type Control_Register is ...;
Cr : constant Address := 8#150000#;
Int_Id : constant Interrupt_Id := Names.User_Clock;
One_Tick : constant Fine_Duration := 0.000004;
  -- granularity of the clock
Clock_Priority : constant Interrupt_Priority := 63;


protected type Timer(Control_Reg : access Control_Register) is
  procedure Set_Alarm(For_Time : Fine_Duration;
                      Sync : access Persistent_Signal);
private
  procedure Handler;
  pragma Attach_Handler(Handler, Int_Id);
  pragma Interrupt_Priority(Clock_Priority);
  Waiting : Waiting_Array := (others => (0.0, null, 0));
  First : Next_Range := 0;
end Timer;

Creg : Control_Register := 8#010#;
  -- interrupt and device enabled
for Control_Reg'Address use Cr;
  -- specifies the address of the control register
My_Timer : Timer(Creg'Access);


procedure Set_Alarm(For_Time : Fine_Duration;
                    Sync : access Persistent_Signal) is
begin
  Timer.Set_Alarm(For_Time, Sync);
end;


protected body Timer is

  function Empty_Slot return Index is
  begin
    for I in Index loop
      if Waiting(I).Tell = null then
        Waiting(I).Next_Event := 0;
        return I;
      end if;
    end loop;
    raise Capacity_Exceeded;
  end Empty_Slot;


  procedure Set_Alarm(For_Time : Fine_Duration;
                      Sync : access Persistent_Signal) is
    Slot, Next, Last : Index;
```

```
        Accumulated : Fine_Duration := 0.0;
begin
  if First = 0 then
    -- empty list
    Waiting(1).Interval := For_Time;
    Waiting(1).Tell := Sync;
    Waiting(1).Next_Event := 0;
    First := 1;
    return;
  end if;
  Slot := Empty_Slot;
  if For_Time <= Waiting(First).Interval then
    -- needs to be placed at the front of the list
    Waiting(Slot).Interval := For_Time;
    Waiting(Slot).Tell := Sync;
    Waiting(Slot).Next_Event := First;
    Waiting(First).Interval :=
            Waiting(First).Interval - For_Time;
    First := Slot;
    return;
  end if;
  Accumulated := Accumulated + Waiting(First).Interval;
  Next := First;
  while Waiting(Next).Next_Event /= 0 loop
    if Accumulated + Waiting(Waiting(Next).Next_Event).
                            Interval > For_Time then
      -- place after next
      Waiting(Slot).Interval := For_Time - Accumulated;
      Waiting(Slot).Tell := Sync;
      Waiting(Slot).Next_Event := Waiting(Next).Next_Event;
      Waiting(Next).Next_Event := Slot;
      Next := Waiting(Slot).Next_Event;
      Waiting(Next).Interval := Waiting(Next).Interval -
                                Waiting(Slot).Interval;
      return;
    end if;
    Next := Waiting(Next).Next_Event;
    Accumulated := Accumulated + Waiting(Next).Interval;
  end loop;
  -- place at end of list
  Waiting(Slot).Interval := For_Time - Accumulated;
  Waiting(Slot).Tell := Sync;
  Waiting(Slot).Next_Event := 0;
  Waiting(Next).Next_Event := Slot;
end Set_Alarm;


procedure Handler is
begin
  if First > 0 then
    Waiting(First).Interval :=
            Waiting(First).Interval - One_Tick;
    while Waiting(First).Interval <= 0.0 and First > 0 loop
```

```
                Waiting(First).Tell.Send;
                Waiting(First).Tell := null;
                First := Waiting(First).Next_Event;
              end loop;
            end if;
          end Handler;
        end Timer;
    end User_Timer;
```

11.3 Task identifiers

If the Systems Programming Annex is being supported, all tasks have
a unique identifier which can be accessed and manipulated by the
Ada.Task_Identification package:

```
package Ada.Task_Identification is

    type Task_Id is private;
    Null_Task_Id : constant Task_Id ;

    function "="(Left, Right : Task_Id) return Boolean;

    function Image(T : Task_Id) return String;
        -- Returns an implementation defined string representing
        -- the task, the null task returns the null string.

    function Current_Task return Task_Id;
        -- Returns an unique id of the calling task; it is
        -- a bounded error to call this function from an
        -- interrupt handler or a protected entry body: either
        -- Program_Error will be raised or an implementation
        -- defined value of type Task_Id will be returned.
        -- Instead, the attribute 'Caller should be used for
        -- protected entries (see below)

    procedure Abort_Task(T : in out Task_Id);
        -- Has the same effect as aborting a task using
        -- the abort statement.
        -- Raises Program_Error if a Null_Task_Id is passed.

    function Is_Terminated(T : Task_Id) return Boolean;
        -- Equivalent to the 'Terminated attribute.
        -- Raises Program_Error if a Null_Task_Id is passed.

    function Is_Callable(T : Task_Id) return Boolean;
        -- Equivalent to the 'Callable attribute.
        -- Raises Program_Error if a Null_Task_Id is passed.
private
    -- not specified by the language
end Ada.Task_Identification;
```

A program is deemed erroneous if an attempt is made to use the Task_Id of a task which no longer exists.

In addition to the above package, the Systems Programming Annex also supports the following two attributes:

* T'Identity:

    for a given task, yields a value of type Task_Id that identifies the task denoted by T.

* E'Caller:

    for a given entry, yields a value of type Task_Id that identifies the task whose call is now being serviced. The attribute can only be used inside the accept or entry body denoted by E.

11.3.1   Secure resource control

An example of using task identifiers was given in Chapter 7, where it was used to ensure that all tasks in a group received a multicast. In this section a simpler example is given: one of secure resource allocation.

Consider a simple resource which can be allocated and freed. It is difficult to ensure that the task which frees the resource is the one to which it was allocated without the use of task identifiers. For example, the following package unsuccessfully attempts to provide secure resource allocation. It uses a limited private key to attempt to ensure that the key cannot be assigned or copied. On release of the resource, the key is set to zero:

```
package Insecure_Resource_Allocation is
   type Key is limited private;
   Null_Key : constant Key;

   protected Controller is
      entry Allocate(K : out Key);
      procedure Free(K : in out Key);
   private
      Allocated : Boolean := False;
      Current_Key : Key;
   end Controller;

   Not_Allocated : exception;
      -- raise by Free
private
   type Key is
      record
         Value : Natural := 0;
      end record;
   Null_Key : Key := (Value => 0);
end Insecure_Resource_Allocation;
```

```ada
package body Insecure_Resource_Allocation is

  protected body Controller is
    entry Allocate(K : out Key) when not Allocated is
    begin
      if Current_Key.Value = Natural'Last then
        Current_Key.Value := 1;
      else
        Current_Key.Value := Current_Key.Value + 1;
      end if;
      Allocated := True;
      K := Current_Key;
    end Allocate;

    procedure Free(K : in out Key) is
    begin
      if K /= Current_Key then
        raise Not_Allocated;
      else
        K := Null_Key;
        Allocated := False;
      end if;
    end Free;
  end Controller;
end Insecure_Resource_Allocation;
```

Although this approach will ensure that the resource will only be released once, it is still possible for the wrong task to issue the 'free' call. This can occur by passing a parameter to Allocate which is in scope to more than one task.

The following secure resource allocator solves the above problem:

```ada
with Ada.Task_Identification; use Ada.Task_Identification;
package Secure_Resource_Allocation is

  protected Controller is
    entry Allocate;
    procedure Free;
  private
    Allocated : Boolean := False;
    Current_Owner : Task_Id := Null_Task_Id;
  end Controller;

  Not_Allocated : exception;
    -- raised by Free
end Secure_Resource_Allocation;


package body Secure_Resource_Allocation is

  protected body Controller is
```

```
entry Allocate when not Allocated is
begin
  Allocated := True;
  Current_Owner := Allocate'Caller;
end Allocate;

procedure Free is
begin
  if Current_Task /= Current_Owner then
    raise Not_Allocated;
  else
    Allocated := False;
    Current_Owner := Null_Task_Id;
  end if;
end Free;
end Controller;
end Secure_Resource_Allocation;
```

The above code ensures that the task allocated the resource is the one that
returns it.

11.4   Task attributes

Not only is it useful to associate a unique identifier with a particular task, it
can also be beneficial to assign other attributes. The Systems Programming
Annex therefore provides a generic facility, Task_Attributes, for associating
user-defined attributes with tasks:

```
with Ada.Task_Identification; use Ada.Task_Identification;
generic
  type Attribute is private;
  Initial_Value : Attribute;
package Ada.Task_Attributes is

  type Attribute_Handle is access all Attribute;

  function Value(T: Task_Id := Current_Task) return Attribute;
    -- returns the value of the corresponding attribute of T

  function Reference(T : Task_Id := Current_Task)
            return Attribute_Handle;
    -- returns an access value that designates
    -- the corresponding attribute of T

  procedure Set_Value(Val : Attribute;
                      T : Task_Id := Current_Task);
    -- performs any finalization on the old value of the
    -- attribute of T and assigns Val to that attribute

  procedure Reinitialize(T : Task_Id := Current_Task);
```

```
                -- as for Set_Value where the Val parameter
                -- is replaced with Initial_Value

       end Ada.Task_Attributes;
```

11.4.1   Periodic scheduling — an example of task attributes

To illustrate the use of the task attribute facility, consider the periodic scheduling of tasks. Typically, a periodic task in Ada is structured as

```
       task Cyclic;
       task body Cyclic is
          Next_Period : Ada.Real_Time.Time := Ada.Real_Time.Clock;
          Period : Time_Span := To_Time_Span(10.0); -- say
       begin
          loop
             -- statements to be executed each period
             Next_Period := Next_Period + Period;
             delay until Next_Period;
          end loop;
       end Cyclic;
```

In some applications (for example, high integrity systems), it is necessary to separate the details of the scheduling from the task itself. In these systems, the task simply wishes to execute a `Wait_Until_Next_Schedule` call. The following package uses task attributes and task identifiers to schedule a set of periodic tasks:

```
       with Ada.Task_Identification; use Ada.Task_Identification;
       with Ada.Real_Time; use Ada.Real_Time;
       package Periodic_Scheduler is
          procedure Set_Characteristic(T : Task_Id; Period : Time_Span;
                                       First_Schedule : Time);
          procedure Wait_Until_Next_Schedule; -- potentially suspending
       end Periodic_Scheduler;
```

```
       with Ada.Task_Attributes;
       package body Periodic_Scheduler is
          Start_Up_Time : Time := Clock;
          type Task_Information is
             record
                Period : Time_Span := Time_Span_Zero;
                Next_Schedule_Time : Time :=
                      Time_Of(100000,Time_Span_Zero);
             end record;
          Default : Task_Information;
             -- a default object needs to be provided
             -- to the following package instantiation
```

```
package Periodic_Attributes is new
        Ada.Task_Attributes(Task_Information, Default);
use Periodic_Attributes;

procedure Set_Characteristic(T : Task_Id; Period : Time_Span;
                             First_Schedule : Time) is
begin
   Set_Value((Period,First_Schedule), T );
end;

procedure Wait_Until_Next_Schedule is
   Task_Info : Task_Information := Value;
   Next_Time : Time;
begin
   Next_Time := Task_Info.Period +
                Task_Info.Next_Schedule_Time;
   Set_Value((Task_Info.Period,Next_Time));
   delay until Next_Time;
end Wait_Until_Next_Schedule;
end Periodic_Scheduler;
```

Periodic tasks can now be encoded as

```
task Cyclic;
task body Cyclic is
begin
   loop
      -- statements to be executed each period
      Periodic_Scheduler.Wait_Until_Next_Schedule;
   end loop;
end Cyclic;
```

and some other component of the application can allocate the period.

11.5   Summary

This chapter has addressed the additional issues, for concurrent programming, that arise if an implementation supports the Systems Programming Annex. One set of issues addresses low level programming, the other is concerned with the extra facilities that the Annex provides.

Embedded systems must often include code for interacting with special purpose input and output devices. Of particular interest to the topic of this book are those devices that generate interrupts. This chapter has presented a model for interrupt handling that maps an interrupt on to a parameterless protected procedure. A standard task, released by the action of the protected procedure, is used to code the response to the interrupt.

The Systems Programming Annex also defines a couple of useful packages. One provides access to a unique identifier for each task. This can be used to write general purpose routines, such as secure resource controllers. The other package enables task attributes to be defined and used in an efficient way.

11.6   Further reading

A. Burns and A.J. Wellings, *Real-time Systems and their Programming Languages*, Addison Wesley, Wokingham, 1990.
C.C. Foster, *Real Time Programming — Neglected Topics*, Addison Wesley, Wokingham, 1981.
D. Whiddett, *Concurrent Programming for Software Engineers*, Ellis Horwood, Chichester, 1987.

Chapter 12 —————————————————

Real-Time Programming

tt It has been mentioned several times already in this book that real-time programming represents a major application area for Ada, and particularly for Ada tasking. The Real-Time Systems Annex specifies additional characteristics of the language which facilitate the programming of embedded and real-time systems. If an implementation supports the Real-Time Systems Annex then it must also support the Systems Programming Annex (see previous chapter). All issues discussed in the Real-Time Systems Annex affect the tasking facilities of the language. They can be grouped together into the following topics:

* Task priorities.
* Synchronisation control.
* Optimisation rules.
* Immediacy of abort.
* Restricted tasking model.
* Monotonic time — described in Chapter 2.
* Delay accuracy.

All of these topics (apart from those concerned with time) are discussed in this chapter.

12.1   Task priorities

The functional correctness of a concurrent program should not depend on the exact order in which tasks are executed. It may be necessary to prove that the non-determinism of such programs cannot lead to deadlock or livelock (i.e. progress is always taking place), but it is not necessary to program the order in which all actions must occur explicitly.

Non-determinism in Ada programs comes from the behaviour of the run-time dispatcher (i.e. the order in which tasks are released), the queues on entries, the choice mechanism of the select statement (when more than one alternative could be taken) and the behaviour of protected objects.

Although functional correctness should not depend upon the behaviour of these non-deterministic constructs, real-time programs do require control over this behaviour. A real-time program has temporal requirements that dictate the order in which events must occur and be handled. In an Ada program, this means that the programmer must be able to control (implicitly or explicitly) the order in which tasks execute, and hence the order in which they complete their work. Once these completion patterns are known, and the resource requirements (e.g. processor load) of each task have been estimated (or measured), it is possible to analyse a program and decide if it will meet all its timing requirements. This analysis determines the schedulability of the program. The timing requirements themselves usually take the form of deadlines on the completion of a set of actions of particular tasks.

Where more than one task is runnable, the actual order of execution can be determined by assigning a unique priority to each task. If two, or more, tasks are contending for the same processor, then the one with the highest priority will be the one that is actually dispatched. Priority can also be used to order entry queues and determine the choices made by the select statement and protected objects.

The use of priority at the language level is merely a mechanism for ordering executions. The meaning, or semantics, of the notion of priority is an issue solely for the programmer. In some applications, priority will be used to imply criticality: hence the most critical tasks will always execute, and finish, first. In the domain of real-time programming, priority is used to represent the urgency by which tasks must complete. Urgency is, thus, a reflection of the timing characteristics of each task.

Different scheduling methods use priority in different ways. One important distinction between alternative approaches is whether each task has a fixed static priority or a dynamic changing priority. An example of the latter approach is *earliest deadline scheduling*. Here, the priority of a task is a function of its impending deadline. As its deadline gets closer, its relative priority is raised so that it becomes the highest priority task when it has the closest deadline. The alternative, fixed priority scheduling, has been the subject of considerable research over the last decade. It now represents a mature engineering technique for real-time programming. Priorities are assigned by some appropriate algorithm (such as rate monotonic, or deadline monotonic) and then scheduling tests are applied to the task set to see if the complete program is schedulable (see further reading section for details on priority allocation algorithms and schedulability tests).

12.1.1   Base priorities

Scheduling theories themselves are beyond the scope of this book. The provisions of the Real-Time Systems Annex allow priorities to be assigned to tasks (and protected objects). Hence consideration here will focus on these facilities. First, static priorities are defined. In package System there are the following declarations:

```
subtype Any_Priority is Integer range implementation-defined;
subtype Priority is Any_Priority range
                    Any_Priority'First .. implementation-defined;
subtype Interrupt_Priority is Any_Priority range
                    Priority'Last+1 .. Any_Priority'Last;

Default_Priority : constant Priority :=
                    (Priority'First + Priority'Last)/2;
```

An integer range is split between standard priorities and (the higher) interrupt priority range. An implementation must support a range for System.Priority of at least 30 values and at least one distinct System.Interrupt_Priority value. Most scheduling theories work optimally if each task has a distinct priority. Hence, ranges in excess of 30 are beneficial.

A task has its initial priority set by including a pragma in its specification:

```
task Controller is
    pragma Priority(10);
end Controller;
```

If a task-type definition contains such a pragma, then all tasks of that type will have the same priority unless a discriminant is used:

```
task type Servers(Task_Priority : System.Priority) is
    entry Service1(...);
    entry Service2(...);
    pragma Priority(Task_Priority);
end Servers;
```

For entities acting as interrupt handlers, a special pragma is defined:

```
pragma Interrupt_Priority(Expression);
```

or simply

```
pragma Interrupt_Priority;
```

The definition, and use, of a different pragma for interrupt levels improves the readability of programs and helps to remove errors that can occur if task and interrupt priority levels are confused. However, the expression used in Interrupt_Priority evaluates down to Any_Priority and hence it is possible to give a relatively low priority to an interrupt handler. If the expression is actually missing, the highest possible priority is assigned.

A priority assigned using one of these pragmas is called a *base priority*. A task may also have an active priority that is higher — this will be explained in due course.

The main program, which is executed by a notional environmental task, can have its priority set by placing the Priority pragma in the main subprogram. If this is not done, the default value, defined in System, is used. Any other task that fails to use the pragma has a default base priority equal to the base priority of the task that created it.

12.1.2 Priority ceiling locking

In Chapter 7, it was explained that protected objects have the fundamental property of ensuring mutually exclusive access to the internal data of the object. It was not explained how an implementation should ensure this mutual exclusion. In this section, it is shown how an inappropriate implementation scheme (i.e. one without inheritance) can undermine the priority model used for ensuring timely behaviour. The difficulties with this scheme motivate the use of the locking protocol defined in the Real-Time Systems Annex.

Consider, for illustration, a three-task system. The tasks have high, medium and low priority, and will be identified by the labels H, M and L. Assume that H and L share data which is encapsulated in a protected object, P. The following execution sequence is possible:

1.   L is released, executes and enters P.

2.   M is released and preempts L while it is executing in P.

3.   H is released and preempts M.

4.   H executes a call on P.

Now, H cannot gain access to P as L has the mutual exclusion lock. Hence H is suspended. The next highest priority task is M and hence M will continue. As a result, H must wait for M to finish before it can possibly execute again (see Figure 12.1). This phenomenon is known as *priority inversion*, as the rules regarding priority seem to have been turned around: in effect, M is holding up the higher priority task H.

To limit the detrimental effect of priority inversion, some form of *priority inheritance* must be used. This allows a task to execute with an enhanced priority if it is blocking (or could block) a higher priority task. There are a number of priority inheritance protocols; the one defined below corresponds to that supported by the Real-Time Systems Annex. It is known as the *Immediate Ceiling Priority Protocol* (ICPP), or *Ceiling Priority Emulation*.

First, a ceiling priority is defined for each protected object. This priority represents the maximum priority of any task that calls the object. Whenever a task executes within a protected object it does so with the ceiling priority

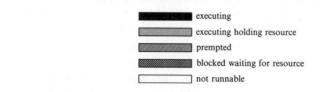

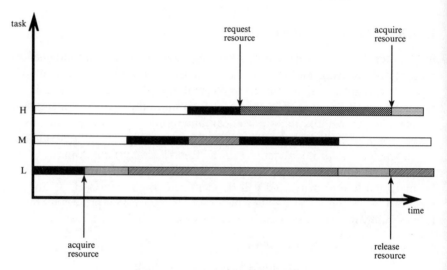

Figure 12.1: Priority Inversion.

(i.e. its priority is potentially raised). The simple three-task system will now behave as follows (see Figure 12.2):

1. L is released, executes and enters P; its priority is raised to that of H (at least).

2. M is released but does not execute as the priority of M is less than the current priority of L.

3. H is released but does not execute as its priority is not higher than L at this time.

4. L exits P and has its priority lowered.

5. H can now execute and will enter and leave P when required.

The result is that H is blocked for the minimum time. Priority inversion cannot be entirely removed as the integrity of the protected data must be ensured. Hence L must be able to block H for the time it is actually within P.

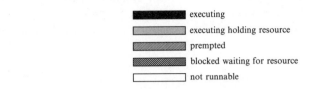

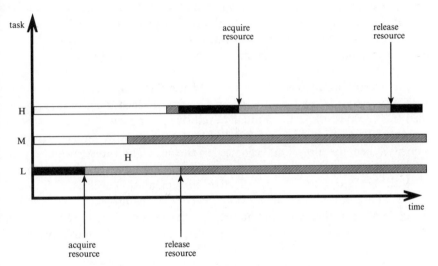

Figure 12.2: Ceiling Priority Inheritance.

The use of the ICPP has a number of benefits in addition to minimising priority inversion. On a single processor-system, the protocol will itself ensure mutual exclusion. While a task is executing within the protected object, it must have a priority higher than any other task that may wish to call that object. [1] Hence no other user of the object can call the object, and mutual exclusion is ensured. ICPP also has three other useful properties:

- A task can only be blocked at the very beginning of its execution (e.g. when it has just been made runnable).

- A task can only suffer a single block (i.e. when it is released there is at most one lower priority task holding a resource that it requires).

- If all resources are accessed by protected objects, with appropriate ceiling priorities, then deadlocks cannot occur.

---

[1]There are two ways of implementing ceiling priorities; either the protected object has a priority greater than any calling task, or it has a priority equal to the highest priority caller. In the latter case, the task with priority equal to the ceiling cannot preempt another task with the same priority.

These properties only apply to single-processor systems. Their derivation is beyond the scope of this chapter.

In order to make use of ICPP, an Ada program must include the following pragma: [2]

```
pragma Locking_Policy(Ceiling_Locking);
```

An implementation may define other locking policies; only Ceiling_Locking is required by the Annex. The default policy, if the pragma is missing, is implementation defined. To specify the ceiling priority for each object, the Priority and Interrupt_Priority pragmas defined in the previous section are used. If the pragma is missing, a ceiling of System.Priority'Last is assumed.

The exception Program_Error is raised if a task calls a protected object with a priority greater than the defined ceiling. If such a call were allowed, then this could result in the mutually exclusive protection of the object being violated. If it is an interrupt handler that calls in with an inappropriate priority, then the program becomes erroneous. This must eventually be prevented through adequate testing and/or static analysis of the program.

With Ceiling_Locking, an effective implementation will use the thread of the calling task to execute not only the code of the protected call, but also the code of any other task that happens to have been released by the actions of the original call. For example, consider the following simple protected object:

```
protected Gate_Control is
   pragma Priority(28);
   entry Stop_And_Close;
   procedure Open;
private
   Gate: Boolean := False;
end Gate_Control;
```

```
protected body Gate_Control is
   entry Stop_And_Close when Gate is
   begin
      Gate := False;
   end Stop_And_Close;

   procedure Open is
   begin
      Gate := True;
   end Open;
end Gate_Control;
```

---

[2]Locking policy (and other such policies) are actually defined on a per-partition basis. Partitions are units of configuration used mainly in distributed programs, see Chapter 14.

Assume a task T, priority 20, calls Stop_And_Close and is blocked. Later, task S (priority 27) calls Open. The thread that implements S will undertake the following actions:

(a)   execute the code of Open for S;

(b)   evaluate the barrier on the entry and note that T can now proceed;

(c)   execute the code of Stop_And_Close for T;

(d)   evaluate the barrier again;

(e)   continue with the execution of S after its call on the protected object.

As a result, there has been no context switch. The alternative is for S to make T runnable at point (2); T now has a higher priority (28) than S (27) and hence the system must switch to T to complete its execution within Gate_Control. As T leaves, a switch back to S is required. This is much more expensive.

12.1.3   Active priorities and dispatching policies

As a task enters a protected object, its priority may rise above the base priority level defined by the Priority or Interrupt_Priority pragmas. The priority used to determine the order of dispatching is the *active priority* of a task. This active priority is the maximum of the task's base priority and any priority it has inherited. The use of a protected object is one way in which a task can inherit a higher active priority. There are others, for example:

• During activation — a task will inherit the active priority of the parent task that created it; remember the parent task is blocked waiting for its child task to completion, and this could be a source of priority inversion without this inheritance rule.

• During a rendezvous — the task executing the accept statement will inherit the active priority of the task making the entry call (if it is greater than its own priority).

Note that the last case does not necessarily remove all possible cases of priority inversion. Consider a server task, S, with entry E and base priority L (low). A high priority task makes a call on E. Once the rendezvous has started, S will execute with the higher priority. But before S reaches the accept statement for E, it will execute with priority L (even though the high priority task is blocked). This, and other candidates for priority inheritance, can be supported by an implementation. The implementation must, however, provide a pragma that the user can employ to select the additional conditions explicitly.

The Real-Time Systems Annex attempts to provide flexible and extensible features. Clearly, this is not easy. Ada 83 suffered from being too prescriptive. However, the lack of a defined dispatching policy would be unfortunate as it would not assist software development or portability. If base priorities have been defined, then it is assumed that preemptive priority based scheduling is to be employed. On a multi-processor system, it is implementation defined whether this is on a per-processor basis or across the entire processor cluster.

To give extensibility, the dispatching policy can be selected by using the following pragma:

pragma Task_Dispatching_Policy(Policy_Identifier);

The Real-Time Systems Annex defines one possible policy: Fifo_Within_Priority. Where tasks share the same priority, then they are queued in FIFO order. Hence, as tasks become runnable, they are placed at the back of a notional run queue for that priority level. One exception to this case is when a task is preempted; here the task is placed at the front of the notional run queue for that priority level.

If a programmer specifies the Fifo_Within_Priority option, then it must also pick the Ceiling_Locking policy defined earlier. Together, they represent a consistent and usable model for building, implementing and analysing real-time programs.

12.1.4   Entry queue policies

A programmer may also choose a queuing policy for a task or protected object entry queue, and the behaviour of the selection policy for open entries in a protected object and the select statement. Again, a pragma is used:

pragma Queuing_Policy (Policy_Identifier);

There are two predefined policies with this pragma: Fifo_Queuing and Priority_Queuing. An implementation may define other policies. Note that the default policy is Fifo_Queuing.

The priority policy behaves as expected: tasks are queued, and hence serviced, in priority order. With the select statement or protected objects, an entry that is open and has the highest priority task queued (across all open entries) is chosen. If two open entries have tasks at the head of their queues with equal priority, then the alternative which is textually first is selected. Although this latter rule seems a little arbitrary, it is a compromise between needing to define the exact semantics of the select and not wishing to add extra syntax. Note that, if FIFO queuing is chosen, the selection process remains arbitrary.

The active priority of the calling task is used to place the task in the correct position in the priority-ordered queue. If the active priority changes while the calling task is suspended, then this has no effect. However, if its base priority changes (see next section), then the task is logically removed from the entry queue and subsequently replaced in a new position that corresponds to its new priority (but behind tasks with the same priority).

12.2   Dynamic priorities

All the above discussions have assumed that the base priority of a task remains constant during the entire existence of the task. This is an adequate model for many scheduling approaches. There are, however, situations in which it is necessary to alter base priorities. For example:

(a)   to implement mode changes;

(b)   to implement dynamic scheduling schemes such as earliest deadline scheduling.

In the first example, base priority changes are infrequent and correspond to changes in the relative temporal properties of the tasks after a mode change (e.g. a task running more frequently in the new mode). The second use of dynamic priorities allows programmers to construct their own schedulers. An example of this will be given shortly.

To facilitate dynamic priorities, the language defines the following library package:

```
with Ada.Task_Identification;
with System;
package Ada.Dynamic_Priorities is

   procedure Set_Priority(Priority : System.Any_Priority;
                  T : Ada.Task_Identification.Task_Id :=
                  Ada.Task_Identification.Current_Task);
      -- raises Tasking_Error if either the task has
      -- terminated or T is a null task

   function Get_Priority(T : Ada.Task_Identification.Task_Id :=
                  Ada.Task_Identification.Current_Task)
                  return System.Any_Priority;
      -- raises Tasking_Error if either the task has
      -- terminated or T is a null task
private
   ... -- not specified by the language
end Ada.Dynamic_Priorities;
```

Note that the package uses task identifiers to identify the designated task. The function Get_Priority returns the current base priority of the task; this can be changed by the use of Set_Priority.

A change of base priority should take effect as soon as is practical. This might seem a little vague; however, it is difficult to be more precise because the implementation of Ada might be running on top of a standard operating system, and task priorities might be mapped to operating system priority levels. Hence, the priority change might well depend on the operating system. An implementation of Ada should document when priority changes take effect.

Base priority changes can affect the active priority of the task and hence have an impact on dispatching and queuing. With the predefined scheduling policies, the effect of calling Set_Priority with the existing priority level is to move the task to the back of the sequence of tasks with that priority.

Although calls to completed or abnormal tasks are allowed, a call to a terminated task will cause Tasking_Error. Arguably, this should be a null operation as it is not necessarily an error to attempt to raise the priority of a terminated task (indeed, the motivation behind the priority change may have been to speed up, or slow down, the task's progress towards completion).

With the mode change example, a number of tasks need to have their priorities changed. Typically, these changes should take place atomically (i.e. all changed together). To achieve this, a protected object with a high ceiling priority could be used. For example, in the following, a group of N tasks can exist in one of four modes. A call of Set_Mode will change the priorities of the tasks. Each task must, however, first call Register, so that its identity can be held:

```
with Ada.Task_Identification;
with Ada.Dynamic_Priorities;
use Ada.Dynamic_Priorities;
with System;
package Flight_Management is
  N : constant Positive := ...;
  type Task_Range is range 1..N;
  type Mode is (Taxiing, Take_Off, Cruising, Landing);

  Mode_Priorities : array(Task_Range, Mode) of System.Priority;
  -- priorities are set during an
  -- initialisation phase of the program

  type Labels is array(Task_Range) of
        Ada.Task_Identification.Task_Id;

  protected Mode_Changer is
    pragma Priority(System.Priority'Last);
    procedure Register(Name : Task_Range);
    procedure Set_Mode(M : Mode);
  private
    Current_Mode : Mode := Taxiing;
    Task_Labels : Labels;
```

```
      end Mode_Changer;
   end Flight_Management;
```

The body of Mode_Changer will be

```
protected body Mode_Changer is
   procedure Register(Name : Task_Range) is
   begin
      Task_Labels(Name) :=
                  Ada.Task_Identification.Current_Task;
   end Register;

   procedure Set_Mode(M : Mode) is
   begin
      if M /= Current_Mode then
         Current_Mode := M;
         for T in Task_Range loop
            Set_Priority(Mode_Priorities(T,M),Task_Labels(T));
         end loop;
      end if;
   end Set_Mode;
end Mode_Changer;
```

Note that this will only work if all the tasks first register and none of them
has terminated. If termination is possible, protection against Tasking_Error
must be programmed:

```
procedure Set_Mode(M : Mode) is
begin
   if M /= Current_Mode then
      Current_Mode := M;
      for T in Task_Range loop
         begin
            Set_Priority(Mode_Priorities(T,M),Task_Labels(T));
         exception
            when Tasking_Error => null;
         end;
      end loop;
   end if;
end Set_Mode;
```

The use of both dynamic priorities and ceiling locking opens up the possibility
of a task having its priority raised above that of the ceiling of some object it
uses. This would be particularly dramatic if the task happened to be inside
the object when its priority is raised. Clearly, care must be taken to ensure
that these potential hazards cannot occur. Note that a protected object
cannot have its ceiling priority changed dynamically, and hence it must have
a ceiling no lower than any calling task in any mode.

12.2.1 Earliest deadline scheduling

As indicated earlier, the provision of dynamic priorities allows programmer defined schedulers to be used. Earliest deadline scheduling is the most common alternative to fixed priority scheduling. The following code illustrates one way that this could be implemented for a single-processor system. Note that the tasks schedule themselves via a protected object, Scheduler. No active scheduling task is needed. A task attribute is used to hold the current deadline (in absolute time) of the task.

A complete program using this scheme could be written as follows. The program assumes a maximum of N tasks to be scheduled by the earliest deadline scheme:

```
with Ada.Task_Identification;
with Ada.Task_Attributes;
with Ada.Real_Time; use Ada.Real_Time;
with Ada.Dynamic_Priorities;
with System;
use Ada;
procedure Earlist_Deadline_Scheduling is -- main program
  pragma Locking_Policy (Ceiling_Locking);
  pragma Task_Dispatching_Policy (Fifo_Within_Priority);

  N : constant Positive := ...;
  subtype Active_Range is Natural range 0 .. N;
  subtype Task_Range is Active_Range range 1..N;

  High : constant System.Priority := System.Priority'Last;
  Medium : constant System.Priority := High - 1;
  Low : constant System.Priority := High - 2;

  package Deadline_Attributes is new
                  Task_Attributes(Time, Time_Last);
    -- time_last is the furthest time into the future the
    -- implementation can give, it is defined in Real_Time

  type Labels is array(Task_Range) of Task_Identification.Task_Id;

  protected Scheduler is
    pragma Priority(High);
    procedure Register;
    procedure Reschedule;
        -- called by tasks coming off delay queue
    procedure Remove;
        -- called by tasks completing their execution
  private
    Task_Labels : Labels;
    Number_Of_Tasks : Active_Range := 0;
    Shortest_Deadline : Time := Time_Last;
    Running_Task : Task_Identification.Task_Id :=
                    Task_Identification.Null_Task_Id;
```

```
end Scheduler;

task type Worker is
   pragma Priority(High);
end Worker;

protected body Scheduler is ...
task body Worker is ...

-- declaration of N workers

end Earlist_Deadline_Scheduling;
```

Note that the registration scheme is different from the one used in the mode change example.

The tasks to be scheduled are assumed to be periodic. When such tasks are runnable but do not have the shortest deadline, they will be allocated a base priority of Low. The task with the shortest deadline has a Medium priority. When this task completes, it will call Scheduler.Remove.

The only difficulty with this scheme is that a task coming off the delay queue may have a shorter deadline than the current running task. There are a number of ways of dealing with this problem. The following simple (although probably not the most efficient) scheme forces each task to execute when it is released from the delay queue. This is done by ensuring that it comes off the delay queue with a High priority. Its priority is then lowered inside the Scheduler. The worker tasks would thus have the following form:

```
task body Worker is
   -- internal declarations
   Period : Time_Span := -- some value;
   Deadline : Time_Span := -- some value;
   Next_Release : Time;
begin
   Scheduler.Register;
   Next_Release := Clock + Period;
   Dynamic_Priorities.Set_Priority(High);
   loop
      delay until(Next_Release);
      Deadline_Attributes.Set_Value(Next_Release+Deadline);
      Scheduler.Reschedule; -- lowers priority from High

      -- code of application

      Dynamic_Priorities.Set_Priority(High);
      Deadline_Attributes.Set_Value(Time_Last);
      Scheduler.Remove; -- retains priority at High
      Next_Release := Next_Release + Period;
   end loop;
end Worker;
```

The code for the Scheduler is as follows:

```
protected body Scheduler is
  procedure Register is
  begin
    Number_Of_Tasks := Number_Of_Tasks + 1;
    Task_Labels(Number_Of_Tasks) :=
                  Task_Identification.Current_Task;
  end Register;

  procedure Reschedule is
  begin
    if Deadline_Attributes.Value < Shortest_Deadline then
      Dynamic_Priorities.Set_Priority(Medium);
      Dynamic_Priorities.Set_Priority(Low,Running_Task);
      Shortest_Deadline := Deadline_Attributes.Value;
      Running_Task := Task_Identification.Current_Task;
    else
      Dynamic_Priorities.Set_Priority(Low);
    end if;
  end Reschedule;

  procedure Remove is
  begin
    Shortest_Deadline := Time_Last;
    Running_Task := Task_Identification.Null_Task_Id;
    for T in 1 .. Number_Of_Tasks loop
      if Deadline_Attributes.Value(Task_Labels(T)) <
                  Shortest_Deadline then
        Shortest_Deadline :=
                  Deadline_Attributes.Value(Task_Labels(T));
        Running_Task := Task_Labels(T);
      end if;
    end loop;
    if Shortest_Deadline < Time_Last then
      -- found a runnable task
      Dynamic_Priorities.Set_Priority(Medium,Running_Task);
    end if;
  end Remove;
end Scheduler;
```

When procedure Remove is called, the next task to execute is found by searching through all tasks (including those currently delayed). Clearly, this is inefficient; tasks could be queued according to their deadlines, although this would make the procedure Reschedule more complicated.

12.3   Synchronisation primitives

During the development of Ada 95 there was a long running debate as to the right level of abstraction for the language synchronisation primitives.

Low level primitives are efficient but do not lend themselves to effective use (from a software engineering viewpoint). But Ada 83's support of only a very high level rendezvous structure was strongly criticised for not facilitating the production of efficient real-time applications. It also leads to what is called abstraction inversion. This is when programmers take a high level abstraction and use it to construct lower level services such as semaphores. These services are then used in the rest of the program.

This debate over the language is further complicated by the realisation that the simple provision of both high and low level abstractions is not appropriate, as the interactions between the levels of abstraction would have to be defined. And this has not proved to be easy.

The compromise that has emerged is the definition of two packages in the Real-Time Systems Annex. One package (synchronous task control) allows a task to suspend itself. This can be viewed as a special protected type (although it would probably not be implemented as such). The other package (asynchronous task control) allows a task to suspend other tasks. The semantics for this more controversial feature are expressed in terms of priorities. These two packages will now be described.

12.3.1   Synchronous task control

The predefined package provides a simple binary-semaphore-like construct:

```
package Ada.Synchronous_Task_Control is
   type Suspension_Object is limited private;
   procedure Set_True(S : in out Suspension_Object);
   procedure Set_False(S : in out Suspension_Object);
   function Current_State(S : Suspension_Object) return Boolean;
   procedure Suspend_Until_True(S: in out Suspension_Object);
      -- raises Program_Error if more than one task tries
      -- to suspend on S at once.
      -- Potentially suspending.
private
   -- not specified by the language
end Ada.Synchronous_Task_Control;
```

An object of this type has two notional values: true and false. The first three subprograms are non-suspending and atomic with respect to one another. They simply allow a Suspension_Object to be set or interrogated.

The procedure Suspend_Until_True will suspend a calling task until the value of S is true. On return from this procedure, the value of S will be false.

Using a Suspension_Object, it is possible to program mutual exclusion between two tasks by simply encapsulating their critical sections with the following:

```
Mutex : Suspension_Object;
```

```
   ...

Set_True(Mutex);

   ...

Suspend_Until_True(Mutex);
   -- critical section
Set_True(Mutex);
```

Suspension objects can also be used inside protected objects to implement condition synchronisation.

12.3.2   Asynchronous task control

The ability to suspend another task is fraught with difficulties. For example, what should happen if the designated task is currently executing inside a protected object? A number of people have argued that if "suspend others" is to be allowed, then it must be supported in such a way as to be consistent with the other parts of the language. One interpretation of "suspend task T" is to lower its priority to below that of other tasks in the system. In effect this is what was done, in the previous section, to implement earliest deadline scheduling using dynamic priorities. Hence, a potentially consistent way of obtaining asynchronous task control is to express the required semantics in terms of priorities. This is the approach taken in the Real-Time Systems Annex by the provision of the following package:

```
with Ada.Task_Identification;
package Ada.Asynchronous_Task_Control is
   procedure Hold(T : Ada.Task_Identification.Task_Id);
   procedure Continue(T : Ada.Task_Identification.Task_Id);
   function Is_Held(T : Ada.Task_Identification.Task_Id)
              return Boolean;
end Ada.Asynchronous_Task_Control;
```

For each processor there is a conceptual idle task which can always run (but has a priority below any application task). A call of Hold lowers the base priority of the designated task to below that of the idle task. It is said to be *held*. If the designated task is executing its own code (i.e. is not inheriting a priority), then it will be suspended immediately. A call of Continue restores the task's priority.

As only the base priority of the held task is affected, it is possible to give clear semantics to the consequences of calling Hold on a task which may be in one of a number of states. For example, if the designated task is executing inside a protected object (i.e. it has inherited the ceiling priority) then it will continue executing until it leaves the object — it will then become held.

Similarly, a held caller of a rendezvous will not affect the rendezvous taking place (although the rendezvous' priority will now be only that of the task that does the accepting).

Two further rules clarify the behaviour of a held task:

- If the held task is currently suspended on an accept statement (or a select), and a call comes in on an (open) entry, then the accept statement is executed. This rule follows from the accepting task inheriting the priority of the caller and is slightly counterintuitive (given that the task is meant to be suspended!).

- If the held task is currently suspended on a protected object's barrier, then it will execute the entry when the barrier comes true (open). This rule follows from the use of ceiling priorities and also the implementation scheme that allows the entry to be executed by the task that lowered the barrier (on behalf of the suspended task).

The use of Hold and Continue, although it does not give "suspend NOW under all circumstances", does provide a safe abstraction for what some real-time programmers feel is a critically important feature.

12.4 Immediacy of abort

The ultimate "suspend others" is abort (with no provision for continue!). The Real-Time Systems Annex requires that abort be immediate on single-processor systems. It also gives other metrics and conditions for implementing this language feature.

Of course, an abort cannot be immediate if the task is currently in an abort-deferred region, such as a protected action. There is thus a uniformity of approach to abort and "suspend others" (i.e. Hold in the above discussion). In a real-time system it is not necessary for things to be immediate. They must, however, be bounded and under programmer control.

12.5 Restricted tasking

Where it is necessary to produce very efficient programs, it would be useful to have run-time systems (kernels) that are tailored to the particular needs of the program actually executing. As this would be impossible to do in general, the Real-Time Systems Annex defines a set of restrictions that a run-time system should recognise and 'reward' by giving more effective support. The following restrictions are identified by pragmas, and are checked and enforced before run-time:

No_Task_Hierarchy
    All (non-environment) tasks depend directly on the
    environment task.

No_Nested_Finalization
    Objects with controlled parts and access types that
    designate such objects shall be declared only at
    library level.

No_Abort_Statement
    There are no abort_statements.

No_Terminate_Alternatives
    There are no selective_accepts with terminate
    alternatives.

No_Task_Allocators
    There are no allocators for task types or types
    containing task subcomponents.

No_Implicit_Heap_Allocation
    There are no operations that implicitly require heap
    storage allocation to be performed by the implementation.

No_Dynamic_Priorities
    There are no semantic dependences on the package
    Dynamic_Priorities.

No_Asynchronous_Control
    There are no semantic dependences on the package
    Asynchronous_Task_Control.

The following restrictions are also defined:

Max_Select_Alternatives
    Specifies the maximum number of alternatives in a
    selective_accept.

Max_Task_Entries
    Specifies the maximum number of entries per task. The
    maximum number of entries for each task type (including
    those with entry families) shall be determinable at
    compile-time. A value of zero indicates that no
    rendezvous are possible.

Max_Protected_Entries
    Specifies the maximum number of entries per protected
    type. The maximum number of entries for each protected
    type (including those with entry families) shall be
    determinable at compile-time.

Subject to the implementation permissions given below, the following restrictions are checked at run-time. If a check fails, Storage_Error is raised at the point where the respective construct is elaborated:

Max_Storage_At_Blocking
    Specifies the maximum portion (in storage elements)
    of a task's Storage_Size that can be retained by
    a blocked task.

Max_Asynchronous_Select_Nesting
    Specifies the maximum dynamic nesting level of
    asynchronous_selects. A value of zero prevents the use
    of any asynchronous_select_statement.

Max_Tasks
    Specifies the maximum number of tasks, excluding the
    environment task, that are allowed to exist over the
    lifetime of a partition.

Note that the Safety and Security Annex sets all the above restrictions to zero
(i.e. *no tasking*). It also introduces a further restriction that disallows protected
types and objects. Current practice, in the safety critical application area,
forbids the use of tasks or interrupts. This is unfortunate, as it is possible to
define a subset of the tasking facilities that is both predictable and amenable
to analysis. It is also possible to specify run-time systems so that they can
be implemented to a high level of integrity. One of the challenges facing
Ada practitioners over the coming decade is to demonstrate that concurrent
programming is an effective and safe technique for even the most stringent
of requirements.

12.6 Other provisions

In addition to the features described so far in this chapter, the Real-Time
Systems Annex defines a number of implementation requirements, documen-
tation requirements and metrics. The metrics allow the costs (in processor
cycles) of the run-time system to be obtained. They also indicate which
primitives can lead to blocking, and which must not.

The timing features (i.e. real-time clock and delay primitives) are defined
precisely. It is thus, for example, possible to know the maximum time
between a task's delay value expiring and it being placed on the run queue.
All this information is needed for the analysis of real-time programs.

12.7 Summary

Many concurrent systems are required to execute in real-time (and almost
all real-time systems are inherently concurrent). To support real-time applications, Ada defines a number of facilities in the Real-Time Systems Annex
of the ARM.

In a non-real-time system, it is acceptable for any task that is executable
to use the available processor resources. With real-time systems, control must

be exercised over the use of system resources. The easiest way to do this is to give priorities to tasks and to use the notion of priority to obtain deterministic behaviour that can be analysed. One popular scheduling scheme uses fixed priorities for tasks and ceiling priorities for protected objects. This model is directly supported by the provisions of the Real-Time Systems Annex. Other scheduling approaches can be programmed with the help of routines that allow dynamic priorities to be used.

This chapter has also reviewed the other provisions for real-time programming and the need for fast implementations. Issues considered include the immediacy of abort and various low level (but efficient) synchronisation routines. If an application restricts itself to a subset of the tasking facilities, then it is possible to obtain much more efficient implementations. This subsetting is allowed by the Real-Time Systems Annex; it defines allowable restrictions on the tasking model.

12.8   Further reading

A. Burns and A.J. Wellings, *Real-time Systems and their Programming Languages*, Addison Wesley, Wokingham, 1990.

H. Gomaa, *Software Design Methods for Concurrent and Real-Time Systems*, Addison Wesley, Massachusetts, 1993.

W.A. Halang and A.D. Stoyenko (editors), *Real Time Computing*, Springer Verlag, Heidleberg, 1994.

M.H. Klein, T. Ralya, B. Pollak, R. Obenza, M. Gonzalez Harbour, *A Practitioner's Handbook for Real-Time Analysis*, Kluwer, Boston, 1993.

S.H. Son (editor), *Advances in Real-Time Systems*, Prentice Hall, New Jersey, 1994.

Chapter 13

Object-Oriented Programming and Tasking

The Ada language addresses many aspects of software engineering, and it is beyond the scope of this book to discuss in detail its support for such topics as programming in the large, reuse, etc. Rather, the goal of this book is to discuss, in depth, the Ada model of concurrency and how it is affected by other areas of the language, such as exception handling. This chapter explores the interaction between the object-oriented programming (OOP) facilities and tasking.

Ada 83 was defined long before object-oriented programming became popular, and it is a credit to the new Ada language designers that they have managed to introduce OOP facilities without having to alter the basic structure of an Ada program. However, it should be emphasised that appropriate techniques for object oriented programming within a concurrent programming language context are still very much the subject of research. In particular, there is currently no satisfactory solution for the inheritance anomaly where objects containing synchronisation code cause difficulties for derived objects (Matasuoka, 1993). Ada 95 has avoided these problems by integrating protected types into the model of type extensibility, albeit with some loss of generality.

This chapter first describes the Ada support for OOP briefly; it then considers the interactions with protected units and tasks.

13.1   An overview of Ada's support for OOP

The following sections provide a brief introduction to object-oriented programming in Ada; only the basic mechanisms are described.

Ada supports object-oriented programming through two complimentary mechanisms which provide type extensions and dynamic polymorphism: tagged types and class-wide types.

13.1.1   Tagged types

In Ada, a new type can be *derived*   from an old type and some of the
properties of the type changed using subtyping. For example, the following
declares a new type and a subtype called Setting which has the same
properties as the Integer type but a restricted range. Setting and Integer
are distinct and cannot be interchanged:

> **type** Setting **is new** Integer **range** 1 .. 100;

New operations manipulating Setting can be defined; however no new
components can be added. Tagged types remove this restriction and allow
extra components to be added to a type. Any type that might potentially be
extended in this way must be declared as a tagged type. Because extending
the type inevitably leads to the type becoming a record, only record types
(or private types which are implemented as records) can be tagged.

Consider the example of a package to calculate the cost of heating a
house. The type in this package will then be extended to include modern
energy saving devices:

```
with Money;
package Heating is
   type House is tagged
      record
         Number_Of_Rooms : Natural;
         Number_Of_Bedrooms : Natural;
         Number_Of_Bathrooms : Natural;
         Number_Of_Receptions : Natural;
      end record;

   function Cost_Of_Heating(H : House) return Money.Pounds;
   -- calculates average cost of heating a house using, say,
   -- gas central heating
end Heating;
```

The type House shows the typical characteristics which affect the cost of
heating. The function returns the average cost of heating a particular house,
and is called a primitive operation of the type House [1] The package assumes
no forms of energy saving.

Now suppose that this package is to be extended to take into account
roof (loft) insulation. A child package can be declared which extends the
type and redefines the Cost_Of_Heating function. (Strictly, the package does
not need to be a child package, but this is a common paradigm.)

---

[1]A primitive operation of a tagged type is a subprogram defined with the type declaration
that takes an instance of the type (or access to the type) as a parameter or a result. A
subprogram can only be a primitive operation for a single tagged type.

```
with Data_Types; use Data_Types;
package Heating.Loft_Insulation is

   type Partially_Insulated_House is new House with
      record
         Thickness_Of_Loft_Insulation : Centimetre;
      end record;
   Saving_On_Loft : constant Percentage := 19;

   function Cost_Of_Heating(H : Partially_Insulated_House)
              return Money.Pounds;
end Heating.Loft_Insulation;
```

Here the type `Partially_Insulated_House` is equivalent to the following type definition:

```
type Partially_Insulated_House is
   record
      Number_Of_Rooms : Natural;
      Number_Of_Bedrooms : Natural;
      Number_Of_Bathrooms : Natural;
      Number_Of_Receptions : Natural;
      Thickness_Of_Loft_Insulation : Centimetre;
   end record;
```

The function `Cost_Of_Heating` has been redefined so that it can calculate the cost savings of loft insulation.

Further savings on heating costs can be obtained by installing double glazing; hence this package can be extended further:

```
package Heating.Loft_Insulation.Double_Glazing is

   type Double_Glazing is (PVC, Aluminium);
   Saving_Per_Window : constant Percentage := 2;

   type Insulated_House is new Partially_Insulated_House with
      record
         Glazing : Double_Glazing;
         Number_Of_Windows : Natural;
      end record;

   function Cost_Of_Heating(H : Insulated_House)
              return Money.Pounds;
   function Saving_On_Maintenance(H : Insulated_House)
              return Money.Pounds;
end Heating.Loft_Insulation.Double_Glazing;
```

As well as extending the type and redefining the `Cost_Of_Heating` function, a new subprogram has been added which provides an additional operation. This operation only applies to houses with double glazing and reflects the

fact that older wooden or metal window frames typically require yearly maintenance, whereas modern double glazed windows are, in theory, maintenance
free.

Finally, the type can be extended even further for brick houses with cavity
walls to take cavity wall insulation into account:

```
package Heating.Loft_Insulation.Double_Glazing.Wall_Insulation is
   type Wall_Insulation is (Rockwool, Foam);
   Saving_For_Walls : constant  Percentage := 25;

   type Energy_Efficient_House is new Insulated_House  with
      record
         Cavity_Insulation : Wall_Insulation;
      end record;

   function Cost_Of_Heating(H : Energy_Efficient_House)
                    return Money.Pounds;
end Heating.Loft_Insulation.Double_Glazing.Wall_Insulation;
```

Note that the Saving_On_Maintenance function is not redefined, as there
are no further savings on house maintenance.

In the above example, the Cost_Of_Heating function has been overridden.
However, it is clear that one way of calculating the cost of heating a house
with loft insulation is to take the cost of heating the house without loft
insulation and subtract a percentage saving. A similar method could be used
for other extensions. Hence, the functions may be implemented as follows:

```
function Cost_Of_Heating(H : House) return Money.Pounds is
begin
   -- calculate average cost of heating;
end Cost_Of_Heating;

function Cost_Of_Heating(H : Partially_Insulated_House)
            return Money.Pounds is
   C : Money.Pounds;
begin
   C := Cost_Of_Heating(House(H));
   if H.Thickness_Of_Loft_Insulation > 4 then
       return C - C*Saving_On_Loft/100;
   else
       return C - C*Saving_On_Loft/200;
   end if;
end Cost_Of_Heating;
```

By converting the parameter, H, of type Partially_Insulated_House to type
House, the previous Cost_Of_Heating function can be called to calculate the
cost of heating an un-insulated house. This cost can then be adjusted. The
other functions can be implemented similarly.

```
function Cost_Of_Heating(H : Insulated_House)
        return Money.Pounds is
  C : Money.Pounds;
begin
  C := Cost_Of_Heating(Partially_Insulated_House(H));
  -- calculate % saving
  return C;
end Cost_Of_Heating;

function Cost_Of_Heating(H : Energy_Efficient_House)
        return Money.Pounds is
  C : Money.Pounds;
begin
  C := Cost_Of_Heating(Insulated_House(H));
  return C - C*Saving_For_Walls/100;
end Cost_Of_Heating;
```

13.1.2 Class-wide types

Tagged types provide the mechanism by which types can be extended incrementally. The result is that a programmer can create a hierarchy of related types. Other parts of the program may now wish to manipulate that hierarchy for their own purposes without being too concerned which member of the hierarchy it is processing at any one time. Ada is a strongly typed language and therefore a mechanism is needed by which an object from any member of the hierarchy can be passed as a parameter. For example, consider a local government which wishes to raise money to pay for local services by taxing homes in its area. It wants to be able to write a subprogram that deals with houses of any type.

Class-wide programming is the technique which enables programs to be written which manipulate families of types. Associated with each tagged type there is a type T'Class which comprises all the types which are in the family of types starting at T. For example, House'Class includes the following specific types:

```
House,
Partially_Insulated_House,
Insulated_House,
Energy_Efficient_House
```

On the other hand, the type Partially_Insulated_House'Class includes just:

```
Partially_Insulated_House,
Insulated_House,
Energy_Efficient_House
```

Given the mechanism to define a class-wide type, it is now possible to write programs which manipulate the type. For example, consider the following function to calculate the tax demand on a house:

```
function Tax_Owed(H : House'Class) return Money.Pounds is
begin
   -- calculate the tax owed according to the number of
   -- rooms in the house
end Tax_Owed;
```

To call this function requires

```
Number6 : Insulated_House;
M : Money.Pounds;
   ...
M := Tax_Owed(Number6);
```

The current definition of the Tax_Owed function only makes use of the number of rooms and thus it could have been defined as

```
function Tax_Owed(H : House) return Money.Pounds;
```

and a call could have been written:

```
M := Tax_Owed(House(Number6));
```

However, it is possible that the Tax_Owed function might make use of some of the operations defined on the family of House types. For example, suppose that the local government wished to penalise those occupiers who do not insulate their houses adequately. The formula for calculating the tax owed might now include a component which measures the average energy consumption per room:

```
function Tax_Owed(H : House'Class) return Money.Pounds is
   Average_Cost_Per_Room : Money.Pounds;
begin
   -- calculate the tax owed according to the number of
   -- rooms in the house and the energy consumed per room
   Average_Cost_Per_Room :=
      Cost_Of_Heating(H)/H.Number_Of_Rooms;
   ...
end Tax_Owed;
```

Here the call to Cost_Of_Heating will call the appropriate function associated with the actual type of the parameter passed to Tax_Owed. This is called dynamic dispatching (or run-time polymorphism). The actual parameter passed has a tag which indicates which type it is, and thus at run-time the corresponding operation is called.

An object of type 'Class can be converted to any type in the same hierarchy; however, when this conversion is done it is necessary to perform a run-time check to ensure that the tagged type is in fact compatible. For example, within the Tax_Owed function above, it would be possible to convert H to an object of type Energy_Efficient_House by

```
-- assuming
E : Energy_Efficient_House;
...


E := Energy_Efficient_House(H);
```

If the parameter passed to the procedure were of a type House, Partially_Insulated_House, or Insulated_House, then the conversion would cause a Constraint_Error to be raised. It is possible to check whether a class-wide type is within a particular subclass by using a membership test, For example,

```
if H in Energy_Efficient_House'Class then
  ...
elsif H in Insulated_House'Class then
  ...
else
  ...
end if;
```

Class-wide programming can be performed using access types as well. For example,

```
type House_Address is access House'Class;
```

enables the programmer to construct (say) a list of heterogeneous houses and then dynamically dispatch to the appropriate operation per house. Alternatively, arrays of access variables can be constructed:

```
type Street is array (Positive range <>) of House_Address;

Main_Street : Street(1..52);
```

and dispatching will occur when the access variables are de-referenced:

```
function Heating_Per_Street(S : Street) return Money.Pounds is
  Total_Cost :  Money.Pounds := 0;
begin
  for J in S'Range loop
    Total_Cost := Total_Cost + Cost_Of_Heating(S(J).all);
  end loop;
  return Total_Cost;
end Heating_Per_Street;
```

Access parameters

As well as dispatching on primitive subprograms which have a tagged type
parameter, Ada also allows dispatching to occur on access parameters.
An access parameter is a special type of In parameter which specifies
an anonymous access type. For example, the primitive operations on the
hierarchy of the House tagged type could have been specified using an access
parameter:

```
function New_Cost_Of_Heating(H : access House) return Money.Pounds;
```

A similar approach could have been taken for all primitive operations in the
hierarchy.

The primitive subprograms can be called either by using an access pointer
to a static object or one that is allocated on the heap:

```
type House_Address is access House;
Number6 : aliased Insulated_House;
Minster_View : House_Address := new House;
M1, M2 : Money.Pounds;
    ...
M1 := New_Cost_Of_Heating(Number6'Access);
        -- dispatching occurs
M2 := New_Cost_Of_Heating(Minster_View);
        -- dispatching occurs
```

13.1.3   Abstract types and subprograms

So far, a hierarchy of types has been rooted in a type which has some data
fields. For example, the type House had some fields defining characteristics
common to all types of house. Often it is necessary to define a type
hierarchy where there is no common data, only common properties or
common operations. For example, consider the general type hierarchy
based on buildings. Here the concern is not with any of the details of the
building, only with (for example) the cost of insuring against fire, that is
the market value of the building and the cost of rebuilding. In this case
the type representing a building can be defined as an abstract type, and the
operations as abstract subprograms:

```
with Money; use Money;
package Buildings is

    type Building is abstract tagged null record;

    function Premium(B : access Building) return Pounds is abstract;
    function Market_Value(B : access Building)
```

```
               return Pounds is abstract;
    function Rebuilding_Cost(B : access Building)
               return Pounds is abstract;

end Buildings;
```

This type is defined to be extended (in the normal way) and not for declaring objects; it would be illegal to declare an object of type Building.

As with other class hierarchies, if a subprogram is not concerned with the particular type of building, then it can be defined to operate on parameters of Building'Class type.

Another use of abstract subprograms and types is to allow more than one implementation of the same abstract data type. For example, a Building may be implemented using many different materials:

```
with Money; use Money;
with Buildings; use Buildings;
package Wood_Buildings is
   type Wood_Building is new Building with private;

   function Premium(B : access Wood_Building) return Pounds;
   function Market_Value(B : access Wood_Building) return Pounds;
   function Rebuilding_Cost(B : access Wood_Building)
            return Pounds;
private
   type Wood_Building is new Building with
      record
         -- details of wood technology used
         -- to construct the building
      end record;
end Wood_Buildings;
```

```
with Money; use Money;
with Buildings; use Buildings;
package Brick_Buildings is
   type Brick_Building is new Building with private;

   function Premium(B : access Brick_Building) return Pounds;
   function Market_Value(B : access Brick_Building) return Pounds;
   function Rebuilding_Cost(B : access Brick_Building)
            return Pounds;
private
   type Brick_Building is new Building with
      record
         -- details of Brick technology used
         -- to construct the building
      end record;
end Brick_Buildings;
```

Although each type of building has a completely different implementation, they can all be referred to by the base type name Building, and any subprogram which is not concerned with the implementation technique used can be defined to work on parameters of type Building'Class:

```
procedure Deliver_Mail(B : Building'Class) is
begin
   -- deliver mail to building B
end Deliver_Mail;
```

13.2   Synchronisation, protected units and tagged types

This section discusses the relationship between the Ada OOP model and the facilities for data oriented synchronisation. Consider, first, a package which defines an extensible type:

```
package Object is
   type Obj_Type is tagged limited private;

   procedure Op1(O : in out Obj_Type);
   procedure Op2(O : in out Obj_Type);

private
   type Obj_Type is tagged limited
      record
         . . .
      end record;
end Object;
```

Where objects of this type are destined for a concurrent execution environment, they may be accessed under various conditions. In some cases an object may be required by one task only; in other cases it may be required by more than one task. Also, it may be that different instances of the same object type may be used in different circumstances (one instance may be used by only one task, another by more than one task). For example, consider the case of an object which encapsulates a resource such as a user's visual display unit (VDU). If more than one task wishes to access the VDU, then synchronisation is required to ensure that the tasks' outputs do not become intermingled. However, if only a single task outputs to the display, no synchronisation is required. On some occasions an object, by its very nature, will always be used by more than one task. For example, an object which provides a transient signal (see Section 9.3) will be shared by the sender and the recipient of the signal.

There are at least three basic ways in which objects in a concurrent environment can be constructed:

- Synchronisation is added if and when it is required by extending the object.
- Synchronisation is provided by the base (root) object type.
- Synchronisation is provided as a separate protected type and the data is passed as a discriminant.

The following sections discuss these approaches in detail.

13.2.1 Synchronisation added if and when required by extending the object

Consider again the following type declaration:

```
package Object is
  type Obj_Type is tagged limited private;
  procedure Op1(O : in out Obj_Type);
  procedure Op2(O : in out Obj_Type);

private
  type Field_Type is ...;
  type Obj_Type is tagged limited
    record
      F1 : Field_Type1;
    end record;
end Object;
```

Assume now that an object of this type is to be used by more than one task and that Op1 and Op2 require mutually exclusive access to the object. Assume also that there exists the following protected type which provides a simple mutual exclusion lock (i.e. a call to Lock is held if there has been a previous call to Lock and no associated call to Unlock):

```
protected type Mutex is
  entry Lock;
  procedure Unlock;
end Mutex;
```

Obj_Type can be extended to include an instance of the lock, and the operations redefined to implement the required synchronisation:

```
package Object.Synchronised is
  type Protected_Type is new Obj_Type with private;

  procedure Op1(O : in out Protected_Type);
  procedure Op2(O : in out Protected_Type);

private
  type Protected_Type is new  Obj_Type with
```

```
         record
           L : Mutex;
         end record;
       end Object.Synchronised;
```

where

```
       procedure Op1(O :  in out Protected_Type) is
       begin
         O.L.Lock;
         Op1(Obj_Type(O));
         O.L.Unlock;
       exception
         when others =>
           O.L.Unlock;
           raise;
       end Op1;
```

A similar approach can be taken with Op2. Note that the "catch all" exception handler is required to ensure that any unhandled exceptions raised by the operations do not leave the object locked. [2]

There are two potential problems that will occur in *any* concurrent object-oriented programming language which supports this general approach:

1. The system is inherently unsafe. The data can be accessed without protection by simply converting the data to the type Obj_Type and calling Object.Op1.

2. If at a later stage the type is extended and the mutual exclusion retained, then the following would lead to deadlock at run-time:

```
       package Object.Synchronised.Extended is
         type Extended_Protected_Type is new Protected_Type with private;

         procedure Op1(O : in out Extended_Protected_Type);
         procedure Op2(O : in out Extended_Protected_Type);

       private
         type Extended_Protected_Type is new Protected_Type with
           record
             F2 :Field_Type2;
           end record;
       end Object.Synchronised.Extended;
```

---

[2]Note that, to make this approach resilient to abort or ATC, the lock and unlock operation could be encapsulated in the initialisation and finalisation subprograms of a dummy controlled type. This technique was used in Section 6.6.1.

where

```
procedure Op1(O :  in out Extended_Protected_Type) is
begin
   O.L.Lock;
   -- potentially some extra manipulation of the data
   Op1(Protected_Type(O));
   -- potentially some extra manipulation of the data
   O.L.Unlock;
exception
   when others =>
      O.L.Unlock;
      raise;
end Op1;
```

Here the Op1 procedure locks the data and then carries out some operations associated with the extension. It then calls the original Synchronised.Op1; unfortunately this also tries to lock the data which is already locked (and hence deadlock will occur).

One possible, yet flawed, solution to this problem is for Synchronised.Extended.Op1 to unlock the data before calling Synchronised.Op1. However, this would potentially allow another task to obtain the lock before the call to Synchronised.Op1. Alternatively, a protected unit could be used which allows the same task to acquire the lock more than once.

If the type is extended and then the locking procedure re-introduced, the system is still inherently insecure. For example,

```
package Object.Extended is
   type Extended_Obj_Type is new Obj_Type with private;

   procedure Op1(O :  in out Extended_Obj_Type);
   procedure Op2(O :  in out Extended_Obj_Type);

private
   type Extended_Obj_Type is new Obj_Type with
      record
         F2 :Field_Type2;
      end record;
end Object.Extended;


package Object.Extended.Synchronised is
   type Protected_Extended_Obj_Type is
           new Extended_Obj_Type with private;

   procedure Op1(O :  in out Protected_Extended_Obj_Type);
   procedure Op2(O :  in out Protected_Extended_Obj_Type);
```

```
      private
        type Protected_Extended_Obj_Type is new Extended_Obj_Type with
        record
          L : Mutex;
        end record;
      end Object.Extended.Synchronised;
```

where

```
      procedure Op1(O : in out Protected_Extended_Obj_Type) is
      begin
        O.L.Lock;
        Op1(Extended_Obj_Type(O));
        O.L.Unlock;
      end Op1;
```

Here, the protection can be violated by calling the existing object directly.

13.2.2 Synchronisation provided by the base (root) object type

If the object introduced in the previous section requires mutually exclusive access to its data, then, ideally, it should now be a protected type. However, the Ada language does not allow a protected type to be extended. This restriction is necessary to keep the semantics of the language and the implementation simple. For example, it is not clear what the semantics of an overridden entry should be, particularly in the context of requeue.

To circumvent this restriction, a lock object is again required; this time it is included in the root type definition:

```
      package Protected_Object is
        type Protected_Type is tagged limited private;

        procedure Op1(O : in out Protected_Type);
        procedure Op2(O : in out Protected_Type);

      private
        type Protected_Type is tagged limited
          record
            F1 : Field_Type1;
            L  : Mutex;
          end record;
      end Protected_Object;
```

where

```
      procedure Op1(O :  Protected_Type) is
      begin
        O.L.Lock;
```

```
      -- perform operation
      O.L.Unlock;
   exception
      when others =>
         O.L.Unlock;
         raise;
   end Op1;
```

This approach suffers from the same problems as those identified in the previous section; if the type is extended, then obtaining mutual exclusion over the new operations is difficult.

An alternative approach is to define the base type to contain only the lock, and to have the actual operations abstract and private. The only operations exported from the package are thus class-wide ones. This means that only child library units can extend the object:

```
package Protected_Object is
   type Protected_Type is abstract tagged limited private;

   procedure Class_Wide_Op1(O : in out Protected_Type'Class);
   procedure Class_Wide_Op2(O : in out Protected_Type'Class);

private
   type Protected_Type is abstract tagged limited
      record
         L : Mutex;
      end record;

   procedure Op1(O : in out Protected_Type) is abstract;
   procedure Op2(O : in out Protected_Type) is abstract;
end Protected_Object;
```

It is now possible to define the operation which acts on the class-wide type as

```
package body Protected_Object is
   ...

   procedure Class_Wide_Op1(O : in out Protected_Type'Class) is
   begin
      O.L.Lock;
      Op1(O); -- dispatch to correct operation
      O.L.Unlock;
   exception
      when others =>
         O.L.Unlock;
   end Class_Wide_Op1;

end Protected_Object;
```

Now the type can be extended without being concerned with protection issues, and the tree of types still maintains its protected status *if the user calls the operations with the class-wide parameter*:

```
Class_Wide_Op1(Some_Type_Derived_From_Protected_Type);
```

Of course, this solution is still not secure as the user could call a child operation directly. However, the interface can protect against this by making these operations private as well:

```
package Protected_Object.Extended is
  type Extended_Protected_Type is new Protected_Type with private;

  procedure Class_Wide_Op3(O : in out Extended_Protected_Type'Class);
private
  procedure Op1(O : in out Extended_Protected_Type);
  procedure Op2(O : in out Extended_Protected_Type);
  procedure Op3(O : in out Extended_Protected_Type);
  type Extended_Protected_Type is new Protected_Type with
    record
      ...
    end record;
end Protected_Object.Extended;
```

where further operations can be added, for example Op3:

```
procedure Op3(O : in out Extended_Protected_Type) is
begin
  ...
end Op3;

procedure Class_Wide_Op3(O : in out
                         Extended_Protected_Type'Class) is
begin
  O.L.Lock;
  Op3(O); -- dispatch to correct operation
  O.L.Unlock;
exception
  when others =>
    O.L.Unlock;
end Class_Wide_Op3;
```

Although this approach allows both the type and the operations to be extended, it can become difficult to program the required synchronisation between the operations. Suppose, for example, that concurrent Op3 calls are allowed (but not concurrent with Op1 or Op2). It would be necessary to implement another type of lock which allows shared and exclusive modes. Further problems arise if the synchronisation is user defined. This is an example of inheritance anomaly.

Also, it should be stressed that the users of these protected data structures would be unable to apply time-outs directly (as they would if the data type were a true protected type) but would have to pass a time-out value as a parameter to each operation. Asynchronous transfer of control operations would also not be possible.

13.2.3 Synchronisation using a protected type with the data passed as a discriminant

The third way of providing an extensible protected type is to define the base type to be protected first, along with all its potentially protected operations. A protected type can then be constructed whose operations mirror those of the type and have a class-wide access discriminant:

```
package Object is
   type Obj_Type is abstract tagged null record;

   protected type Controller (O : access Obj_Type'Class) is
      procedure Op1;
      procedure Op2;
   end Controller;
private
   procedure Op1(O : in out Obj_Type) is abstract;
   procedure Op2(O : in out Obj_Type) is abstract;
end Object;


package body Object is
   protected body Controller  is
      procedure Op1 is
      begin
         Op1(O.all);
      end Op1;

      procedure Op2 is
      begin
         Op2(O.all);
      end Op2;
   end Controller;
end Object;
```

With this approach, the full power of protected types can be used to obtain the required synchronisation between the operations. An example of its use is as follows:

```
package Object.My_Object is
   type Obj is private;
private
```

```
type Obj is new Obj_Type with record ... end record;
procedure Op1(O : in out Obj);
procedure Op2(O : in out Obj);
end Object.My_Object;

   ...

O : aliased Obj;
Cont : Controller(O'Access);
   ...
Cont.Op1;
```

In the above example, mutually exclusive access is guaranteed; alternatively the operations could have been implemented as protected functions or protected entries.

The advantage of this approach is that the types can be easily extended and securely accessed under the required synchronisation constraints (as long as the original operations are kept private) and, if appropriate, timed and conditional entry calls can be used. The main problem is that extra synchronised operations cannot be added because it is not possible to extend the protected controller.

Note that, with this approach, it is also possible to make the protected type private and to provide a procedure interface. However, timed and conditional entry calls would then not be directly available to the clients, thereby nullifying one of the main advantages of this approach over the previous two approaches.

13.3   Reusable and extensible communication abstractions

In Chapter 9, several communication and synchronisation abstractions were defined using protected units. Some of those abstractions were for synchronisation only; others required data flow as well. This section will consider those which require data flow:

* a bounded buffer,

* a blackboard,

* a multicast,

and will show how the abstractions can be implemented within the framework of the extensible types.

The previous section considered the various ways in which protected types and the Ada OOP model could be used. In this section, the model of passing the data as an access type to a protected type is adopted.

Previously, these abstractions have been implemented as generics, and it is appropriate to consider first why the implementation model should be changed. Consider the buffer example; this was previously defined as

```
generic
   type Message is private;
package Buffers is

   Max_Capacity : constant Natural := Maximum;
      --set to some appropriate value
   subtype Capacity_Range is Natural range 0..Max_Capacity - 1;
   subtype Count is Natural range 0..Max_Capacity;
   type Buffer_Array is array(Capacity_Range) of Message;

   protected type Buffer(Capacity : Capacity_Range) is
      entry Get(Item: out Message);
      entry Put(Item: in Message);
      function Buffer_Capacity return Capacity_Range;
   private
      First : Capacity_Range := Capacity_Range'First;
      Last : Capacity_Range := Capacity_Range'First;
      Number_In_Buffer : Count := 0;
      Store : Buffer_Array;
   end Buffer;
end Buffers;
```

There are two basic limitations with this approach:

1. It is not possible to define a single buffer type of, say, integers which can have different implementations (say, an array or a linked list). The above definition allows an integer array-based buffer to be instantiated, but a new definition would be required to create a link-based buffer. Even if this were done there would be no relationship between the two buffers implemented and the protected type interfaces.

2. It is not possible to define a procedure which simply wants to manipulate a buffer (without regard to the actual data stored in the buffer), for example a buffer name server. Different instantiations of the buffer have different data types.

However, as will be illustrated below, it is not always straightforward to combine a completely abstract data type with a synchronisation controller.

13.3.1 Bounded buffers

An object, in general, is defined by its internal state (often called *instance variables*) and its operations (and their parameters). In the following package, the type Buffer represents the instance variables of the bounded buffer object, and the type Data is the type of data to be stored in the buffer.

These two types are related, in that the Buffer will need to store data of
type Data. However, the two types are clearly not identical. The buffer
and its operations are all abstract; note that the operations are primitive
operations on the Buffer *not* on the Data (remember, Ada only allows a
given subprogram to be a primitive operation for one tagged type). It is
therefore necessary to pass the data parameter as a class-wide type.

A shared buffer is defined by using a protected type to provide the required
synchronisation. Note that, as the protected type can store a pointer to
the buffer implementation, it is possible to pass this pointer as an access
discriminant to the Buffer_Controller rather than with each operation:

```
package Buffers is

    type Data is abstract tagged null record;

    type Buffer is abstract tagged private;

    -- Basic protected Buffer
    protected type Buffer_Controller (B : access Buffer'Class) is
        entry Put(D :  in  Data'Class);
        entry Get(D :  out Data'Class);
    end Buffer_Controller;
private
    type Buffer is abstract tagged null record;
    procedure Put(D : Data'Class; B : access Buffer) is abstract;
    procedure Get(D : out Data'Class; B : access Buffer) is abstract;
    function Buffer_Not_Full(B : access Buffer)
                    return Boolean is abstract;
    function Buffer_Not_Empty(B : access Buffer)
                    return Boolean is abstract;

end Buffers;

package body Buffers is

    protected body Buffer_Controller is
        entry Put(D : in Data'Class) when Buffer_Not_Full(B.all) is
            -- note buffer_not_full(B) is a dispatching operation
        begin
            Put(D,B); -- dispatching operation
        end Put;

        entry Get(D : out  Data'Class)
                when Buffer_Not_Empty(B.all) is
            -- note buffer_Not_Empty(B) is a dispatching operation
        begin
            Get(D,B); -- dispatching operation
        end Get;
    end Buffer_Controller;
end Buffers;
```

The implementation of the Buffer_Controller simply calls the non-synchronised operations on the buffer, which dispatch to the correct routines.

To use the protected buffer requires the buffer data type and its implementation to be defined. By defining the implementation first (and keeping the buffer as abstract), it is possible to reuse the basic implementation strategy for a range of buffer types:

```
package Buffers.Array_Based_Buffers is

  type Array_Buffer is abstract new Buffer with private;

private
  Buffer_Size : constant Natural := 10;
    -- The package could be made generic, and the size
    -- passed as a generic parameter
  subtype Index is Natural range 0 .. Buffer_Size - 1;
  subtype Count is Natural range 0 .. Buffer_Size;

  type Array_Buffer is abstract new Buffer with record
    First : Index := Index'First;
    Last : Index := Index'First;
    Number_In_Buffer : Count := 0;
  end record;
  procedure Put(D : Data'Class; B : access Array_Buffer)
          is abstract;
  procedure Get(D : out Data'Class; B : access Array_Buffer)
          is abstract;
  function Buffer_Not_Full(B : access Array_Buffer) return Boolean
          is abstract;
  function Buffer_Not_Empty(B : access Array_Buffer) return Boolean
          is abstract;
end Buffers.Array_Based_Buffers;
```

Note that it is not possible to define the actual buffer data storage within the above package, as the data type is unknown still. Therefore, a new package must be created to give the element type and the buffer implementation; for example, in the following an integer buffer using an array-based implementation is defined:

```
package Buffers.Array_Based_Buffers.Integer_Buffers is

  type Integer_Data is new Data with record
    X : Integer;
  end record;

  type Integer_Array_Buffer is new Array_Buffer with private;

private
  -- a bounded buffer

  type Integer_Array is array (Index) of Integer_Data;
```

```
-- child package has visibility of
-- the private part of the parent


type Integer_Array_Buffer is new Array_Buffer with record
  Mb1 : Integer_Array;
end record;


procedure Put(D : Data'Class; B : access Integer_Array_Buffer);
procedure Get(D : out Data'Class; B : access Integer_Array_Buffer);
function Buffer_Not_Full(B : access Integer_Array_Buffer)
        return Boolean;
function Buffer_Not_Empty(B : access Integer_Array_Buffer)
        return Boolean;


end Buffers.Array_Based_Buffers.Integer_Buffers;
```

Integer_Data is derived from the Data and an integer field is added. The
buffer type Integer_Array_Buffer is derived from Array_Buffer and is
made private, so that the user is still unaware of the implementation. The
buffer itself can then be declared, as can the buffer controller. Note that the
buffer must be aliased as an access value is required by the buffer controller.
The primitive operations on the new buffer are declared as 'private' to ensure
that clients cannot access the buffer except through the buffer controller.

The implementation of the package can now be given:

```
package body Buffers.Array_Based_Buffers.Integer_Buffers is

  procedure Put(D : Data'Class;
                B : access Integer_Array_Buffer) is
  begin
    B.Mb1(B.Last) := Integer_Data(D);
                     -- may generate Constraint_Error
    B.Last := (B.Last + 1) mod Buffer_Size;
    B.Number_In_Buffer := B.Number_In_Buffer + 1;
  exception
    when Constraint_Error =>
      -- potential error recovery
      raise;
  end Put;

  procedure Get(D : out Data'Class;
                B : access Integer_Array_Buffer) is
  begin
    D := B.Mb1(B.First);
    B.First := (B.First + 1) mod Buffer_Size;
    B.Number_In_Buffer := B.Number_In_Buffer - 1;
  end Get;

  function Buffer_Not_Full(B : access Integer_Array_Buffer)
          return Boolean is
```

```
      begin
         return B.Number_In_Buffer = Buffer_Size;
      end Buffer_Not_Full;

      function Buffer_Not_Empty(B : access Integer_Array_Buffer)
               return Boolean is
      begin
         return B.Number_In_Buffer /= 0;
      end Buffer_Not_Empty;
   end Buffers.Array_Based_Buffers.Integer_Buffers;
```

Note that, although the buffer is for the Integer_Data type, it must be prepared to receive a request for any data in the class hierarchy; hence the following situation could occur because the buffer controller is defined in terms of the class-wide type:

```
with Buffers.Array_Based_Buffers.Integer_Buffers;
with Character_Buffers;
with Buffers;
   ...

   Mb1 : aliased Buffers.Array_Based_Buffers.
                 Integer_Buffers.Integer_Array_Buffer;
   Pb1 : Buffers.Buffer_Controller(Mb1'Access);

   Mb2 : aliased Buffers.Array_Based_Buffers.Character_Buffers.
                 Character_Array_Buffer;
   Pb2 : Buffers.Buffer_Controller(Mb2'Access);

   D1 : Integer_Buffers.Integer_Data;
   D2 : Character_Buffers.Character_Data1;

begin

      Pb1.Put(D1); -- valid call
      Pb2.Put(D2); -- valid call
      Pb1.Put(D2);  -- raises Constraint_Error
      Pb2.Put(D1);  -- raises Constraint_Error
      -- similarly a Get from the buffer might raise
      -- Constraint_Error if the types are incompatible
   end;
```

As the above illustrates, with this approach it is possible to get the buffers confused and to attempt to obtain character data from an integer buffer! This will result in a run-time exception being raised.

In spite of the problem noted above, this approach is quite elegant and allows the type to be extended. *However, as previously mentioned, this overall approach does not allow new protected operations to be added using inheritance.* For example, the user is unable to add an operation which reads the next item in the buffer without extracting it.

13.3.2   Blackboards

An extensible Blackboard is presented below. The example first assumes that the user provides the storage for the blackboard but that the controller provides a flag which indicates whether the data is valid. Strictly, the implementation of the valid/invalid abstraction should be left to the user. However, in this example there is little scope for an alternative implementation of this flag; consequently the controller maintains the status. Furthermore, allowing the implementation to become completely abstract often complicates the interface. To illustrate this, the completely abstract blackboard is also presented.

The blackboard abstraction is similar to the buffer abstraction in that it requires both the data and the implementation to be passed. As with the buffer, the operations are primitive for the blackboard implementation rather than the blackboard data type (which is defined to be class-wide):

```
package Blackboards is

    type Message is abstract tagged null record;
    type Blackboard is abstract tagged private;

    type Blackboard_State is (Valid, Invalid);

    protected type Blackboard_Controller
                    (Bs : access Blackboard'Class) is
        procedure Display(M : Message'Class);
        procedure Clear;
        function State return Blackboard_State;
        entry Read(M : out Message'Class);
    end Blackboard_Controller;
private
    type Blackboard is abstract tagged record
        Status : Blackboard_State := Invalid;
    end record;
    procedure Display(M : Message'Class;
                        S: access Blackboard) is abstract;
    procedure Read(M : out Message'Class;
                        S: access Blackboard) is abstract;

end Blackboards;


package body Blackboards is

    protected body Blackboard_Controller is
        procedure Display(M : Message'Class) is
        begin
            Display(M, Bs); -- dispatches
            Bs.Status := Valid;
        end Display;
```

```
    procedure Clear is
    begin
      Bs.Status := Invalid;
    end Clear;

    function State return Blackboard_State is
    begin
      return Bs.Status;
    end State;

    entry Read(M : out Message'Class) when Bs.Status = Valid is
    begin
      Read(M, Bs); -- dispatches
    end;
  end Blackboard_Controller;

end Blackboards;
```

Use of the blackboard might take the following form:

```
package Blackboards.My_Blackboard is

  type My_Message is new Message with
    record
      -- Data to be displayed
    end record;

  type My_Implementation is new Blackboard with private;

private
  type My_Implementation is new Blackboard with
    record
      S : My_Message;
    end record;
  procedure Display(M : My_Message'Class;
                    Bs: access My_Implementation);
  procedure Read(M : out My_Message'Class;
                    Bs: access My_Implementation );
end Blackboards.My_Blackboard;


package body Blackboards.My_Blackboard is

  procedure Display(M : My_Message'Class;
                    Bs: access My_Implementation) is
  begin
    Bs.S := My_Message(M); -- possible Constraint_Error
  end Display ;

  procedure Read (M : out My_Message'Class;
                    Bs: access My_Implementation) is
```

```
      begin
         M:= Bs.S;
      end Read ;
   end Blackboards.My_Blackboard;


   with Blackboards.My_Blackboard; use Blackboards.My_Blackboard;
   with Blackboards; use Blackboards;

      ...
   My_Blackboard : aliased My_Implementation;
   Controller : Blackboard_Controller(My_Blackboard'Access);
```

A completely abstract blackboard

When the implementation of an abstract synchronised data type is left open,
the abstract interface becomes more complex. For example, consider the case
of the blackboard where the valid/invalid implementation is to be provided
by the user. It is now necessary to provide two extra subprograms: one
for determining if the status is valid, and another for setting the status to
invalid:

```
   package Blackboards is

      type Message is abstract tagged null record;
      type Blackboard  is abstract tagged private;
      type Blackboard_State is (Valid, Invalid);

      protected type Blackboard_Controller
                     (B: access Blackboard'Class) is
         procedure Display(M : Message'Class);
         procedure Clear;
         function State return Blackboard_State;
         entry Read(M : out Message'Class);
      end Blackboard_Controller;
   private
      type Blackboard is abstract tagged null record;
      procedure Display(M : Message'Class; B:
                        access Blackboard) is abstract;
      procedure Read(M : out Message'Class;
                     B: access Blackboard) is abstract;

      function Valid(B: access Blackboard) return Boolean is abstract;
      procedure Clear(B: access Blackboard) is abstract;
   end Blackboards;


   package body Blackboards is
```

```
      protected body Blackboard_Controller is
        procedure Display(M : Message'Class) is
        begin
          Display(M, B);
        end Display;

        procedure Clear is
        begin
          Clear(B); -- dispatches
        end Clear;

        function State return Blackboard_State is
        begin
          if Valid(B) then return Valid; -- Valid(B) dispatches
          else
            return Invalid;
          end if;
        end State;

        entry Read(M : out Message'Class) when Valid(B) is
        begin
          Read(M, B);
        end;
      end Blackboard_Controller;

    end Blackboards;
```

Use of the blackboard might take the following form:

```
    package Blackboards.My_Blackboard is

      type My_Message is new Blackboards.Message with
        record
          -- Data to be displayed
        end record;

      type My_Implementation is new
          Blackboards.Blackboard with private;

    private
      type My_Implementation is new Blackboards.Blackboard with
        record
          The_Message : My_Message;
          Status : Blackboards.Blackboard_State;
          -- could use an alternative implementation
          -- if the user wished
        end record;

      procedure Display(M : Message'Class;
                        B: access My_Implementation);
      procedure Read(M : out Message'Class;
                     B: access My_Implementation);
      function Valid(B: access My_Implementation) return Boolean;
```

```ada
     procedure Clear(B: access My_Implementation);
  end Blackboards.My_Blackboard;


  package body Blackboards.My_Blackboard is

    procedure Display(M : My_Message'Class;
                      B: access My_Implementation) is
    begin
      B.The_Message := My_Message(M);
    end Display ;

    procedure Read(M : out My_Message'Class;
                   B: access My_Implementation) is
    begin
      M:= B.The_Message;
    end Read;

    function Valid(B: access My_Implementation) return Boolean is
    begin
      return (B.Status = Valid);
    end Valid;

    procedure Clear(B: access My_Implementation) is
    begin
      B.Status := Invalid;
    end Clear;

  end Blackboards.My_Blackboard;


  with Blackboards.My_Blackboard; use Blackboards.My_Blackboard;
  with Blackboards; use Blackboards;

    ...

  My_Blackboard : aliased My_Implementation;
  Controller : Blackboards.Blackboard_Controller(
                      My_Blackboard'Access);
```

13.3.3   Multicasts

With the multicast communication abstraction,   there might be various
alternative implementations for keeping track of which task has received the
data. Consequently, the controller should ideally be completely abstract;
however, the interactions between the controller and the implementation
approach are quite complex and would require many extra subprograms
to be defined. This is left as an exercise for the reader. Here a simpler
version is presented which is abstract in its message type but concrete in its
implementation of the Group.

The package uses task identifiers to keep track of tasks. The subprograms Save and Get are abstract and are used to access the variables provided by the user to store a message whilst it is being multicast. The Multicast_Controller protected type provides the required synchronisation:

```
with Ada.Task_Identification; use Ada.Task_Identification;
package Multicasts is

   type Message is abstract tagged null record;
   type Group is abstract tagged private;

   Already_Member, Not_Member, Group_Too_Large,
   Group_Empty : exception;

   procedure Save(M : Message'Class;
                  Gs: access Group) is abstract;

   procedure Get(M : out Message'Class;
                 Gs: access Group) is abstract;


   Max_Group_Size : constant Positive := Maximum;
                      --set to some appropriate value
   type Group_Size_Range is range 1 .. Max_Group_Size;
   Default_Group_Size : constant Group_Size_Range := ...;
                      --set to some appropriate value

   type Task_Status is private;
   Default_Status : constant Task_Status;

   type Group_Tasks is
        array(Group_Size_Range range <>) of Task_Status;


   protected type Multicast_Controller
        (Storage : access Group'Class := null;
         Max_Size : Group_Size_Range := Default_Group_Size) is
      procedure Join_Group;
        -- raises Already_Member, Group_Too_Large
      procedure Leave_Group;
        -- raises Not_Member

      entry Send(This_Message : Message'Class);
        -- raises Group_Empty

      entry Receive(A_Message : out Message'Class);
        -- raises Not_Member

   private
      entry Wait_Next_Message(A_Message : out Message'Class);
```

```
      Message_Available : Boolean := False;
      New_Message_Arrived : Boolean := False;
      Ok_To_Send : Boolean := True;
      Group : Group_Tasks(1 .. Max_Size) :=
             (others => Default_Status);

   end Multicast_Controller;



private
   type Group is abstract tagged null record;

   type Task_Status is
      record
         Id : Task_Id;
         Received : Boolean;
      end record;
   Default_Status : constant Task_Status :=
                       (Null_Task_Id, False);
end Multicasts;



package body Multicasts is
   protected body Multicast_Controller is

      function All_Received return Boolean is
      begin
         -- check if all tasks in the Group
         -- have received the data
      end All_Received;

      function Already_Received(Id : Task_Id) return Boolean is
      begin
         -- check if task has received the data
      end Already_Received;


      procedure Log_Received(Id : Task_Id) is
      begin
         -- log that task has received the data
      end Log_Received;

      procedure Clear_Received is
      begin
         -- set all Boolean flags in Group array to False
      end Clear_Received;

      procedure Join_Group is
      begin
         -- save ID of Current_Task in Group array and set
         -- up receive value; raise Already_Member,
```

```ada
   -- or Group_Full if appropriate
end;



procedure Leave_Group is
begin
  -- delete ID of Current_Task in Group array
  -- raise Not_Member if appropriate
  if Message_Available and All_Received then
    Message_Available := False;
    Ok_To_Send := True;
    Clear_Received;
  end if;
end;



entry Send(This_Message: Message'Class) when Ok_To_Send is
begin
  -- if empty group raise Group_Empty
  Ok_To_Send := False;
  New_Message_Arrived := True;
  Save(This_Message, Storage);
end Send;



entry Receive(A_Message : out Message'Class) when True is
  Id :Task_Id :=  Receive'Caller;
begin
  -- if not member raise exception
  if Message_Available then
    if Already_Received(Id) then
      requeue Wait_Next_Message;
    else
      Log_Received(Id);
      Get(A_Message, Storage);
      if All_Received then
        Ok_To_Send := True;
        Message_Available := False;
        Clear_Received;
      end if;
    end if;
  else
    requeue Wait_Next_Message;
  end if;
end Receive;



entry Wait_Next_Message(A_Message : out Message'Class)
              when New_Message_Arrived is
  Id :Task_Id :=  Wait_Next_Message'Caller;
```

```
      begin
        Log_Received(Id);
        Get(A_Message, Storage);
        if All_Received then
          Ok_To_Send := True;
          New_Message_Arrived := False;
          Clear_Received;
        elsif Wait_Next_Message'Count=0 then
          New_Message_Arrived := False;
          Message_Available := True;
        else
          null;
        end if;
      end Wait_Next_Message;
    end Multicast_Controller;
  end Multicasts;
```

A user of the multicast facility would contain the following code:

```
with Multicasts; use Multicasts;
package My_Multicasts is

  type My_Message is new Message with
    record
      ...
    end record;

  type My_Group is new
      Group with private;

private
  type My_Group_Implementation is new Group with
    record
      M : My_Message;
    end record;

  procedure Save(M : Message'Class; Gs: access My_Group);
  procedure Get(M : out Message'Class; Gs: access My_Group);

end My_Multicasts;


package body My_Multicasts is

  procedure Save(M : Message'Class; Gs: access My_Group) is
  begin
    Gs.M := My_Message(M);
  end Save;

  procedure Get(M : out Message'Class; Gs: access My_Group) is
  begin
    M := Gs.M;
```

```
    end Get;

end My_Multicasts;

with My_Multicasts; use My_Multicasts;
with Multicasts; use Multicasts;

    ...

Storage : aliased My_Group;

Controller : Multicast_Controller(Storage'Access);
```

13.4   Tasks and tagged types

In Chapter 4, it was noted that tasks could have discriminants which could either be of a discrete type or an access type. It is the latter which enables tasks to make use of the Ada OOP facilities (in a similar fashion to protected types presented in the previous section).

This section presents a single example which illustrates how reusable tasks can be constructed. Consider, for example, a parallel sorting algorithm (similar to that given by Andrews (1991) and Magee *et al.* (1993)). A group of tasks are connected by bounded buffers and between them they sort data. The algorithm for sorting is independent of the data to be sorted: all that is required is a subprogram which, given two data items, indicates if one is "less than" the other.

The algorithm is illustrated in Figure 13.1.

If there are Number_Of_Data_Items_To_Sort then there are Number_Of_Data_Items_To_Sort - 1 tasks. Each task is connected to three channels: two input channels and one output channel. Data on an input channel is assumed to be sorted. The task merges two sorted channels to a single output channel. Obviously, a task must be able to detect the end of an input stream.

The algorithm makes use of the Buffers package developed in Section 13.3.1. Each buffer represents a channel with a capacity (to allow the tasks to run as asynchronously as possible). Consider, first, the following package specification:

```
with Buffers; use Buffers;
package Parallel_Sort is

    type Sortable_Data is abstract new Data with
    record
       Terminator : Boolean;
    end record;
```

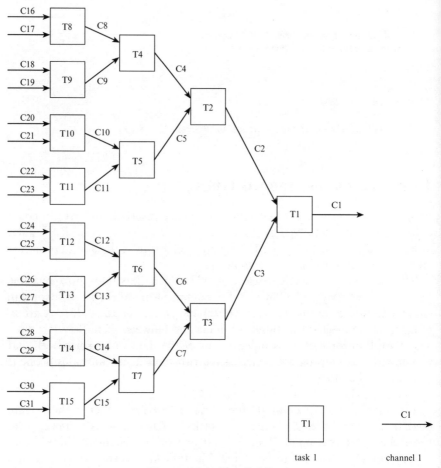

Figure 13.1: Parallel Sort.

```
function "<" (Lhs, Rhs : Sortable_Data)
    return Boolean is abstract;

task type Merge(In_Chan1, In_Chan2,
                Out_Chan : access Buffer_Controller;
                Actual_Data : access Sortable_Data'Class);
end Parallel_Sort;
```

To detect the end of data on a channel requires a special data item. The package thus extends the abstract data type Data to have a boolean which, when set, indicates that there is no more data. An abstract function "¡" is also defined so that the package is independent of the data to be sorted.

Finally, a task type is defined which has three access discriminants (one for each of the channels) and an access value to a dummy data item whose type will correspond to the type of the data which will actually be sorted. This is needed to initialise class-wide variables in the task's body.

The body of the package is given below: D1 and D2 are class-wide values and can therefore contain any data derived from Sortable_Data. However, they must be initialised so that the compiler can determine the size of the data. The algorithm itself is reasonably self-explanatory. The tasks merge the two channels until there is no data left:

```
package body Parallel_Sort is
   task body Merge is
      -- the following dummy assignments are required to
      -- determine the size of the data item to be sorted
      D1 : Sortable_Data'Class := Actual_Data.all;
      D2 : Sortable_Data'Class := Actual_Data.all;
      Term : Sortable_Data'Class := Actual_Data.all;
   begin
      Term.Terminator := True;
      In_Chan1.Get(D1);
      In_Chan2.Get(D2);
      while not D1.Terminator and not D2.Terminator loop
         if D1 < D2 then
            Out_Chan.Put(D1);
            In_Chan1.Get(D1);
         else
            Out_Chan.Put(D2);
            In_Chan2.Get(D2);
         end if;
      end loop;
      if D1.Terminator then
         while not D2.Terminator loop
            Out_Chan.Put(D2);
            In_Chan2.Get(D2);
         end loop;
      else
         while not D1.Terminator loop
            Out_Chan.Put(D1);
            In_Chan1.Get(D1);
         end loop;
      end if;
      Out_Chan.Put(Term);
   end Merge;
end Parallel_Sort;
```

Having defined the parallel sorter, it is now necessary to provide the data to be sorted. The following package does this. My_Data is the data to be sorted, and is an extension of Sortable_Data. The storage type for the bounded buffers is defined:

```
with Buffers.Array_Based_Buffers;
use Buffers.Array_Based_Buffers;
with Buffers; use Buffers;
with Parallel_Sort; use Parallel_Sort;
package Sorter is

   type My_Data is new Sortable_Data with
     record
       ....
     end record;

   type Buf is array (1 .. 5) of My_Data;

   type My_Buffer is new Array_Buffer with
     record
        B : Buf;
     end record;

private
   procedure Put(D : Data'Class; B : access My_Buffer);
   procedure Get(D : out Data'Class; B : access My_Buffer);
   function Buffer_Not_Full(B : access My_Buffer) return Boolean;
   function Buffer_Not_Empty(B : access My_Buffer) return Boolean;
   function "<" (Lhs, Rhs : My_Data) return Boolean;
end Sorter;
```

The body of the package creates the buffers, which are then associated with
the buffer controllers (note that it is necessary to use functions with side
effects as Ada does not allow a suitable way of initialising discriminants in
an array). Note that the details of the buffer implementation variables and
access routines are not of interest in this example.

Once the buffers have been created, the sorter tasks can be created and
initialised with their correct channels. The package then simply reads the
data to be sorted and outputs each data item to the appropriate input
channels, followed by a terminator data item:

```
package body Sorter is

   Number_Of_Data_Items : constant Positive := 8; -- say
   Num_Of_Chans : Positive := 2*Number_Of_Data_Items - 1;

   Buf_Number : Natural := 0;
   Out_Chan_Number : Natural := 0;
   In1_Chan_Number : Natural := 0;
   In2_Chan_Number : Natural := 1;

   Terminated : aliased My_Data;

   Bufs : array(1 .. 2*Number_Of_Data_Items - 1) of
            aliased My_Buffer;
```

```
function Next_Buf return Integer is
  -- used for array initialisation
begin
  Buf_Number := Buf_Number + 1;
  return Buf_Number;
end Next_Buf;

Channels : array(1 .. 2*Number_Of_Data_Items - 1) of
           aliased Buffer_Controller(Bufs(Next_Buf)'Access);


function Outchan return Integer is
  -- used for array initialisation
begin
 Out_Chan_Number := Out_Chan_Number + 1;
 return Out_Chan_Number;
end Outchan;

function Inchan1 return Integer is
  -- used for array initialisation
begin
 In1_Chan_Number := In1_Chan_Number + 2;
 return In1_Chan_Number;
end Inchan1;

function Inchan2 return Integer is
  -- used for array initialisation
begin
 In2_Chan_Number := In2_Chan_Number + 2;
 return In2_Chan_Number;
end Inchan2;



Sorters : array(1 .. Number_Of_Data_Items - 1) of
          Merge(Channels(Inchan1)'Access,
                Channels(Inchan2)'Access,
                Channels(Outchan)'Access,
                Terminated'Access);

procedure Put(D : Data'Class; B : access My_Buffer)
          is separate;
procedure Get(D : out Data'Class; B : access My_Buffer)
          is separate;
function Buffer_Not_Full(B : access My_Buffer) return Boolean
          is separate;
function Buffer_Not_Empty(B : access My_Buffer) return Boolean
          is separate;
function "<" (Lhs, Rhs : My_Data) return Boolean
          is separate;

begin
  Terminated.Terminator := True;
```

```
     for I in 0 .. Number_Of_Data_Items - 1 loop
        -- get data_item to be sorted
        Channels(Num_Of_Chans-I).Put(...);
        Channels(Num_Of_Chans-I).Put(Terminated); -- terminator
     end loop;
  end Sorter;
```

13.5   Summary

Ada gives direct support to object-oriented programming and concurrent programming, and is therefore unique amongst those languages intended for large-scale industrial software engineering. This chapter has given an overview of the OOP facilities and has addressed the interactions between the two programming paradigms. In particular, attention has been focused upon the need to support synchronisation abstractions that are extensible. Possible paradigms have been explored for using protected types in an object-oriented environment:

* Synchronisation is added if and when it is required by extending the object.

* Synchronisation is provided by the base (root) object type.

* Synchronisation is provided as a separate protected type and the data is passed as a discriminant.

The most elegant approach is to pass class-wide data to the protected type. This does not suffer from the inheritance anomaly and it allows the types to be extended. However, the operations on the protected type cannot be extended using inheritance. This technique was used to construct reusable and extensible communication abstractions. The examples chosen were bounded buffers, blackboards and multicasts.

13.6   Further reading

C. Atkinson, *Object-Oriented Reuse, Concurrency and Distribution: An Ada-Based Approach*, Addison-Wesley, Wokingham 1991.
B. Meyer, *Eiffel The Language*, Prentice Hall, New Jersey, 1992
J. Skansholm, *Ada from the Beginning*, 2nd Edition, Addison-Wesley, Wokingham, 1994.

Chapter 14 —————————————————

Distributed Systems

The full tasking model described so far in this book can be implemented on single-processor or multi-processor systems (the latter being systems with more than one processor, each having access to shared memory). This chapter considers the use of Ada for programming distributed systems. It reviews that part of the language definition contained in the *Distributed Systems Annex*.

There are many reasons why an application might need to be physically distributed. The potential advantages of distribution include the following:

* some applications by their very nature are distributed, for example production control systems; dispersing computing power to the location of equipment enables timely control and avoids complex wiring;

* improving the performance of an application through the exploitation of parallelism;

* increasing availability and reliability through the exploitation of redundancy;

* facilitating incremental growth through the addition or enhancement of processors and communications links.

Ada 83 was widely criticised for its lack of support for programming distributed systems. During the 1980s, many academic and industrial research projects attempted to find the most appropriate approach to developing distributed Ada systems. Most have revolved around the concept of the *virtual node*, which is a software component intended to serve as a unit of allocation in a network. A virtual node encapsulates strongly cohesive components and is guaranteed to run in a single node (where a node is one or more processing units having access to common memory). It interacts with other virtual nodes forming the complete system.

While virtual nodes have been used successfully to construct distributed Ada 83 systems, the solutions offered by the various research projects all suffer from limitations arising from the nature of the language. In particular, the structures used are awkward and unable to provide the capability of dynamic reconfiguration following failure, which is one of the main purposes of distributing software in many embedded, safety critical applications. The current version of Ada has built upon the concept of virtual nodes and provides some support for them. However, the scope of changes allowed within the Ada revision process has meant that this support has its limitations.

The production of a distributed software system to execute on a distributed hardware system involves several steps which are not required when programs are produced for a single processor:

- *Partitioning* is the process of dividing the system into parts (units of distribution) suitable for placement onto the processing elements of the target system.

- *Configuration* takes place when the partitioned parts of the program are associated with particular processing elements in the target system.

- *Allocation* covers the actual process of turning the configured system into a collection of executable modules and downloading these to the processing elements of the target system.

The Ada language provides support for the partitioning process but not for the configuration and allocation processes, which it assumes will be provided by an implementation.

This chapter first considers the Ada model of partitioning and then discusses three potential paradigms for programming distributed systems: the client/server model, filter partitions and the distributed object model. An example is also given of using the Ada model in a shared memory distributed environment. The chapter then considers issues of fault tolerance and whether partitions can be replicated to achieve tolerance of processor failure. Finally, the chapter summarises the strengths and weaknesses of the Ada approach.

14.1   The Ada model of distribution

The ARM defines a distributed system as an "interconnection of one or more processing nodes (a system resource that has both computational and storage capabilities), and zero or more storage nodes (a system resource that has only storage capabilities, with the storage addressable by more than one processing nodes)".

The Ada model for programming distributed systems specifies a *partition* as the unit of distribution. Partitions are not first-class language entities (in the sense that they cannot be declared as types and instances created). Instead, they comprise aggregations of library units (separately compiled library packages or subprograms) that collectively may execute in a distributed target execution environment. It is this inability to declare partition types which is the main limitation of the Ada model. Later discussions show how generics can be used to create instances of partitions; however, arrays of partitions are not expressible within the language.

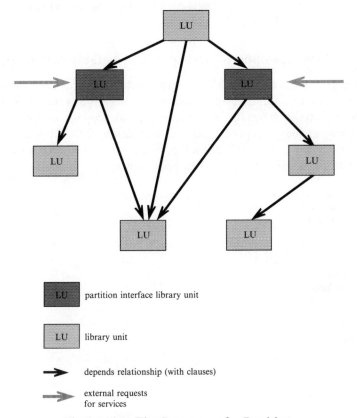

Figure 14.1: The Structure of a Partition.

Each partition resides at a single execution site where all its library units occupy the same logical address space. More than one partition may, however, reside on the same execution site. Figure 14.1 illustrates one possible structure of a partition. The arrows represent the dependencies between library units. The principal interface between partitions consists of one or more package specifications (each labelled "partition interface library unit" in Figure 14.1).

Partitions may be either *active* or *passive*. The library units comprising an active partition reside and execute upon the same processing element. In contrast, library units comprising a passive partition reside at a storage element that is directly accessible to the nodes of different active partitions that reference them. This model ensures that active partitions cannot directly access variables in other active partitions. Variables can only be shared directly between active partitions by encapsulating them in a passive partition.

Communication between active partitions is defined in the language to be via remote subprogram calls (however, an implementation may provide other communication mechanisms).

14.1.1   Data types and objects in a distributable Ada program

In order to understand how distributable Ada programs are constructed, it is necessary to appreciate how data types and objects are viewed. Ada is a strongly typed language with name equivalence; if two identical type declarations appear in separate parts of a program, these types are distinct. Furthermore, if a generic unit has a type declaration, then each instantiation of the unit produces a different type. For example,

```
generic
package X is
   type Y is ...
end X;

   ...
declare
   package X1 is new X;
   package X2 is new X;
   I : X1.Y;
   J : X2.Y;
begin
   ...
   I := J; -- ILLEGAL, I and J are not of the same type
   ...
end;
```

Similarly, with object declarations, each instantiation of a generic has its own copy of all its declared objects.

In constructing partitions, it is possible that the same library unit will need to be available in each partition; for example most partitions will require their own copy of Text_Io. Some library units may thus exist at more than one processing element in the distributed system. A key issue is whether any type declared in these 'replicated' library units is considered to be a single type or a group of distinct types; and similarly whether conceptually only a single instance of each data object exists. To be consistent with generics, types and data objects should be distinct. However, this may cause some structural problems within the distributed program and make it difficult for partitions to communicate. For example, passing tagged type objects between partitions where the same derived type is declared in each partition will fail.

14.1.2   Categorisation pragmas

To resolve the type and object issues, Ada distinguishes between different categories of library units, and imposes restrictions on these categories to maintain type consistency across the distributed program. The categories (some of these are useful in their own right, irrespective of whether the program is to be distributed) are designated by the following pragmas:

Preelaborate

A preelaborable library unit is one that can be elaborated without execution of code at run-time. For example, an elaborable construct is preelaborable if its elaboration does not execute a statement (other than a null statement) and does not require the creation of an object of a task type, a protected type with entry declarations or a controlled type.

Preelaborated library packages are useful for two purposes:

1.   They define which packages must be elaborated before all other non-preelaborable packages.

2.   They are essential in time-critical systems, which must begin their execution with minimal delay. Run-time elaboration can introduce unacceptable delays; preelaboration is intended to allow certain structures to be set up at link time rather than at run-time.

Pure

Pure packages are preelaborated packages with further restrictions which enable them to be freely replicated in different active or passive partitions without introducing any type inconsistencies. These restrictions concern the declaration of objects and types; in particular, variables and named access types are not allowed unless they are within a subprogram, generic subprogram, task unit or protected unit.

A type declared in a pure package is considered to be a single declaration, irrespective of how many times the package is replicated in the distributed system (the package is replicated once for each partition that references it). Hence, pure packages enable types to be declared which can subsequently be used in the communication between partitions.

Remote_Types

A Remote_Types package is a preelaborated package that must not contain any variable declarations within the visible part. An access type declared in the visible part of a Remote_Types package (or, in a Remote_Call_Interface library unit) is called a *remote access type* (see discussion below).

Any types declared in a Remote_Types package are considered to be single declarations, as with Pure packages.

Shared_Passive

Shared_Passive library units are used for managing global data shared
between active partitions. They are therefore configured on storage nodes in
the distributed system. Consequently, they are not allowed to contain tasks,
task types, protected objects or types with entry declarations, or library-level
access-type declarations that designate class-wide types. The restrictions
ensure that the packages are preelaborable and are compatible with the
properties of storage nodes.

A Shared_Passive library unit's body can only exist within a single
passive partition.

Remote_Call_Interface

A Remote_Call_Interface package defines the interface between active
partitions. Its body exists only within a single partition. All other occurrences
will have stubs allocated.

The specification of a Remote_Call_Interface package must be preelaborable; in addition the following restrictions apply:

•   It shall not contain the definition of a variable (to ensure no remote
    data access).

•   It shall not contain the declaration of a limited type (i.e. one for which
    the assignment operator is not available).

•   It shall not contain a nested generic type declaration (again to ensure
    no remote variable access).

•   Any parameters to subprograms (or access to subprograms) which are
    limited types shall have Read and Write attributes (see Section 14.3).

•   It shall not contain any subprograms which have access parameters.

•   It can only contain the declaration of access types if they are general
    access types that designate class-wide limited private types (declared in
    a Pure or Remote_Types package). Moreover, the primitive operations
    on the class-wide type can only have controlling access types, and all
    other parameters must have Read and Write attributes (see Section
    14.3); these access types are called remote access types and they can
    only be converted to other remote access types.

•   Any access-to-subprogram types declared are considered to be remote
    access types and can only be converted to other (subtype conformant)
    remote access-to-subprogram types.

A package which is not categorised by one of the above pragmas is called a
normal library package. If it is included in more than one partition, then it

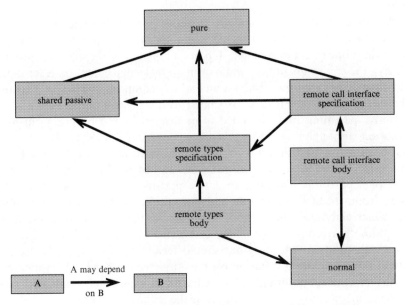

Figure 14.2: Allowed Dependencies Between Library Units.

is replicated and all types and objects are viewed as distinct. For example, the Calendar package is, in this regard, normal.

Those library units which are categorised can only depend on certain other types of library unit. In general, a library unit can always 'with' a library unit of the same category as itself (e.g. a Shared_Passive can depend on another Shared_Passive). Figure 14.2 shows the allowable dependencies between library units used for distribution. Of course, normal library units may depend on any other type of library unit.

The above pragmas facilitate the distribution of an Ada program and ensure that illegal partitionings (which allow direct remote variable access between partitions) are easily identifiable.

The grouping of library units into partitions is specified after their compilation, although the mechanisms for doing this are outside the language.

14.2 Program elaboration and termination

Each partition is elaborated independently of all other partitions. Any remote subprogram calls to a partition which has yet to finish elaborating are held until elaboration is complete. Deadlock may occur if cyclic elaboration dependencies are introduced by the programmer. If this is detected by the implementation, then Program_Error can be raised in one or more partitions to break the deadlock.

The library units which comprise an active partition are elaborated by the environment task devoted to the partition, and then, if present, the body of the main subprogram is executed. Upon completion of the main subprogram (if any), the environment task waits until all tasks dependent on it terminate, and then it finalises the library units which comprise the active partition. There is no environment task associated with a passive partition.

Active partitions may be added to or deleted from a program during its execution, although it is not specified how this can be achieved. It is assumed that each active partition has an associated partition identifier (see below) and implementation defined subprograms can be used to query or alter the state of a partition. Deleting an active partition is equivalent to aborting its environment task. Adding an active partition creates a new environment task which elaborates the partition and executes its main subprogram, if any.

Because partitions can be added or created at any time, it is not defined when a distributed Ada program should terminate. In general, a program should not terminate if it has active partitions which have not terminated.

Any remote subprogram call to a partition which has terminated raises the Communication_Error exception in the calling partition.

As a non-distributed program is, in effect, a single partition, a number of language features have so far been described as if they apply to the complete program. In fact, task identifiers and the pragmas that control dispatching and queuing policy do not affect the entire program but, rather, only the partition in which they are used. Thus different task scheduling schemes can be used simultaneously (although in different partitions).

14.3   Remote communication

The only predefined way in which active partitions can communicate directly is via remote subprogram calls. They can also communicate indirectly via data structures in passive partitions.

There are three different ways in which a calling partition can issue a remote subprogram call:

(a)   by calling a subprogram which has been declared in a remote call interface package of another partition directly;

(b)   by dereferencing the value of a remote access-to-subprogram type;

(c)   by calling a primitive operation of a tagged type where the controlling parameter designates a value of a remote access-to-class-wide type.

Examples of systems using each of these remote communication approaches are given in Section 14.4. It is important to note that, in the first type of communication, the calling and the called partitions are statically bound at compile time. However, in the latter two, the partitions are dynamically bound at run-time.

14.3.1 Asynchronous remote procedure calls

Many remote calls contain only 'in' or 'access'parameters (i.e. data that is being passed in the same direction as the call) and a caller may wish to continue its execution as soon as possible. In these situations it is sometimes appropriate to designate the call as an asynchronous call. Whether a procedure is to be called synchronously or asynchronously is considered by Ada to be a property of the procedure and not of the call. This is indicated by using a pragma `Asynchronous` when the procedure is declared. The pragma can also be applied to a remote subprogram access type, and to an access-to-class-wide type. In the latter case, all dispatching calls based on the type which only have 'in' parameters are asynchronous.

Any exceptions raised by the remote call, or by the implementation supporting the remote call, are lost (although some exception may be raised prior to the call returning; for example, `Communication_Error` may be raised if the destination is known to be unreachable).

14.3.2 The partition communication subsystem

Ada has defined how distributed programs can be partitioned and what forms of remote communication must be supported. However, the language designers were keen not to overspecify the language and not to prescribe a distributed run-time support system for Ada programs. They wanted to allow implementors to provide their own network communication protocols and, where appropriate, allow other ISO standards to be used; for example the ISO Remote Procedure Call standard. To achieve these aims, the Ada language assumes the existence of a standard implementation-provided package for handling all remote communication (the Partition Communication Subsystem, PCS). This allows compilers to generate calls to a standard interface without being concerned with the underlying implementation.

The following package defines the interface to a remote procedure (subprogram) call (RPC) support system:

```
with Ada.Streams;
package System.RPC is

    type Partition_ID is range 0 .. implementation_defined;

    Communication_Error : exception;

    type Params_Stream_Type(
            Initial_Size : Ada.Streams.Stream_Element_Count) is
```

```
         new Ada.Streams.Root_Stream_Type with private;

procedure Read(
         Stream : in out Params_Stream_Type;
         Item : out Ada.Streams.Stream_Element_Array;
         Last : out Ada.Streams.Stream_Element_Offset);

procedure Write(
         Stream : in out Params_Stream_Type;
         Item : in Ada.Streams.Stream_Element_Array);

-- Synchronous call
procedure Do_RPC(
         Partition    : in Partition_ID;
         Params       : access Params_Stream_Type;
         Result       : access Params_Stream_Type);

-- Asynchronous call
procedure Do_APC(
         Partition    : in Partition_ID;
         Params       : access Params_Stream_Type);

-- The handler for incoming RPCs
type RPC_Receiver is access procedure(
         Params       : access Params_Stream_Type;
         Result       : access Params_Stream_Type);

procedure Establish_RPC_Receiver(Partition : Partition_ID;
         Receiver : in RPC_Receiver);

private
   ... -- not specified by the language
end System.RPC;
```

The type Partition_Id is used to identify partitions. For any library-level declaration, D, D'Partition_Id yields the identifier of the partition in which the declaration was elaborated.

The exception Communication_Error is raised when an error is detected by System.RPC during a remote procedure call. Note: only one exception is specified even though many sources of error might exist, since it is not always possible to distinguish among these errors. In particular, it is often impossible to differentiate between a failing communication link and a failing processing element. The function Exception_Information may be used by an implementation to provide more detailed information about the cause of the exception, such as communication errors, missing partitions, etc.

An object of stream type Params_Stream_Type is used for marshaling (translating data into an appropriate stream-oriented form) and unmarshaling the parameters or results of a remote subprogram call, for the purposes of sending them between partitions. The object is also used to identify the particular subprogram in the called partition.

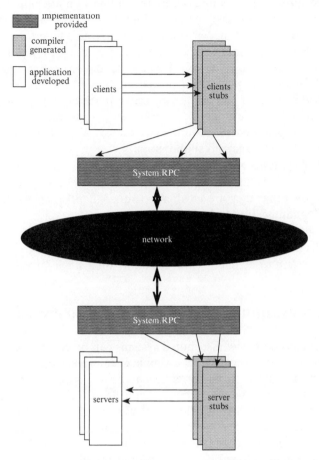

Figure 14.3: Relationship between Components in a Distributed Ada System.

Two abstract operations are defined in a standard package called Streams to support the interface: 'Write and 'Read. The operation 'Write marshals an object so that its representation is suitable for transmission across the network. Operation 'Read rebuilds the object once it has been transmitted.

The compiler will enforce restrictions on the Remote_Call_Interface packages, and will provide stubs to be called from remote active partitions. These stubs pack the parameters, invoke the user-provided communication subsystem and process any **in** and **in out** parameters or exceptions from the acknowledgement messages when the RPC completes. Corresponding routines are generated to handle the RPC at the server site. They receive the RPC messages, invoke the normal Ada subprograms, and report back the results. The process is illustrated in Figure 14.3

The procedure Do_RPC is invoked by the calling stub after the parameters are flattened into the message. After sending the message to the remote partition, it suspends the calling task until a reply arrives. The procedure Do_APC acts like Do_RPC except that it returns immediately after sending the message to the remote partition. It is called whenever the Asynchronous pragma is specified for the remotely called procedure. Establish_RPC_Receiver is called immediately after elaborating an active partition, but prior to invoking the main subprogram, if any. The Receiver parameter designates an implementation-provided procedure that receives a message and calls the appropriate RCI package and subprogram.

If a package is assigned to the same partition as a Remote_Call_Interface package, then it is valid for an implementation to optimise all calls to the RCI package so that they are local calls (rather than going via the PCS — Partition Communication Subsystem).

The pragma All_Calls_Remote, when applied to a package, indicates that all calls must be routed through the PCS. This allows, for example, a distributed system to be debugged more easily on a single-processor system.

14.4   Programming paradigms for distributed systems

This section considers how distributed systems can be constructed using the partition model. First, it considers a simple client/server model where there are many clients and a single server; each client is statically bound to the server by issuing direct remote subprogram calls. It then discusses how filter partitions can be used; here the filters are dynamically bound using remote access-to-subprogram types. Next, dynamic binding using remote access-to-class-wide types is illustrated using the distributed object model of program construction. Finally, shared partitions are illustrated.

An implementation of Ada for distributed systems will provide mechanisms for configuring a distributed system. For the purpose of illustration, this section will assume the following entities:

```
type Partition_Id is range 0 .. Max;

type Library_Unit_Names is ...;

type Library_Units is array(Units_Index range <>) of
     Library_Unit_Names;

procedure Partition(Ptn : Partition_Id; Assign : Library_Units);
```

The Partition procedure assigns the named library units to a partition and identifies the partition as Ptn. Any normal, Pure or Remote_Types library units which are 'withed' by the named library units are also included.

14.4.1 Client/Server model

To illustrate how a distributed system can be constructed, consider a simple disk block server partition which exists in a distributed environment. The disk block server provides a basic service whereby its remote clients can request a particular disk block. However, each client also wishes to cache recently accessed blocks in its own partition in order to avoid an excessive amount of communication across the network.

First, some basic types are defined for communication between several clients and a server. These are defined in a Pure package as they must be freely replicated in each partition:

```
package Disk_Block_Server_Types is
  pragma Pure;

  type Block_Id is new Natural;

  type Byte is mod 256; -- an unsigned byte
  for Byte'Size use 8;

  type Disk_Block_Size is range 1 .. 1024;

  type Disk_Block is array (Disk_Block_Size) of Byte;

end Disk_Block_Server_Types;
```

The Disk_Block_Server partition can now be defined. Server partitions are easily constructed by first considering their interfaces. In this case the partition has two simple subprograms: a procedure for reading a disk block and a procedure for writing a disk block. The body of the package can include support packages for accessing the disk, etc. Its implementation is not of interest here:

```
with Disk_Block_Server_Types; use Disk_Block_Server_Types;
package Disk_Block_Server is
  pragma Remote_Call_Interface;

  procedure Read_Block(From: Block_Id; Data : out Disk_Block);
  procedure Write_Block(To: Block_Id; Data : Disk_Block);
  pragma Asynchronous(Write_Block);

end Disk_Block_Server;

with Disk_Driver; ...
package body Disk_Block_Server is
  ...
end Disk_Block_Server;
```

Each client partition will require its own local disk block server for caching disk blocks. The local server interface consists of a normal package:

```
with Disk_Block_Server_Types; use Disk_Block_Server_Types;
package Local_Disk_Block_Server is

  procedure Read_Block(From: Block_Id; Data : out Disk_Block);
  procedure Write_Block(To: Block_Id; Data : Disk_Block);

end Local_Disk_Block_Server;
```

Its body provides an in-memory cache, and, if necessary, calls the remote file server:

```
with Disk_Block_Server;
package body Local_Disk_Block_Server is

  type Cache_Element is
    record
      ID : Block_ID;
      Block : Disk_Block;
    end record;
  subtype Cache_Index is Integer range 1 .. 100;
  Local_Cache : array (Cache_Index) of Cache_Element;

  procedure Read_Block(From: Block_ID; Data : out Disk_Block) is
    LRU : Cache_Index;
  begin
    -- look to see if required Block is in Cache,
    -- if not, find empty Cache Element or Least Recently
    -- Used One and if necessary write the
    -- Block back to the server
    Disk_Block_Server.Read_Block(From, Local_Cache(LRU).Block);
      -- remote call
    Data := ...;
  end Read_Block;


  procedure Write_Block(To: Block_ID; Data : Disk_Block) is
    E : Cache_Index;
    Write_Through : Boolean := ..;
  begin
    -- update cache
    if Write_Through then
      Disk_Block_Server.Write_Block(To, Data); -- remote call
    end if;
  end Write_Block;

end Local_Disk_Block_Server;
```

Finally, each client, which will be a partition without an interface, can now 'with' the local disk block server. (Client partitions are best constructed by considering a root subprogram.)

```
with Local_Disk_Block_Server; use Local_Disk_Block_Server;
procedure Main_Client1 is
begin
   -- issue requests to local file server
end Main_Client1;

with Local_Disk_Block_Server; use Local_Disk_Block_Server;
procedure Main_Client2 is
begin
   -- issue requests to local file server
end Main_Client2;

   ...
```

As the local file server is a normal package it is replicated in each partition which 'withs' it.

Using the example configuration language introduced earlier, the system can be configured:

```
Partition(Ptn => 1, Assign => (1 => Disk_Block_Server));

Partition(Ptn => 2, Assign => (1 => Main_Client1));
Partition(Ptn => 3, Assign => (1 => Main_Client2));
```

Figure 14.4 illustrates the logical structure of the system diagrammatically, and Figure 14.5 the partitioned structure.

As there is only one file server, static binding between the clients and the servers has been used. If more then one file server exists in the network, then it is necessary to define the server as a generic and use a name server to connect the clients to their servers dynamically. The approach is similar to that given in the following sections for filter partitions (where each filter partition can be considered as a server, albeit without a direct interface).

14.4.2   Filter partitions

A filter task is a task which continuously reads from its input, performs some transformation on the data and writes the results to its output. Consider, for example, using a pipeline of filter tasks to produce prime numbers using the Sieve of Eratosthenes. This requires dynamic binding between the filter partitions. The solution in Ada for a single processor or multi-processor is straightforward and was presented in Section 4.1.2. To turn this solution into a distributed one is not easy because partitions are not dynamic objects; they cannot be created from within an executing distributed Ada program (unless extra implementation-dependent features are provided).

To construct a distributed program which is composed of filter partitions, it is necessary to use the Ada generic facility and to provide mechanisms

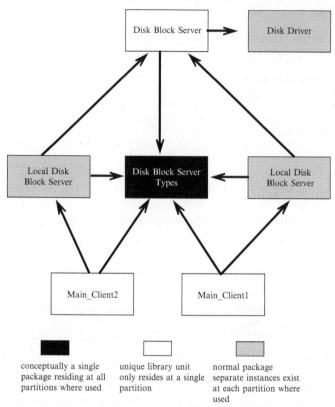

Figure 14.4: Structure of a Disk Server and its Clients.

for the run-time linking of partitions (via a name server). First, however, it must be remembered that active partitions can only call subprograms in other active partitions. They can neither make rendezvous nor protected subprogram/entry calls. Consequently, the channels which usually connect the tasks must be represented as procedures. As data is only passed one way, these procedures can be called asynchronously.

The following Sieve_Server package provides an interface to an active partition which defines a remote subprogram access type and indicates that all subprogram calls that dereference this access type are asynchronous. It then declares two subprograms which can be called at run-time to link the filter tasks. Register is called by a filter partition to indicate that it wishes to participate in the pipeline; it passes a procedure to be used as its input channel. Allocate is called by a filter partition to indicate that it wishes to be allocated an output channel. The Sieve_Server is thus able to set up the pipeline dynamically. Finally, a Print procedure is callable (asynchronously)

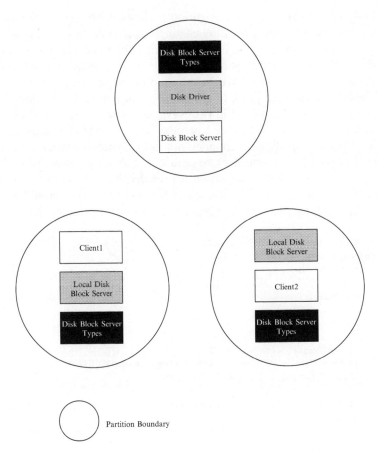

Figure 14.5: The Partitioned Disk Server and its Clients.

by each filter partition:

```
package Sieve_Server is

  pragma Remote_Call_Interface;

  type Channel is access procedure (I : Integer);
  pragma Asynchronous(Channel);
  Limit : constant Integer := ...;

  procedure Register(C : Channel);
  function Allocate return Channel;

  procedure Print(I : Integer);
  pragma Asynchronous(Print);
end Sieve_Server;
```

The body of the Sieve_Server partition declares the bodies of the subprograms for registering and allocating channels. It also declares a task which is responsible for generating the input to the first filter (i.e. the odd numbers). Clearly, as the filter partitions become active in an unsynchronised order, it is necessary to provide some synchronisation in the package, for example to stop the Odds task attempting to send data to an uninitialised channel.

Synchronisation is provided in two ways; firstly the Odds task declares an entry which is called by Register when the first filter partition announces its arrival. This sets up the first channel. Secondly, synchronisation is required by the filter partitions themselves, to ensure that an output channel is always available. This latter synchronisation is provided by making use of a buffer abstraction (which has been discussed in Section 9.5). The Channel_Buffer ensures that a filter partition is blocked until an output channel is available:

```
with Buffers; -- see Section 9.5
package body Sieve_Server is
  task Odds is
    entry First_Client(F : Channel);
  end Odds;

  First : Boolean := True;

  Sieve_Count : constant := 7;
  package Channel_Buffers is new Buffers(Channel, Sieve_Count);
  Channel_Buffer : Channel_Buffers.Buffer;

  procedure Register(C : Channel) is
  begin
    if First then
      Odds.First_Client(C);
      First := False;
    else
      Channel_Buffer.Put(C);
    end if;
  end Register;


  function Allocate return Channel is
    C : Channel;
  begin
    Channel_Buffer.Get(C);
    return C;
  end Allocate;

  procedure Print(I : Integer) is
  begin
    ...
  end Print;
```

```
task body Odds is
  Value : Integer;
  First_Chan : Channel;
begin
  Print(2);
  Value := 3;
  accept First_Client(F : Channel) do
    First_Chan := F;
  end First_Client;

  while Value < Limit loop
    First_Chan(Value);  -- remote call
    Value := Value + 2;
  end loop;
end Odds;
  ...
end Sieve_Server;
```

A filter partition is declared as a generic partition:

```
generic
  Limit : Integer;
package Sieve_Of_Eratosthenes is
  pragma Remote_Call_Interface;

  procedure Input(I : Integer);
end Sieve_Of_Eratosthenes;
```

The Input procedure will represent the input channel; as it will be called remotely it must be declared in the interface.

The body of the package is given below. The Input procedure uses another bounded buffer to implement the required channel synchronisation protocol. The initialisation section of the package is responsible for setting the input and output channels correctly:

```
with Sieve_Server; use Sieve_Server;
with Buffers;
package body Sieve_Of_Eratosthenes is

  Max_Buf_Size : constant Integer := 10;

  package My_Buffers is new Buffers(Integer, Max_Buf_Size);
  My_Buffer : My_Buffers.Buffer;

  procedure Input(I : Integer) is
  begin
    My_Buffer.Put(I);
  end Input;

  task Sieve is
    entry Assign_Output_Channel(C : Channel);
  end Sieve;
```

```
task body Sieve is
  Prime, Value : Integer;
  Output: Channel;
begin
  My_Buffer.Get(Prime);
  Print(Prime);
  accept Assign_Output_Channel(C : Channel) do
    Output := C;
  end Assign_Output_Channel;
  loop
    My_Buffer.Get(Value);
    if Value rem Prime /= 0 then
      Output(Value);  -- remote call
    end if;
    exit when Value >= Limit;
  end loop;
end Sieve;
begin
  Register(Input'Access);  -- remote call
  Sieve.Assign_Output_Channel(Allocate);
  -- a remote call is required to evaluate the parameter
end Sieve_Of_Eratosthenes;
```

Finally, a number of filter partitions can be created as instantiations of the generic:

```
with Sieve_Server; with Sieve_Of_Eratosthenes;
package Sieve1 is new Sieve_Of_Eratosthenes(Sieve_Server.Limit);

with Sieve_Server; with Sieve_Of_Eratosthenes;
package Sieve2 is new Sieve_Of_Eratosthenes(Sieve_Server.Limit);

    ...

with Sieve_Server; with Sieve_Of_Eratosthenes;
package Sieve7 is new Sieve_Of_Eratosthenes(Sieve_Server.Limit);
```

The system can then be configured:

```
Partition(Ptn => 1, Assign =>  (1 => Sieve_Server));
Partition(Ptn => 2, Assign =>  (1 => Sieve1));
Partition(Ptn => 3, Assign =>  (1 => Sieve2));
Partition(Ptn => 4, Assign =>  (1 => Sieve3));
Partition(Ptn => 5, Assign =>  (1 => Sieve4));
Partition(Ptn => 6, Assign =>  (1 => Sieve5));
Partition(Ptn => 7, Assign =>  (1 => Sieve6));
Partition(Ptn => 8, Assign =>  (1 => Sieve7));
```

14.4.3 Distributed object model

Chapter 13 discussed the ways in which tasking and the object-oriented programming model could be used together. This section considers an approach to programming distributed systems based on distributed objects (Gargaro, 1993). It illustrates dynamic binding between partitions and remote subprogram calls via remote access-to-class-wide types.

Consider a distributed file system, where a collection of file servers provide file storage for a group of client partitions. Each file server can be viewed as an object, and therefore can be developed using the OOP facilities. To program distributed objects, it is first necessary to define the abstract interface to the objects in a pure package. Assume that the required interface is where a client can issue open, close, read, write and seek requests on a file:

```
with Disk_Block_Server_Types; use Disk_Block_Server_Types;
package File_Server_Objects is
   pragma Pure;

   type File is abstract tagged limited private;
   type Mode is (Reading, Writing);

   procedure Open(F : access File; M : Mode) is abstract;
   procedure Close(F : access File) is abstract;
   procedure Read(F :  access File; Data : out Disk_Block;
                  Size : Disk_Block_Size) is abstract;
   procedure Write(F :  access File; Data : Disk_Block;
                   Size : Disk_Block_Size) is abstract;
   procedure Seek(F :  access File; Position : Integer)
                  is abstract;

private
   type File is abstract tagged limited null record;

end File_Server_Objects;
```

A name server can now be defined to provide a mapping between files and character strings:

```
with File_Server_Objects; use File_Server_Objects;
package Name_Server is
   pragma Remote_Call_Interface;

   type File_Name is new String;

   type File_Id is access all File'Class;
   pragma Asynchronous(File_Id);
   -- File_Id is a remote access-to-class-wide type.
   -- Any primitive operation using this type will result in
   -- dynamic binding and potentially distributed dispatching
```

```
      procedure Register(Fid : File_Id; File : File_Name);
      function Find(File : File_Name) return File_Id;
   end Name_Server;


   package body Name_Server is
      ...
   end Name_Server;
```

With this distributed object model it is not necessary to define the operations that will be called remotely in a Remote_Call_Interface package. The fact that they have controlling operands which are of remote access-to-class-wide type is enough for the compiler to generate the appropriate stubs. Therefore, an actual file server can be defined by extending the basic File type (to include all the information it requires to maintain a file such as the current length, whether the file is open, etc.) in a normal package. It also overrides the primitive subprograms:

```
   with Name_Server; use Name_Server;
   with File_Server_Objects; use File_Server_Objects;
   package Default_File_Server is

      type My_File is new File_Server_Objects.File with private;

      function Create(Fn : File_Name) return File_Id;

      procedure Open(F : access My_File; M : Mode);
      procedure Close(F : access My_File);
      procedure Read(F :   access My_File;
                  Data : out Disk_Block; Size : out Disk_Block_Size);
      procedure Write(F :   access My_File;
                  Data : Disk_Block; Size : Disk_Block_Size);
      procedure Seek(F :   access My_File; Position : Integer);

   private
      type My_File is new File_Server_Objects.File with
         record
            ...
         end record;

   end Default_File_Server;
```

Note that a new operation is defined to create a file at a particular server; it can only be called locally, as there is no operation in the File_Server_Objects package.

The body of the Default_File_Server uses a local disk block manager. The Create routine creates a new file data type and associates a name with it via the Name_Server:

```
with Local_Disk_Block_Server; use Local_Disk_Block_Server;
package body Default_File_Server is

   type My_File_Pointer is access all My_File;

   type Local_Files is array ( 1 .. Max) of My_File_Pointer;
   -- arrays of My_file_Pointer types etc

   Files : Local_Files;

   function Create(Fn : File_Name) return File_Id is
   begin
      -- find empty slot in array, index is I
      Files(I) := new My_File;
      Name_Server.Register(File_Id(Files(I)), Fn);
      ...
   end Create;
   ...

end Default_File_Server;
```

Each partition which 'withs' the Default_File_Server will obtain its own copy.

Alternative file servers can be provided:

```
with File_Server_Objects; use File_Server_Objects;
with Name_Server; use Name_Server;
package Alternative_Server is

   type New_File is new File_Server_Objects.File with private;

   function Create(Fn : File_Name) return File_Id;

   procedure Open(F : access New_File; M : Mode);
   procedure Close(F : access New_File);
   procedure Read(F : access New_File;
                  Data : out Disk_Block; Size : out Disk_Block_Size);
   procedure Write(F : access New_File;
                   Data : Disk_Block; Size : Disk_Block_Size);
   procedure Seek(F : access New_File; Position : Integer);

private
   type New_File is new File_Server_Objects.File with
      record
         ...
      end record;

end Alternative_Server;

package body Alternative_Server is
   ...
end Alternative_Server;
```

Finally, a client of the distributed file system can locate a file by its name, and then call operations on the file without being aware of its location:

```
with File_Server_Objects;
with Name_Server;
procedure Client1 is
  My_File :  Name_Server.File_Id
begin
  -- issue requests
  My_File := Name_Server.Find("My_File");
  File_Server_Objects.Open(My_File, Writing);
  -- dispatches to correct file server
  ...
end Client1;


  ...
```

The dynamic binding provides a powerful mechanism; new file servers can be added at any time without changing the clients.

14.4.4   Passive partitions

To illustrate the use of passive partitions, consider an image-processing system using range images. The image to be processed begins as an array of points whose values represent the distance from the camera to a corresponding point in the scene being viewed. A typical first step in the processing is the calculation of the surface normals at each point of the array. This operation is ideally suited for parallel computation.

The problem is configured so that the image acquisition is performed in a passive partition, Image_Acq, and the data is held in shared memory. Overall control is performed by a Manager partition which allocates segments of the image to be processed to instances of the generic partition, Calc_Seg.

A pure package, Images, contains the type declarations for the images and image segments. The example is illustrated in Figure 14.6:

```
package Images is
  pragma Pure;

  subtype Seg_Index is Positive range 1 .. 8;
  subtype Image_Index is Positive range 1 .. 4;
  type Image_Seg is array(Seg_Index, Seg_Index) of Integer;
  type Image is array (Image_Index, Image_Index) of Image_Seg;
end Images;
```

The Image_Acq package is a shared passive package which will be allocated into a shared memory module of a distributed system. It contains the code to take the picture, and stores the resulting image so that it can be accessed by the worker tasks:

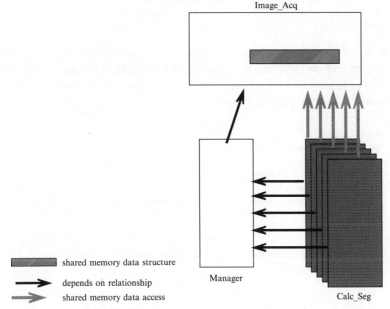

Figure 14.6: Image Processing Example.

```
with Images; use Images;
package Image_Acq is
   pragma Shared_Passive;
   procedure Get_The_Picture;
   Picture : Image;
end Image_Acq;


package body Image_Acq is

   procedure Get_The_Picture is
   begin
      -- take picture and put result in Picture
   end Get_The_Picture;

end Image_Acq;
```

The Manager package contains the interface to a managing partition. Worker tasks can request segments to be processed and return the results. The segments are identified by indices into the Picture image:

```
with Images; use Images;
package Manager is
```

```
        pragma Remote_Call_Interface;
        procedure Get_Segment_Index(I, J : out Image_Index);
        procedure Segment_Completed(I, J : Image_Index);
   end Manager;
```

The body of Manager contains two tasks. The first is responsible for taking the picture and distributing the segments of the image to the worker tasks. The Controller task is responsible for initiating the image acquisition processes and collecting the results:

```
with Image_Acq;
package body Manager is

   task Distribute_Image is
     entry Take_Picture;
     entry Get_Segment_Index(I, J : out Image_Index);
   end Distribute_Image;

   task Controller is
     entry Segment_Completed(I, J : Image_Index);
   end Controller;


   procedure Get_Segment_Index(I, J : out Image_Index) is
   begin
     Distribute_Image.Get_Segment_Index(I,J);
   end Get_Segment_Index;

   procedure Segment_Completed(I, J : in Image_Index) is
   begin
     Controller.Segment_Completed(I,J);
   end Segment_Completed;

   task body Distribute_Image is
   begin
     loop
       accept Take_Picture;
       Image_Acq.Get_The_Picture;
       for Major_Index in Image_Index loop
         for Minor_Index in Image_Index loop
           accept Get_Segment_Index(I, J : out Image_Index) do
             I := Major_Index;
             J := Minor_Index;
           end Get_Segment_Index;
         end loop;
       end loop;
     end loop;
   end Distribute_Image;


   task body Controller is
```

```
    type Seg_Status is array(Image_Index, Image_Index) of Boolean;
    Done : Seg_Status;
    Seg_Done : Seg_Status := (others => (others => True));
begin
  loop
    -- The image acquisition process is often of a repetitive
    -- nature, so some sort of loop structure would often
    -- be used here. The actual nature of the loop is not
    -- of significance to this example, so no details are
    -- given. Whatever computation and communication is
    -- required takes place before image acquisition.
    Distribute_Image.Take_Picture;
    Done := (others => (others => False));
    -- Accept results back from the
    -- individual computation units
    while Done /= Seg_Done loop
      accept Segment_Completed(I, J : in Image_Index) do
        Done(I, J)  := True;
      end Segment_Completed;
    end loop;
    -- Whatever computation and communication takes
    -- place after image processing.
  end loop;
  end Controller;
end Manager;
```

The Calc_Seg package is a generic package which provides the worker tasks which process the image segments and calculate the surface normals:

```
generic
package Calc_Seg is
  pragma Elaborate_Body;
  -- required as there is no syntactical link with the body
end Calc_Seg;

with Images; use Images;
with Manager;
with Image_Acq;
package body Calc_Seg is
  task Do_Normal;
  task body Do_Normal is
    I, J : Image_Index;
  begin
    loop
      -- These calculation segments run continuously,
      -- getting a new segment to process whenever
      -- Image_Acq has a new image to be processed.
      Manager.Get_Segment_Index(I, J);
      -- Get a segment to work on. Do calculation
      -- of normals, leaving result in Picture.
      Picture(I,J) := ...;
      Manager.Segment_Completed(I,J);
```

```
          end loop;
        end Do_Normal;
      end Calc_Seg;
```

A package is initiated for each site in the distributed system which is to have
worker tasks:

```
    with Calc_Seg;
    package Calc1 is new Calc_Seg;

    with Calc_Seg;
    package Calc2 is new Calc_Seg;

    with Calc_Seg;
    package Calc3 is new Calc_Seg;

    with Calc_Seg;
    package Calc4 is new Calc_Seg;

    with Calc_Seg;
    package Calc5 is new Calc_Seg;

    with Calc_Seg;
    package Calc6 is new Calc_Seg;
      ...
```

The system can then be partitioned:

```
    Partition(Ptn => 1, Assign => (Image_Acq));
      -- destined for a shared storage node
    Partition(Ptn => 2, Assign => (Manager));
    Partition(Ptn => 3, Assign => (Calc1));
    Partition(Ptn => 4, Assign => (Calc2));
    Partition(Ptn => 5, Assign => (Calc3));
    Partition(Ptn => 6, Assign => (Calc4));
      ..
```

14.5 Tolerance of processing element failure

One of the prime motivations for using distributed systems is to obtain
a degree of fault tolerance to hardware failure. It is clearly beyond the
scope of the Ada language to define a particular approach to fault tolerance.
However, it is important to understand how/whether common approaches
can be integrated into an Ada environment. This is an area where further
research is required, and so this section discusses issues rather than giving
firm guidelines.

All fault tolerance techniques must be built upon a failure hypothesis.
This describes the ways in which the hardware can fail, and how often

failures may occur. Obviously, any hardware can, in extreme conditions, fail in many different ways; the failure hypothesis defines those failures that the application is concerned about. If the failure hypothesis is poorly defined, then the fault tolerance techniques may be ineffective.

One clear distinction, that must be articulated within the failure hypothesis is whether the processing nodes are deemed to fail in a controlled, or uncontrolled, manner. Most failures are *fail-stop*. Only very rarely will a node continue to work and yet produce results that are 'believable' but actually incorrect. This latter form of failure (which is often known as a Byzantine failure) can usually be ignored in the failure hypothesis. Only truly safety-critical applications, such as air traffic control systems, need to accommodate uncontrolled failures.

The most frequently used technique for tolerating processor failure is replication. In general, replication comes in two forms, active and passive (not to be confused with the Ada terms for its classification of partitions). Active replication takes some executing entity and duplicates it. Passive techniques use a dormant 'alternative' that can take over in the event of the primary failing. These two techniques will be considered, in more detail, in the following sections.

A key issue for distributed Ada programs is whether the application programmer must program the desired forms of replication directly. Or is it possible for some distributed operating system to 'hide' the techniques, so that the application consists of 'normal' code and the production of replicated versions is undertaken transparently? Although this latter approach may in the long term be the correct one to follow, nothing in Ada's definition gives direct support for this type of facility. Rather, Ada has provided features that could be used by the application programmer or system builder to provide replication. For example, the ability to bind to subprogram calls dynamically is a very useful feature.

There is also an important issue in deciding upon the correct unit of replication. Should this be the partition, or is it necessary to work at a higher level (all partitions allocated to the same processing element) or even a lower level (for example, at the task level)?

14.5.1 Active replication

With fail uncontrolled processing elements it is necessary to run a number of identical copies of the code and to vote on the outputs from the various copies. Using two copies it is only possible to recognise a fault; with three copies a single fault can be masked. If the failure hypothesis only recognises controlled failures, then voting is not necessary: any non-failed copy can be assumed to be producing the correct result. Hence replication is employed for availability.

With both of these uses of active replication there is one overriding concern for correct implementation: how to keep active replicas coordinated. In the absence of failure, all active replicas must behave in an identical manner. This is a non-trivial issue. Differing arrival times of external requests and internal events due to varying execution rates between replicas may cause divergence. Even if all incoming RPC requests are ordered using some atomic broadcast facility, it is still possible for different interleavings of internal and external calls to protected objects (or local tasks) to occur. Interactions with time (such as using a delay statement) are another source of divergence.

One way of integrating active replication into the current Ada distribution scheme is to assume that replication occurs at the partition level and to support a broadcast RPC scheme (as a child package of the PCS, Partition Communication Subsystem). Each replicated partition has an associated group identifier which can be used by the system. All remote procedure calls are potentially replicated calls. The body of the package would require access to a bounded reliable atomic broadcast facility:

```
package System.RPC.Atomic is

    type Group_Id is range 0 .. implementation_defined;

    -- Synchronous replicated call
    procedure Do_Replicated_RPC(Group : in Group_Id;
                Service : in Service_Id;
                Params : access Params_Stream_Type;
                Results : out Param_Stream_Access);


    -- Asynchronous call
    procedure Do_Replicated_APC(Group : in Group_Id;
                Service : in Service_Id;
                Params : access Params_Stream_Type);

    type RRPC_Receiver is access procedure (Service : in Service_Id;
                Params : access Params_Stream_Type;
                Results : out Param_Stream_Access);

    procedure Establish_RRPC_Receiver(Receiver : in RRPC_Receiver);

private
    ...
end System.RPC.Atomic;
```

14.5.2   Passive replication

There are two general forms of passive replication: *cold standbys* and *warm standbys*. As these names imply, a cold replica starts its execution with no knowledge of the execution of the system up to the point of the failure; a warm replica does not run (i.e. it is not active) but keeps copies of relevant state information so that it can take over in a much more responsive way. The issue of which form of standby to use (and, for the warm variety, how often it updates its state information) is a matter of the response time required. If a failure must be tolerated without any performance degradation, then a very warm (hot) or active replica is needed. If more time is available, then it may be possible to bring a cold standby "up to speed".

Cold passive replica partitions can be implemented in Ada without any help from the implementation. Essentially, each passive partition may be written as a generic. Consider, for example, the following disk server partition which can access a dual-port disk:

```
type Replica_Type is (Prime, Standby);

with Disk_Block_Server_Types; use Disk_Block_Server_Types;
generic
   Replica : Replica_Type;
package Disk_Block_Server is
   pragma Remote_Call_Interface;

   procedure Read_Block(From: Block_Id; Data : out Disk_Block);
   procedure Write_Block(To: Block_Id; Data : Disk_Block);
   pragma Asynchronous(Write_Block);

   procedure Become_Prime;
   procedure Become_Standby;

end Disk_Block_Server;



with Disk_Driver; ...
with Name_Server;
package body Disk_Block_Server is

   -- internal synchronisation agents, tasks etc
   procedure Become_Prime is
   begin
      -- create tasks etc;
   end Become_Prime;

   procedure Become_Standby is
   begin
      -- abort tasks etc;
   end Become_Standby;

begin
   if Replica = Prime then
      -- create tasks etc;
   end if;
```

```
      Name_Server.Register(Replica, Read_Block'Access);
      Name_Server.Register(Replica, Write_Block'Access);
   end Disk_Block_Server;
```

Both a Prime and a Standby server partition may be created. The clients, on detecting a failure of the primary, can switch to a backup. The approach is not transparent as, in the general case, the cold standby will have to acquire enough state information to take over the role of the primary.

With warm standbys, it would be possible to use a shared memory partition to store the state information about the primary replica. When the warm standby takes over from the primary, it acquires its current state directly from the shared partition.

14.6   Summary

The Ada model for distribution may be summarised by the following points:

- The Ada partition model provides support for distributed execution without introducing additional linguistic constructs. The motivation is to minimise the differences in programming distributed and non-distributed systems without bias towards specific distributed target architectures.

- Partitions elaborate and execute independently. Normal packages elaborate in the partition in which they are referenced; if such packages have state then this state is independent of the state of the same package elaborated in a different partition. For example, package Calendar, when elaborated in different partitions, is not required to maintain a synchronised system-wide clock.

- There is no requirement for a distributed Ada run-time system. Communication among active partitions is through passive partitions or through remote subprogram calls.

- A canonical model for implementing remote subprogram calls is specified through the requirement for all implementations to conform to the Partition Communication Subsystem interface package System.RPC. This model supports both statically and dynamically bound remote subprogram calls in both synchronous and asynchronous form.

- Implementations must define the required postcompilation support to construct partitions and to configure the partitions onto a distributed target system. The construction of partitions allows the explicit assignment of remote call interface packages and shared passive packages to partitions.

The most severe limitation of the Ada partition model is that partitions are not first-class language objects. Partition types cannot be created and therefore instances of partitions, pointers to partitions and arrays of partitions cannot be expressed. In Ada, to create more than one copy of a partition requires the static instantiation of generic remote call interface packages or shared passive packages; each instantiation is assigned to a separate partition. The partition becomes the closure of the library units mentioned in the 'with' clauses of each instantiation. Unless remote access types are used, client partitions are required to reference the name of the instantiated package explicitly in their closure.

Using remote access types it is possible to achieve dynamic binding between partitions, and hence a certain amount of fault tolerance can be obtained by the programmer.

14.7 Further reading

J. Bishop (editor), *Distributed Ada: Development and Experiences*, Cambridge University Press, Cambridge, 1990.
D. Powell (editor), *Delta-4: A Generic Architecture for Dependable Distributed Computing*, Research Reports ESPRIT, Springer-Verlag, Berlin, 1991.

Chapter 15

Conclusion

Ada 83's concurrency facilities were widely criticised, and during the Ada 95 development process some 25 major "revision issues" were raised on the tasking model (Ada 9X, 1990) by the team responsible for generating the requirements for the new language. This chapter briefly reviews these revision issues and considers the extent to which Ada 95 has been successful in addressing the main concerns of the Ada 83 community. Following this, a summary is given of some of the outstanding issues that have been raised during the discussions in this book. Finally, the chapter and book closes with an evaluation of the potential for concurrent programming in Ada 95.

15.1   Ada 83 and Ada 95

The process of evolving from Ada 83 to Ada 95 has been a long and thorough one. The teams responsible for managing this transition conducted the process in a very open manner, involving as wide a selection of the Ada community as possible. Early on, Ada users were requested to articulate their concerns in respect of Ada 83 and to suggest possible solutions. Over 750 observations were received, addressing all aspects of the language. These "revision requests" (RRs) were distilled (by the team responsible for generating the requirements for Ada 95) to revision issues (RIs). Of these, the following groups are most appropriate for discussion in this book:

- Expressive power of the select statement

  There were several RIs which considered the ability of the select statement to express all the required constraints on synchronisation.

  These issues have already been discussed in Chapter 8 of this book in the context of avoidance synchronisation. Ada 95 has provided the requeue mechanism to help solve these problems. Furthermore, protected objects allow more flexible communication structures to be set up.

- Tasking ease-of-use issues

  Although, in general, Ada 83 has a coherent tasking model, there were some minor issues with the ease with which some programming paradigms (expressible within the model) could be written. For example, it was easy to write a function which could return an instance of a task local to the function. However, the task termination rules required the returned task to terminate before the function could return. Another problem was that representation clauses and priority levels were associated with a task type and not the task object. These minor irritations have been corrected in Ada 95.

A final problem articulated in this class of RIs was the inability to pass initialisation data to a task at its creation time. Although this problem has been partly solved by allowing discriminant and access discriminants to tasks, there are still several minor difficulties (see next section).

- Real-time control

One of the main concerns with Ada 83's tasking model was its poor support for real-time systems. The priority and time models were vague and weak, and really not adequate for implementing hard real-time systems. Priority inversion was inevitable because of FIFO entry queues. Periodic tasks were not well supported and relied on the delay statement for their implementation (this suffered from race conditions). Concern was also expressed that the language defined a particular model of scheduling and it was difficult for applications to program their own paradigms.

Ada 95 has resolved all these issues, and now supports a consistent set of facilities for programming all classes of real-time systems.

- Interrupt handling

Ada 83 made a brave attempt to address interrupt handling by providing a mechanism by which an entry call could be associated with an interrupt and by allowing the specification and manipulation of device registers through representation clauses. However, as mentioned above, by tying these facilities to the task type rather than the task object, it made interrupt handling of identical devices very cumbersome. Furthermore, many application programmers felt that the model of an interrupt as an entry call was too complicated and that an interrupt was better thought of as a procedure call.

Ada 95 has a well integrated set of facilities for handling interrupts (as illustrated in Chapter 11). It allows a protected procedure to be called by an interrupt, and has removed the restrictions associated with representation clauses.

- Parallelism

Ada 83 was originally designed when distributed and parallel systems were in their infancy. Consequently, the distribution model was almost non-existent. Furthermore, problems were to be found with implementations of the language on highly parallel computers; there is no way within the language to specify fine-grain parallelism, for example, parallel loops.

Ada 95 has made some effort to correct these problems, but still suffers from a lack of expressive power in this area (see the next section).

- Shared variables

There were various problems in Ada 83 on the topic of sharing variables between tasks. The exact effect of pragma Shared was not clear, and there was confusion over the notion of synchronisation points within a task and between tasks.

Ada 95 has resolved all these issues (see Section 7.10).

- Asynchronous systems

The Ada 83 tasking model was synchronous, and whenever it was necessary for tasks to interact in an asynchronous manner extra agent tasks had to be created. This led to an proliferation of tasks in an application and a perceived loss of efficiency. Promises of optimised task structures (such as monitor or buffer tasks) were never fulfiled by compiler vendors in a standard manner (if at all). Consequently, it was impossible to write portable programs which relied on these optimisations. Furthermore, it was not possible to attract the attention of a task and alter its flow of control. The task had either to be aborted or was forced to poll for the asynchronous communication.

Ada 95 has addressed the issue of asynchronous systems on two fronts. Protected objects allow data-oriented asynchronous communication and the asynchronous select statement allows one task to alter the flow of control in another asynchronously.

- Task termination and abort issues

Several RIs focus on the problems of terminating tasks in Ada 83. Firstly, it is impossible to guarantee the termination of a task using the abort statement if the task does not execute a synchronisation point. Secondly, the terminate option on the select statement does not allow the task any last wishes, and therefore it cannot safely clean up after itself. Other RIs requested a different model of task termination, for example a model of library task termination was requested where the termination of the main program forced the termination of any library tasks, and the necessity of the terminate alternative of the select was questioned.

Ada 95 has more fully defined when aborted tasks must terminate and the Real-Time Systems Annex demands some measure of the immediacy of an abort. Also, finalisation allows a task's last wishes to be executed following the selection of a terminate alternative in a select statement (see Section 6.1.1). The alternative models of task termination were deemed not to be appropriate for Ada.

• Efficiency issues

Perhaps one of the most common complaints against Ada 83 was that the implementations were inherently inefficient due to the complexity of the tasking model. An often articulated requirement was for an efficient mechanism to support mutually exclusive access to shared data.

The upward compatibility requirement on Ada 95 has made it impossible to simplify the tasking model. However, the language designers have made significant efforts to facilitate the production of efficient tasking paradigms by:

— providing data-oriented communication and synchronisation via protected objects;

— allowing alternative tasking models to be implemented in the Real-Time Systems Annex;

— sanctioning 'subsets' of tasking via the introduction of a pragma Restricted;

— requiring the implementation to recognise entry-less protected types for special optimisation.

15.2 Outstanding issues

Throughout this book, several outstanding issues with the Ada tasking model have been identified. Many of these were known during the design of Ada 95, and solutions were available. However, there was great concern about the number of changes to the language and the potential efficiency of real-time programs. Consequently there was a scope reduction exercise where expressive power, run-time efficiency and number of changes were traded off against each other. The issues that remain for the tasking model can be summarised as follows:

1. Task initialisation

In Section 4.1, the difficulty of declaring an array of tasks with discriminants was discussed. This was a known problem during the language design and solutions were proposed. However, the demand to keep the number of language changes as small as possible meant that elegant language-based solutions were not adopted. Instead, the programmer has to resort to a function with side-effects.

It was also noted that task discriminants do not provide a general parameter passing mechanism, as only discrete and access types can be passed. This restriction makes task discriminants consistent with record discriminants.

2.   Expressive power of the select

The addition of a requeue mechanism to Ada has led to an increase in the expressive power of Ada's synchronisation facilities. Ada is now able to express all the criteria discussed in Section 8.1. Only one minor problem remains: that is, that FIFO queuing applies only to a single entry queue and not across more than one entry queue. It is not therefore straightforward to implement a fair selection between entries.

The ARM does allow the implementation to provide other queuing policies, so this problem is easily solved for those applications that need such queuing policies.

3.   Selective entry calls

Ada has introduced very powerful and elegant features for asynchronous communication. It is now possible to construct efficient asynchronous communications paradigms, such as mail boxes, channels, etc. However, the absence of a selective entry call facility does lead to some awkward programming when a task is required to wait for a communication on more than one protected object (see Section 9.9).

Once again, this problem was known during the design of Ada. Given the choice between a more expressive language and a more efficient implementation, it was decided that most users would prefer the efficient implementation.

4.   The asynchronous select

The asynchronous select will probably be as controversial in Ada 95 as the abort statement was in Ada 83. There are many interactions with other aspects of the language and this will no doubt add to its implementation cost.

In the efficiency/expressive power trade-off, the user demand for an asynchronous transfer of control facility outweighed arguments of efficiency.

5.   Object-oriented programming and tasking

Integrating concurrency features within an object-oriented framework is still an open research issue. It is therefore no surprise to find that Ada does not solve all the issues. In particular, it is not possible to create a synchronised object in Ada that can easily be extended in both its data and the operations on the data (see Chapter 13).

6.   Distribution issue

The Ada partition model provides support for distributed execution without introducing additional linguistic constructs. The motivation is to minimise the differences in programming distributed and non-distributed systems without bias towards specific distributed target architectures.

The most severe limitation of the Ada partition model is that partitions are not first-class language objects. Partition types cannot be created and therefore instances of partitions, pointers to partitions and arrays of partitions cannot be expressed. See Chapter 14.

15.3   The future

Ada 95 is now an ISO and ANSI standard. Inevitably, writing concurrent and real-time programs in Ada will be compared with writing them in C++ running under Posix (and Real-time Posix). In our view, the success of Ada will depend on the realisation of two crucial events:

(a)   the success of the current efforts to produce public domain Ada compilers;

(b)   the response of Ada vendors to the challenge to produce highly efficient, tailorable run-time support systems.

If these activities are both successful, then Ada has a promising future as a programming language for concurrent, distributed and real-time applications. What is beyond doubt is that *Concurrency in Ada* will remain a key, but controversial, component of the language.

References

ARM, 1995
Ada 9X Mapping/Revision Team, Intermetrics, *Ada 9X Reference Manual, Draft Version 5.99*, Ada 9X Project Report (December 1994).

ARTEWG, 1993
Ada Run Time Environment Working Group, *A Catalog of Interface Features and Options for the Ada Run Time Environment*, Release 3.1., ACM SIGAda, (1993).

Ada 9X, 1990
Ada 9X Requirements Team, *Ada 9X Revision Issues, Release 2*, Ada 9X Project Report, (May 1990).

Andrews, 1981
G.R. Andrews, Synchronising Resources, *ACM Transactions on Programming Languages and Systems*, **3**(4), 405-431, (October 1981).

Andrews, 1991
G.R. Andrews, Paradigms for Process Interaction in Distributed Programs, *Computing Surveys*, **23**(1), 49-90, (March 1991).

Andrews, 1993
G.R. Andrews and R.A. Olsson, *The SR Programming Language: Concurrency and Practice*, Benjamin/Cummings, California, (1993).

Barnes, 1994
J.G.P. Barnes, *Programming in Ada Plus an Overview of Ada 9X*, Fourth Edition, Addison-Wesley, Wokingham, (1994).

Ben-Ari, 1982
M. Ben-Ari, *Principles of Concurrent Programming*, Prentice Hall, New Jersey, (1982).

Bloom, 1979
T. Bloom, "Evaluating Synchronisation Mechanisms", *Proceedings of the Seventh ACM Symposium on Operating System Principles*, Pacific Grove, 24-32 (December 1979).

Brinch-Hansen, 1972
P. Brinch-Hansen, Structured Multiprogramming, *CACM*, **15**(7), 574-8 (July 1972).

Burns *et al.*, 1987
A. Burns, A.M. Lister and A.J. Wellings, A Review of Ada Tasking, *Lecture Notes in Computer Science*, **262**, Springer-Verlag, Berlin, (1987).

Campbell and Habermann, 1974
R.H. Campbell and A.N. Habermann, The Specification of Process Synchronisation by Path Expressions, *Lecture Notes in Computer Science*, **16**, 89-102, Springer-Verlag, Berlin, (1974).

Dijkstra, 1968
E.W. Dijkstra, Cooperating Sequential Processes, in *Programming Languages*, ed. F. Genuys, Academic Press, 43-112, London (1968).

Dijkstra, 1975
E.W. Dijkstra, Guarded Commands, Nondeterminacy, and Formal Derivation of Programs, *CACM*, **18**(8), 453-7, (August 1975).

Francez and Pnueli, 1978
N. Francez and A. Pnueli, A Proof Method for Cyclic Programs, *ACTA*, **9**, 133-57, (1978).

Francez and Yemini, 1985
N. Francez and A. Yemini, Symmetric Intertask Communication, *ACM Transactions on Programming Languages and Systems*, **7**(4), 622-636, (October 1985).

Gargaro, 1993
A. B. Gargaro, Towards Distributed Objects in Ada 9X, *Ada: Towards Maturity. Proceedings of the 1993 AdaUK Conference*, ed. L. Collingbourne, 20-31, IOS Press, Netherlands (1993).

Gehani, 1984
N.H. Gehani and T.A. Cargill, Concurrent Programming in the Ada Language: The Polling Bias, *Software-Practice and Experience*, **14**(5), 413-27 (May 1984).

Hoare, 1974
C.A.R. Hoare, Monitors — An Operating System Structuring Concept, *CACM*, **17**(10), 549-57, (October 1974).

Hoare, 1979
C.A.R. Hoare, *Subsetting of Ada*, Draft Document (June 1979).

Magee, 1993
Magee, J., Dulay, N. and Kramer, J., Structuring parallel and distributed programs, *Software Engineering Journal*, **8**(2), 73-82, (1993). (March 1993).

Matsuoka, 1993
S. Matsuoka and A. Yonezawa, Analysis of Inheritance Anomaly in Object-Oriented Concurrent Programming Languages, in *Research Directions in Concurrent Object-Oriented Programming*, 107-50, MIT Press (1993).

Simpson, 1990

H. Simpson, Four-Slot Fully Asynchronous Communication Mechanism, *IEE Proceedings*, **137**(Pt.E.1), 17-30, (Jan 1990).

Wellings *et al.*, 1984

A.J. Wellings, D. Keeffe and G.M. Tomlinson, A Problem with Ada and Resource Allocation, *Ada Letters*, **3**(4), 112-23, (January/February 1984).

Index